MY

YEAR

INSIDE

RADICAL ISLAM

MY

YEAR

INSIDE

RADICAL ISLAM

a memoir

DAVEED GARTENSTEIN-ROSS

JEREMY P. TARCHER • PENGUIN
A MEMBER OF PENGUIN GROUP (USA) INC.
NEW YORK

JEREMY P. TARCHER/PENGUIN
Published by the Penguin Group
Penguin Group (USA) Inc., 375 Hudson Street, New York, New York 10014,
USA • Penguin Group (Canada), 90 Eglinton Avenue East, Suite 700, Toronto,
Ontario M4P 2Y3, Canada (a division of Pearson Penguin Canada Inc.) •
Penguin Books Ltd, 80 Strand, London WC2R 0RL, England • Penguin Ireland,
25 St Stephen's Green, Dublin 2, Ireland (a division of Penguin Books Ltd) •
Penguin Group (Australia), 250 Camberwell Road, Camberwell, Victoria 3124, Australia
(a division of Pearson Australia Group Pty Ltd) • Penguin Books India Pvt Ltd,
11 Community Centre, Panchsheel Park, New Delhi–110 017, India • Penguin Group
(NZ), 67 Apollo Drive, Mairangi Bay, Auckland 1311, New Zealand (a division
of Pearson New Zealand Ltd) • Penguin Books (South Africa) (Pty) Ltd,
24 Sturdee Avenue, Rosebank, Johannesburg 2196, South Africa

Penguin Books Ltd, Registered Offices:
80 Strand, London WC2R 0RL, England

Most Tarcher/Penguin books are available at special quantity discounts for bulk purchase
for sales promotions, premiums, fund-raising, and educational needs. Special books or book
excerpts also can be created to fit specific needs. For details, write Penguin Group
(USA) Inc. Special Markets, 375 Hudson Street, New York, NY 10014.

Library of Congress Control Number: 2006939148
ISBN-13: 978-1-58542-551-8

Printed in the United States of America
1 3 5 7 9 10 8 6 4 2

BOOK DESIGN BY SUSAN WALSH

While the author has made every effort to provide accurate telephone numbers and Internet
addresses at the time of publication, neither the publisher nor the author assumes any
responsibility for errors, or for changes that occur after publication. Further, the publisher
does not have any control over and does not assume any responsibility for author or third-
party websites or their content.

This book is dedicated to Amy Elizabeth Powell,
because it is love that saw me through.

*This book is also dedicated to al-Husein Madhany and Mike Hollister,
two men who took it upon themselves to teach me about God.*

AUTHOR'S NOTE

As with any memoir, a large part of this book is dependent on my memory. Given the sensitivity of the subject matter I'm writing about, I've attempted wherever possible to track down eyewitnesses and documents relevant to the events described herein. Generally, any quotes from personal conversations are approximations of what was actually said. I had much better success finding relevant e-mail and Internet postings. Virtually all of the e-mail and Internet postings that I quote from are direct quotes.

In most cases, I have used the actual names of the people discussed in the narrative. In a few instances, however, the names have been changed to protect certain individuals' privacy.

one

SEARCHING FOR GOD
AMONG THE HIPPIES

Before I was an FBI informant, an apostate, and a blasphemer, I was a devout believer in radical Islam who worked for a Saudi-funded charity that sent money to al-Qaeda. At the time, it all seemed pretty normal.

On the inside of a radical Islamic group, there are many rules to remember. A lot of them involve limbs. I could eat using only my right hand. I could never pet a dog or shake hands with a woman. To avoid Allah's wrath, I had to roll up my pants legs above the ankles before prayer. On the other hand, shorts on men had to extend below the knee or they were indecent. I believed in all of this and more. I believed that Jews and other nonbelievers had to be conquered and ruled as the inferiors they are.

Funny thing, I was born Jewish. At twenty-three, with my nose in a wool prayer rug, I had to pray for the humiliation of my parents.

This is a story about the seduction of radical Islam, which, like love, can take its devotees suddenly or by degrees, and the long, dangerous climb out. It is a story of converts trapped by extremist views that once seemed alien, furtive calls to the FBI, and a surprising series of revelations that changed my life.

My name is Daveed Gartenstein-Ross. If you went looking for my child-hood home, you'd snake along I-5 out of California, follow the green-and-white signs to the Elizabethan-themed tourist town of Ashland, Oregon, and wend your way into one of the town's countless subdivi-sions. There, you would find my house at the end of a lazy cul-de-sac. It wouldn't be hard to spot. My neighbors all had perfect green lawns, while we had the rocks and weeds of an old riverbed. In the back, we kept an untamed jungle of trees and flowers. Our neighbors did not com-plain; we were on the hippie end of a hippie town.

Like most people who grow up in Ashland, I would complain con-stantly that there was nothing to do. But I always knew that I would miss the place. Ashland was a liberal oasis in conservative southern Oregon and it brimmed with counterculture. There was an award-winning Shakespearean theater. There was Lithia Park, designed by Golden Gate Park's creator. And there was the telling fact that this hamlet of only fif-teen thousand boasted close to a dozen bookstores.

My parents fell in love with Ashland during a brief visit when I was three years old. For those who are drawn to the town, it is the peaks they see first. The Siskiyou Mountains meet the Cascades in Ashland, one stop along the Cascades' northward crawl to Mount St. Helens. It is these hills that give the best view of town. A short hike would take you to a vantage point above the park where you could see my old childhood haunts: the plaza and ice cream shop, the baseball diamonds, the dirt lot off C Street where my friends and I used to race our bikes.

My family moved a couple of times before settling down at the end of our cul-de-sac. We first lived in a brown ranch house in the Quiet Vil-lage neighborhood before spending half a dozen years in a town house on sloping Wimer Street. Though we moved a few times, every place we lived had the same serene New Age feel inside.

My parents' artwork spoke a great deal about their brand of religion. Various scenes from Jesus' life graced the living room. In the backyard stood a small white statue of Buddha. They were sort of Unitarian Jews who esteemed Jesus and Buddha equally.

Though my parents were from Jewish backgrounds, they weren't happy with traditional Judaism and decided to join a new religion when I was still a toddler. It was known as the "Infinite Way." My dad once described the group as a "disorganized religion," in contrast to organized religion: it had no membership, no dues, no nonprofit corporation, and no enforcement of doctrine. The group was founded by Joel Goldsmith, who was also born Jewish but became a Christian Scientist; he left Christian Science when his ideas diverged from those of Mary Baker Eddy. Joel, whose followers called him by his first name, founded the Infinite Way around 1940, but didn't name it then. Instead, he simply started teaching spiritual principles late that year.

The group's name came seven years later, when Joel published a book called *The Infinite Way*. Joel's teachings focused on awakening people to their unlimited potential that could only be harnessed through spiritual consciousness. As Joel explained: "The necessity for giving up the material sense of existence for the attainment of the spiritual consciousness of life and its activities is the secret of the seers, prophets, and saints of all ages."

In an effort to make the spiritual foremost in their own lives, my parents spent a lot of time meditating. Often I would burst into the living room—excited to share something I had seen or read or some small accomplishment, the way kids so often want to—only to find my parents sitting on the couch silently, their eyes closed, their focus on another world.

My parents' love for spiritual figures and religious traditions didn't end with Jesus, Buddha, and the Old Testament prophets. They also cherished the wisdom of Rumi, St. Augustine, and Ramana Maharshi.

And they drew lessons from Zen, Taoism, and Sufism. Upon hearing of my parents' syncretistic views, a friend once jokingly referred to them as "Jewnitarians."

People often present the stories of their religious conversions as though their lives were completely normal, and then there was some great thunderclap. My experience, and the experience of other converts I have known, suggests that it's not that straightforward. Instead, a religious conversion comprises a series of seemingly unrelated events that are later revealed to have had a purpose: they are pointing toward devotion to a god that you never knew. And strange as it may seem, my debates with fundamentalist Christians were milestones on the path to radical Islam.

These debates came when Christian friends tried to push me on my spiritual views. Mike Hollister is the one I remember best. We met at a debate tournament when I was a high school sophomore. Mike was from the state of Washington. Unlike most high school debaters, he was also an athlete. Six feet tall with light brown hair, Mike played varsity soccer. His athleticism set him apart from other debaters by giving him an unusually strong presence.

Given the geographic distance between us, there's no easy way to explain why our chance meeting grew into a friendship. We shared a passion for policy debate and a similarly quirky sense of humor—but these alone don't make a friendship. The best explanation is that Mike found me interesting because I was unlike his other friends, and I felt the same about him. Mike appreciated my intensely analytic approach to the world, my willingness to debate and discuss every imaginable subject, from politics to economics to baseball. And I was interested in how Mike's worldview differed from that of my other friends. He was traditional and conservative, values alien to my parents' Ashland.

Although we remained friends through college, Mike's descent into fundamentalist Christianity disturbed me. Having been a nominal Christian through high school, he started to become serious about his faith soon after he started classes at Western Washington University, in Bellingham. Christianity became more central to his identity—and I noticed him becoming less fun and less open-minded.

While Mike stayed close to home, I went three thousand miles away for college, to Wake Forest University, in Winston-Salem, North Carolina in the fall of 1994. I was drawn mainly by scholarship money. My parents had more books than dollars, and paying for a private college without a scholarship would have been hard.

With its closely trimmed lawns, tennis courts, and golf course, Wake Forest's campus looked like a country club. While this may seem welcoming, and surely was to the majority of students who would eventually join country clubs, it made me feel all the more the stranger. I did not make the coast-to-coast drive in my beat-up red 1985 Toyota Tercel that it would have taken to have the car on campus. But if I had, the car would have stuck out among the BMWs, Mercedeses, and new sports sedans that packed the parking lots. From the day I arrived on campus in red Chuck Taylor sneakers and a flannel shirt, I stuck out almost as much as my car would have. For my first couple of years there, I felt isolated, alone.

I decided to visit Mike early in the summer of 1996, driving up to Washington to see him. Since Wake Forest's school year ended earlier than Western Washington's, classes were still in session when I arrived. By then Mike had become deeply involved in a group called Campus Christian Fellowship. I hung out with him and his college friends, who were also fundamentalist Christians, for about a week. They were perfectly nice, but struck me as dangerously naive. They seemed to shut themselves off from so much of the richness and ideas that life had to offer.

I met Mike's girlfriend over lunch during that visit. Amy Childers stood about five feet nine and had intense blue eyes. Within the first three minutes of meeting her, she asked me: "So why aren't you Christian?"

I was taken aback and offended. What business of hers was it? Though my identity as a Jew was far from central to my life, I immediately shot back, "Because I don't need to be Christian. Remember, I'm one of God's chosen people."

I found the Old Testament notion that the Jews were the "chosen people" rather absurd, but thought that might be an effective parry.

My response caught her off guard. Amy muttered something about how it was true that I was one of God's chosen people, but she envied Jews who became Christian because they were doubly loved by God. "I mean, God loves everybody," she said, "but Jews who convert get to have a special relationship with Him because they're part of God's chosen people, and also get to accept Christ as their savior. They get to be doubly special."

I managed to steer the discussion in a different direction. We didn't talk about Jesus again for the rest of lunch.

I don't think Mike realized how much Amy's question offended me. He simply would not drop the subject of Christianity.

Like many people, I had adopted most of my parents' spiritual beliefs when growing up. Or, at least, I had adopted as much of these beliefs as I could understand; true to their liberal vision, my parents were careful not to push their views of God onto me. I believed that truth could be found in most religions—that Jesus had an amazing connection to God, but so did Buddha, so did many other religious figures. I rejected the Christian idea that Jesus had been God: no matter how deep a person's spiritual insight, there's a fundamental difference between the Creator and his creation.

Knowing my analytical approach to the world, Mike thought he spotted a logical problem that could make me rethink these ideas. He wanted to make me consider the case for Christianity.

Mike homed in on my respect for Jesus. At the time, Mike's favorite Christian author was Josh McDowell, an apologist with a gift for making his arguments accessible to college-age readers. Mike shared a passage from one of McDowell's books, *Evidence That Demands a Verdict*, with me.

In the passage, McDowell discussed at length C. S. Lewis's claim that there were three possible things Jesus could have been: a liar, a lunatic, or the Lord. Both McDowell and Lewis concluded that those were the only three alternatives, and there could be no middle ground. This is because Jesus claimed to be God in the New Testament. If this claim were true, then one should accept him as Lord. But if Jesus' claim was false, and he knew the claim was false, he would be a liar who had nothing to offer his students. On the other hand, if Jesus believed he was God but wasn't, then he would be a madman. The one thing Jesus could not be, according to this logic, was exactly what I thought he was: a good and wise teacher.

While I found the passage compelling, I was sure that I must be overlooking some fatal flaw. But the argument was put to me forcefully enough that it made me uncomfortable because it suggested that there was some incoherence in my ideas about God.

Contrary to Mike's intentions, this discomfort started me down the path to Islam, and ultimately to radical Islam.

As I was leaving Bellingham a few days later, Mike walked me to my car, past the sloping lawns that dotted Western Washington's campus. The setting sun gave the sky a pink hue. Some of the college kids tossed

Frisbees around. A few people who had been studying outside were folding up their beach towels and heading back to the dorms.

Mike made one last effort. "Have you thought about devoting your life to Christ?"

We had spent enough of the visit discussing Christianity that the question wasn't unexpected. But I was a bit annoyed by it—and still didn't have a good answer. "I'm not ready to do that," I said. "I'm young. I have a lot of living to do before I could commit myself to any religion."

"But you never know what will happen to you. You're driving home to Oregon now. What happens if you have a car crash and die? Will you go to heaven?"

I smiled and shook my head slightly. This was another of Mike's clumsy attempts at evangelism. I was one of the first people with whom he tried to share his faith, and his lack of experience showed. I found myself wondering why he cared which god I worshipped.

I looked Mike dead in the eyes. "I'll take my chances."

When I returned home, I asked my dad about the "liar, lunatic, or Lord" argument. My dad was a short man with a New York accent who liked to discuss big ideas. He had a beard and black hair speckled with patches of white. Although he worked as a physical therapist, he devoted himself to family life. When I was a kid we had endless walks and talks, and constantly created new games to play together.

Although very few topics were off-limits for my dad, I could tell that my question upset him. My dad had certain hot buttons, and apparently I had unwittingly touched one. He wouldn't yell or become belligerent, but there were signs—slight coloration of his face, speaking faster and louder, biting of the lip—that tipped me off to his anger. After I told him Mike's argument, my dad blurted out, "As far as I'm concerned, that's just a kind of idolatry."

My parents had a live-and-let-live attitude toward spiritual matters, so I was surprised by my father's strong reaction. But my thoughts quickly turned to the very first of the Ten Commandments, which barred idolatry. There was a reason, I knew, that it came first. (When I was writing this book, my dad told me that I had misinterpreted his idolatry point. Rather than referring to idolatry in the standard Jewish way, my dad's thinking was that every person and thing is divine: it's idolatry, in his view, to say that one person is divine but nobody else is. His intended meaning speaks volumes about my parents' beliefs.)

Beside Dad's response, Christianity felt wrong. The Christians I knew lived shuttered lives, conforming to a model of morality and political opinion that missed out on so much of the big picture.

But Mike's efforts at evangelism came at a time when I had some intense spiritual questions. Not only did I feel isolated at Wake Forest, but I also came close to dying twice before I turned twenty-one. After a couple of brushes with death, I was acutely aware of the emptiness in my life.

I came down with pneumonia during my final semester of high school. By the time I was admitted to Ashland Community Hospital, I was within a few days of death. I spent ten days in a hospital bed. Perhaps it was my relatively quick recovery or my young age, but I didn't have the life-changing experience that people sometimes do when they almost die. I somewhat generically resolved to live a fuller life, but beyond that I remained a normal kid.

The spiritual questions came after the second time I faced mortality. That happened in the fall of 1996, shortly after I visited Mike in Bellingham. I felt very sick when I returned to North Carolina for the next semester. I tried to go on living a normal life despite feeling like I was in the grip of a disease. I was able to tough it out for almost a month, but the lesions in my mouth kept coming, and my stomach grew angrier and angrier. I felt my body gradually breaking down. I wore a bulky winter coat and was always shivering even though it was a warm September. Some days it was a real challenge just to walk across campus.

I went to Wake Forest's notorious student health services a few times to see what was wrong. On one visit the nurse dismissively told me that I had a fever and gave me some aspirin (charging me five dollars for a couple of tablets). Finally, near the end of a miserable month, one of the doctors in student health services recognized that my condition was beyond their expertise, and transferred me to North Carolina Baptist Hospital, in downtown Winston-Salem.

At North Carolina Baptist, they diagnosed me with a digestive condition called Crohn's disease. I stayed in the hospital for about two weeks and had to withdraw from school for the semester. I went back to Oregon to recover. I lost more than forty pounds while I was sick, and was a 119-pound skeleton by the time I got home.

When you're deprived of something you love for a long time, you're sometimes treated to a wonderful process of rediscovery. In the fall of 1996, my rediscovery was the joy of food. My mom would cook me five or six meals a day to help me put weight back on. I would first smell the aromas wafting from the kitchen. I relished the olfactory experience almost as much as the meal itself. And every time I passed one of Ashland's new restaurants, I'd stop to look at the menu, savoring the thought of applewood smoked bacon or five-spice chicken.

It was just one of the parts of my life that I was reexamining.

I was already asking hard questions because of my illness. My grandfather's death added urgency to them. My grandfather had suffered a stroke about a decade earlier. He had led a brilliant life, eventually becoming the dean of the medical school's clinical campus at Stony Brook University in New York. But everything changed with the stroke.

By the fall of 1996, he stayed in Hearthstone, a single-story brick nurs-
ing home in Medford, Oregon, where my dad worked.

One day we got a phone call. My grandfather was very sick. Shortly
after darkness began to cover the valley, another call informed us that he
had died. My dad and I drove through ten miles of downpour to get
to my grandfather's room. Near the end of his life, Grandpa could no
longer stand the debilitating effects of the stroke. Sometimes he'd cry or
scream. But when we got to his room and saw him lying there with the
warmth fleeing from his body, Grandpa finally looked at peace.

My dad patted his forehead and repeated, "My good dad. My good
dad."

When I returned to Wake Forest in the spring of 1997, I was ready to
find answers.

That was the semester I became friends with al-Husein Madhany, a
tall Kenyan-born man of Indian-American parents (the South Asian
variety of Indian). He was a serious Muslim who prayed five times a day,
but could also date five women at once. It was through al-Husein that I
began to learn about Islam.

My first real interaction with al-Husein came when he was running
to be the student government secretary. At the Wake Forest student TV
studios to watch the televised "debates" among the candidates for office,
I gave him some speaking advice. These debates featured no interaction
between the candidates. Instead, a host interviewed one person at a
time, asking each of them three questions. I had won the national cham-
pionship in policy debate a few weeks before, and was riding high on the
idea that I had mastered the art of public speaking. I noticed that none
of the candidates looked into the camera when answering the questions.
Instead, they looked at the host. The viewers could see only the sides of

their faces. I didn't think this showed enough confidence, so I suggested that al-Husein speak directly into the camera.

If anything, my advice only hurt him. Shortly after the debates, another student complained to me that al-Husein looked "arrogant." She said, "He didn't look at Matt [the host] when Matt asked him questions. He just looked into the camera and acted like Matt wasn't there." Despite my bad advice, al-Husein kept me around to help with the campaign. We became fast friends.

I took to al-Husein quickly because he had a depth that most people lack. This depth was a double-edged sword that often resulted in brooding. Al-Husein generally wanted to focus his conversations and thoughts not on small day-to-day matters, but on big, significant issues. He believed that others should focus on the big issues as well. One night, another student told me that he had decided to write a term paper about Nirvana frontman Kurt Cobain. Al-Husein butted in. "Kurt Cobain? Why aren't you writing about racism?"

The other student stuttered out a bashful explanation, but al-Husein had made his point. Why are you wasting your time writing about some singer when we have real and pervasive social problems? It was classic college thinking.

Al-Husein had a definite sense of the image he projected. He usually spoke slowly and softly, as though parsing every word, as though he had no doubt that he would hold the listener's attention. Although he spoke with a soft voice, his words were like a victory speech, to be savored and passed down for generations.

Al-Husein was also socially daring. One frequent exchange was the unanswered question that he'd return to days later. One day, I saw al-Husein in the hall and asked him to recommend a good book. He looked at me quizzically and walked off without saying a word. When I saw him three days later, he said, without introduction, "The Autobiography of Malcolm X."

"What?" I said.

"You asked me to recommend a book three days ago. That's my recommendation."

"Why didn't you just tell me when I asked?"

"I wanted to think about it."

This habit initially struck me as both rude and impressive. I had never met someone with enough social confidence to ignore people seemingly completely, only to continue the discussion after a few days' hiatus.

My view shifted slightly when I learned more about Sufism, the mystical strain of Islam to which al-Husein adhered. Sufism's emphasis on emptying the heart of attachment to anything but God can produce idiosyncratic behavior in its devotees. As I learned about how Sufis value patience, I realized there may have been a deeper reason for al-Husein's behavior. In a famous story, the Sufi philosopher Ibn 'Arabi was asked by his sheikh to explain the meaning of a specific Qur'anic verse. After some contemplation, Ibn 'Arabi left without saying a word—and didn't return for four years. The sheikh wanted a deeper interpretation than he could give. On Ibn 'Arabi's return, his sheikh said, "Give me your answer. After four years, the time is ripe for it."

Al-Husein may have had this or a similar Sufi example in mind when he decided to wait three days before answering a basic question of mine.

Before I knew al-Husein, I was living in my own world, divorced from other people's needs and struggles. I was an island that longed to be a peninsula. My time was divided between my studies and intercollegiate debate, and little else. The three biggest things that were missing from my life were friendship, a sense of purpose, and a relationship with God.

I had opportunities to get involved in matters of importance to other students, but always let them pass by. Wake Forest is north of downtown

Winston-Salem, a city where crime rates in every major category are worse than the national average. Since a campus crawling with rich kids makes a tempting target for criminals, there was a handful of armed robberies on campus during my sophomore year. When the school announced that it would erect gatehouses staffed with security personnel in response, there was an outcry from student activists. They were concerned that people of color would face greater scrutiny at the gates. I understood their concerns, but when friends asked me to join the protests, I refused. I had far too busy a life, it seemed, to get involved in causes of that kind.

I was also cut off from other people socially. Moving to the South was a culture shock. Also, I wasn't used to or comfortable with the extravagant wealth on display at Wake Forest. So the other students had unfamiliar values that differed immeasurably from those of the hippie mecca of Ashland, Oregon. Even Winston-Salem's restaurants seemed less friendly, less inviting than those that I had known in Ashland.

I flung myself into my work, which was like a many-headed hydra. Whenever I finished one project, two more instantly filled the void. I would drink or go out to movies with friends around campus, but had no confidants. It sometimes seemed that even my surface-level friendships were too much effort. I remember driving home one night from dinner in downtown Winston-Salem. Instead of thinking about the food we had eaten or the conversations we'd had, the only thing on my mind was my looming deadlines. Nothing was due the next day, or even that week—but I wished I had stayed in and worked rather than spending time with my friends. It struck me then that it was always this way: every night out with friends was tinged with feelings of regret rather than fulfillment. Many people go through periods where they feel alone, separated from their surroundings. For me, this lasted through my first two years at Wake Forest.

My friendship with al-Husein Madhany started to bring me outside myself. Al-Husein was aggressive about inserting himself into my life. He would constantly burst into my room without knocking and, seeing me working, would insist that there were more important things to do. Al-Husein often asked me to walk around Wake Forest's idyllic grass-covered quad with him while he smoked a pipe and waxed philosophical. Once he found me playing a game of Risk (the board game where you try to conquer the world with your armies) on my computer. After learning that the game could take multiple players, al-Husein roped in four other students. We played one six-player game of Risk after another until two in the morning.

I never regretted a moment that I spent with al-Husein, and soon came to think of him as my best friend. I couldn't wait until the next time we'd circle the quad together. I couldn't wait to see what new things I'd learn about the world—and about myself.

My first experience with student political activism was a spur-of-the-moment thing in early April 1997. It was a warm day, with a slight breeze rustling the leaves of the magnolia trees dotting campus.

"There's a rally on the quad," al-Husein said as he entered my room unannounced. "You should come."

"What's the rally?" I was looking for an excuse to get out, but was having trouble pulling myself away from my work.

"It's for a new student group called VOICE, Voices Organized in the Interest of Collective Equality. Knox founded the group."

Knox was a wiry, dreadlocked black intellectual with a range of talents and a far-left outlook. He and I were close during my first semester at Wake Forest, when we took an introductory poetry class together. Knox tended to speak as though he were the only person in the room: he was the topic of all his conversations. We had a falling-out later in my freshman year when another friend and I made fun of Knox for his self-centeredness. It was the kind of rough humor with a serious undertone that isn't uncommon among friends, but Knox didn't find it funny. He didn't speak to me for a few months, and we were never close again.

So I hesitated. "I don't know. I'm not sure if going to a student rally is the best way to spend the day."

"Do you care about racism?" al-Husein said, moving into his didactic mode. "Are issues like homophobia, religious discrimination, and white heterosexual Christian male hegemony on campus important to you?" Al-Husein had lost his student government election, but remained a major force in campus politics. Now he was helping to bring me outside of myself in yet another way, by pushing me toward political activism.

"Well, they are, but—"

"Then you should come."

Al-Husein and I walked out the front door of the Huffman dorm and onto the quad. A small knot of people gathered for the rally by the steps of Wait Chapel, which towered over the north end of the quad. Even though it was a rally for diversity, the demonstrators were mostly black and the onlookers were mostly white.

Knox stood on the chapel steps with a megaphone. He seemed disappointed with the lackluster turnout, but mustered all the enthusiasm that a man with a megaphone can.

He asked a few other minority students to address the rally, some of whom pointed to the clutch of campus cops who had come to watch, saying that their presence revealed Wake Forest's racism. "Anyone who doesn't believe that racism exists on this campus need only look at that cop," said an African-American sophomore named Ronetta. "Think about all the scrutiny that black people face next time you're wondering where the cops are when students are getting raped and cars are getting broken into."

After the minority speakers addressed the crowd, Knox said, "Anybody else want to speak? White people, you got anything to say?" While his remark was said with humor, the serious undertone was that white people did not care about racism.

All those walks on the quad and talks with al-Husein had affected me. I found that I had something to say. In response to Knox's call, I climbed the chapel steps and took the megaphone. Despite all my public speaking experience as a college debater, I was nervous. I wasn't making abstract arguments to persuade a judge; instead, I was talking to my peers about something I cared about. My speech was short and disjointed. It was about how white people, as members of the majority culture, needed to confront racism when we saw it. I finished the speech to a mixture of scattered applause and long stares. Still, I felt good.

As I walked down the steps, I felt that I was changing. I was moving from spectator to participant. Al-Husein clapped me on the back. "It's nice to see you taking a stand. We need more people like you involved," he said.

Later that day, al-Husein brought me to a meeting of a group he had founded, the Asian Student Interest Association (ASIA), a minority student group for those of Asian descent. Al-Husein opened the meeting by introducing each attendee. When it was my turn, he jokingly described me as a "token white member," then said I had given a speech at the VOICE rally that caught people's interest. My speech probably caught no one's interest, but this was al-Husein's way: he made people feel that their contributions, however small, were valued. Al-Husein asked me to tell the others why I had decided to address the rally.

I told the group that I had always been aware of racism at Wake Forest, but that I—like too many white people—often shrugged it off as someone else's problem. Over time, I realized that racism *wasn't* someone else's problem. Racism was *everyone's* problem, and it was time for all of us to take a stand. As I spoke those words, I knew that this was the beginning of my stand.

I was also intrigued by al-Husein's religious views. From the beginning, one of the things I liked about him was that he was Muslim. He was, in fact, the first practicing Muslim I knew. The difference between al-Husein's faith and Mike's was pronounced. While fundamentalist Christianity seemed to shut Mike's mind from the rest of the world, al-Husein's practice of Islam spurred him to new levels of inquiry and interest in the world.

Islam, al-Husein told me, is "a simple faith." Its defining characteristic is its steadfast monotheism. I learned that Muslims believe in the same God as Christians and Jews, even though they often use the Arabic term "Allah" to refer to the Lord. Muslims also believe in the same prophets as Christians and Jews. The line of prophets in Islam begins with the first man, Adam, and includes the likes of Noah, Abraham, Moses, and Jesus. Muslims believe that Muhammad was the final prophet. They believe that God revealed Islam's holy book, the Qur'an, to Muhammad, and that the Qur'an is God's direct, literal word. I was also interested to learn that Muslims believe that the Old and New Testaments are earlier holy books inspired by God—but that those books became corrupted over time and are no longer completely reliable.

After my long, intense discussions with Mike about Christianity, I was especially interested in Islam's view of Jesus. Al-Husein explained that Islam holds, similar to what I believed, that Jesus was a prophet of God and had a special relationship with Him, but that Jesus was still just a man. He was in no way divine.

When Mike first told me the "liar, lunatic, or Lord" argument, I was sure that it must have a fatal flaw. Islam seemed to make that flaw explicit. Josh McDowell's argument could only be true if Jesus really did claim to be God—and Islam held that he never did so. Instead, the holy books that purport to show Jesus claiming his own divinity have been corrupted over time and can't be trusted on that point.

The logic underlying the faith appealed to me, as did al-Husein's Sufi-oriented practice of Islam. He had actually undergone a set of religious transformations by the time I met him. Al-Husein was raised as an Ismaili. There are two main branches of Islam, Sunni and Shia, of which Sunnis comprise about 90 percent of the world's Muslims. The Ismaili branch of Islam is Shia, and its adherents follow the Aga Khan. They believe the Aga Khan is Prophet Muhammad's rightful successor, and many Ismailis refer to him as a "living guide" or even "the living Qur'an." Every Ismaili I've known has had a moderate religious outlook. However, Sunni Muslims often regard them as heretics because of the Ismaili notion that the Aga Khan can interpret the Qur'an for his followers. Many Sunni Muslims believe that, rather than showing fidelity to the text of the Qur'an and Islamic traditions, the Ismailis are faithful to a man who changes the religion over time.

Shortly before al-Husein and I became friends, he converted to Sunni Islam. He didn't provide too many details when we discussed it, but apparently he had been briefly sucked into a very conservative practice of Islam. Al-Husein once said that the semester before he met me, he would walk around campus feeling anger and loathing toward the Christians and Jews around him. He would think of the Christians, with their belief in the divinity of Jesus, as polytheists; he would think of the Jews, with their idea that they were God's chosen people, as racists. Because of this, he earned the nickname "angst-ridden al-Husein."

But he abandoned those views before I met him. When I got to know al-Husein, he was a Sufi.

Sufism is a mystical strain of Islam that emphasizes spirituality over religious formalism. One of its defining characteristics is that it doesn't claim to hold a monopoly on religious wisdom. This resonated with the spiritual views with which I had been raised. In his introduction to *Essential Sufism*, Robert Frager explains, "Most Sufis believe that the great religions and mystical traditions of the world share the same essential Truth. The various prophets and spiritual teachers are like the light bulbs that illuminate a room. The bulbs are different, but the current comes from one source, which is God."

I viewed my parents as spiritual outliers when I was growing up, but here was a venerable religious tradition that agreed with them in substance.

When I went to a mosque for the first time, it was al-Husein who took me. I spent the summer of 1997 in Winston-Salem, teaching at Wake Forest's summer debate institute for high school students. It was then that al-Husein brought me to the *juma* prayers (the traditional Friday prayers) at Masjid al-Mu'minun.

Masjid al-Mu'minun was affiliated with the Islamic ministry of W. D. Muhammad, the son of former Nation of Islam leader Elijah Muhammad. When al-Husein asked me to go with him, I was hesitant. There were a couple of mosques in town, and al-Husein had mentioned that he had heard anti-Semitic comments at one. I was also skeptical of Masjid al-Mu'minun's roots in the Nation of Islam, which taught that the white man is the devil.

But I nonetheless joined al-Husein. When we got to the mosque, it didn't stand out from the other nondescript houses dotting Harriet Tubman Drive. Once we were inside, though, the building had an Islamic feel, with a large well-lit prayer room and a poster of the Grand Mosque in Mecca on one of the walls.

There were some two dozen mosque-goers inside, mostly African-

Americans, with a few Middle Easterners mixed in. I noticed that the men sat near the front of the prayer room, facing forward, while the women gathered in the back of the room. Shortly after we arrived, a tall black man stood up and shouted in melodic Arabic: *"Allahu Akbar! Allahu Akbar! Allahu Akbar! Allahu Akbar! Ashadu laa ilaha il Allah! Ashadu laa ilaha il Allah!"* I realized that this was the start of the call to prayer, signaling that the services were beginning.

A short Middle Eastern man with a humble demeanor delivered the sermon, which is known as a *khutbah* in Arabic. Al-Husein whispered that this was a guest imam who normally didn't give the *khutbah*. He obviously wasn't used to public speaking and seemed bashful about it. But I listened attentively.

The sermon was devoted to apologetics for Islam, explaining why it could shed light where other religions proved deficient. He started out by rebutting the Christian notion of the Trinity, pointing out that the Qur'an says of God, "He begetteth not, nor is he begotten."

"So," the speaker said, "Allah has no son. Allah is only one, which leaves no room for a son or a trinity of gods." I was puzzled that his only evidence came from the Qur'an. But I nonetheless sympathized with his argument, as I was unwilling to accept the idea that a man could be God.

It made me nervous when the sermon's refutations moved from Christianity to Judaism. I recalled what al-Husein told me about his stint as a fundamentalist, when he thought of every Jew as a racist. I became even more concerned when the discussion of Judaism immediately homed in on the concept of the chosen people. Although the speaker rejected the notion that the Jews were God's chosen people, the speech didn't become an anti-Semitic screed. Instead the guest imam simply said, "But this isn't so. The Holy Qur'an rejects any race's superiority when it states in Sura [chapter] 49:13: 'O mankind! We created you from a single pair of a male and a female, and made you into nations and tribes, that ye may know each other, not that ye may despise each other. Verily the most honored of you in the sight of Allah is he who is the most righteous of you.' So Allah doesn't prefer people because of their race, but only because of their righteousness."

That was it; no extra digs at the Jews.

I found that my other hesitation, the mosque's roots in the racist Nation of Islam, proved equally unjustified. While the attendees were predominantly black, I didn't feel out of place. Instead, I noticed a spirit of brotherhood in faith that united the believers regardless of race.

I had found myself absorbed by the question of race since moving to the South, as I was uncomfortable with the racial tension that I witnessed in North Carolina. But my visit to Masjid al-Mu'minun reminded me of the moving passage in Malcolm X's autobiography when he went on the hajj, the Islamic pilgrimage to Mecca. It is there that Malcolm X experienced a reversal in his thoughts about race:

Packed in the plane were white, black, brown, red, and yellow people, blue eyes and blond hair, and my kinky red hair—all together, brothers! All honoring the same God, all in turn giving equal honor to each other. . . . That is when I first began to re-appraise the "white man." It was when I first began to perceive that "white man," as commonly used, means complexion only secondarily; primarily it described attitudes and actions. In America, "white man" meant specific attitudes and actions toward the black man, and toward all other non-white men. But in the Muslim world, I had seen that men with white complexions were more genuinely brotherly than anyone else had ever been. That morning was the start of a radical alteration in my whole outlook about "white" men. There were tens of thousands of pilgrims, from all over the world. They were of all colors, from blue-eyed blonds to black-skinned Africans.

But we were all participating in the same ritual displaying a spirit of unity and brotherhood that my experiences in America had led me to believe never could exist between the white and the non-white.

I sensed echoes of the same spirit in Masjid al-Mu'minun. There was a greater ease of interaction between the races than I had encountered since moving to North Carolina.

Al-Husein had assured me before we left for the mosque that it was okay if I took part in *salat*, the Islamic ritual prayer. He said that some of the other Wake Forest students who had gone with him found *salat* to be a deeply moving experience. I merely found it confusing. I followed along as best I could when I stood in line for prayer, trying to imitate the bowing and prostration. I didn't even try to repeat the Arabic words.

My confusion about what to do during *salat* helped tip off the other mosque-goers that I wasn't Muslim. When the prayers ended, al-Husein and I stood around talking with some of the worshippers. One of the Muslims came up to me and said he wanted to give me something, then headed to the back rooms.

When he returned, he handed me an audiotape of a previous sermon, along with a short book by Imam Muhammad Armiya Nu'Man called *What Every American Should Know About Islam and the Muslims*. It was a touching gesture, one that marked my transition from mere intellectual curiosity about Islam to actually considering the faith for myself.

With each new layer I peeled back in my study of Islam that summer, the faith seemed more inviting.

Although the book by Muhammad Armiya Nu'Man that had been given to me was grammatically challenged, it verified much of what al-Husein had told me about the true, peaceful Islam. I was again struck by the respect displayed for other religions. In a section somewhat absurdly titled "Do Muslims Hate Christians and Jews?" Nu'Man quoted Sura 2:62 of the Qur'an:

> Those who believe (in the Qur'an)
> And those who follow the Jewish (Scriptures)
> And the Christians and the Sabians,
> And who believe in Allah and the
> Last Day, and work righteousness
> Shall have their reward with their Lord;
> On them shall be no fear, nor shall
> They grieve.

Nu'Man commented on the verse: "This verse lets us know that Jews, Christians, and Sabians (an ancient religious sect), who believe in Almighty God and do good works, will have their reward with their Lord. As Muslims we accept this." To me, Sura 2:62 left no room for ambiguity: one did not have to be Muslim to reach heaven. Righteous Jews and Christians would also have their reward with the Lord.

This reminded me of a conversation I had with my dad while I was considering Mike's argument for Christianity. My dad said that the idea that believing in Jesus' divinity was necessary for salvation was wrong, and added, "I'll *prove* it to you." He said that if you were in "heaven," but knew that many other people—even your friends and family—were being eternally tormented just because they called God the wrong name, that wouldn't really be heaven. How could you be happy in a place like that? In contrast to Mike's fundamentalist Christianity, verse 2:62 of the Qur'an offered a strikingly nonexclusivist view of salvation.

Even before 9/11, I knew that a lot of non-Muslims feared Islam because of so-called "Islamic terrorism." But as I read more, I decided that terrorism was separable from the religion itself. I was convinced of this by people like Nu'Man, the average Muslim on the street who could testify to the impact that the faith had on him. I was also convinced by some of the Western scholarship I came across. John Esposito's *The Islamic Threat: Myth or Reality?* discussed at length terrorism and Islam. Firmly rejecting what he dubbed "the temptation . . . to view Islam through the prism of religious extremism and terrorism," Esposito elegantly summarized a conclusion I was rapidly reaching: "The demonization of a great religious tradition due to the perverted actions of a minority of dissident and distorted voices remains the real threat."

There was also Huston Smith, the eloquent scholar of comparative religion. In *The World's Religions*, Smith addressed four crucial areas of Islam's social teachings. In each area, Smith either defended Islam against the charges leveled against it or else found it superior to the West. He concluded that Islamic economics wasn't incompatible with capitalism, but that "[t]he equalizing provisos of the Koran would, if duly applied, offset" capitalism's excesses. Smith defended Islam against the charge of degrading women. Of Islam and race relations, Smith wrote, "Islam stresses racial equality and 'has achieved a remarkable degree of interracial coexistence.'" Here, Smith explained that Malcolm X discovered in his 1964 pilgrimage to Mecca "that racism had no precedent in Islam and could not be accommodated to it." Finally, Smith defended Islam against the common Western stereotype of being a warrior religion. While he admitted that the Qur'an "does not counsel turning the other cheek, or pacifism," Smith wrote that the Qur'an only countenanced warfare that was defensive or else intended "to right a wrong."

My studies convinced me that the true Islam was moderate. There were undoubtedly some Muslim extremists, but Christianity had its own dark periods, and one couldn't impute the actions of a few extremists to the entire body of believers. The faith felt not only comfortable, but thanks to my childhood in a hippie town and the religious views of my "Jewnitarian" parents, also *familiar*.

The respect for other religions was familiar. The conception of Jesus was familiar. Islam's position on warfare, as explained by Huston Smith and others, was sensible. And Muslims were encouraged to search for greater social and economic justice. Islam's success in eliminating racism in its adherents was one proof of the faith in action. The religion had so many deep insights relevant to modern life.

As the summer came to end, I no longer wondered if I would become a Muslim. Rather, it seemed only to be a question of when.

two

CAMPUS RADICAL

Al-Husein gave me a ride to the Piedmont Triad International Airport in Greensboro and waited with me for my flight. We played a few games of pinball in the airport's game room before saying our good-byes. It was fitting that al-Husein was the last friend I would see before I left the country, since the new ideas and concepts to which he had introduced me would profoundly influence the course of my time in Europe.

It was fall of 1997, and I was heading to study abroad in Venice, a city of canals where I would find a bridge to a new life.

En route to Italy, I saw a Saudi Arabian businessman making *salat* in the Chicago O'Hare Airport. When he finished his prayers, I showed him the books I had been reading about Islam. We conversed for as long as his broken English could carry him. I felt a real warmth from him.

While in the Chicago airport, I called my home in Oregon. My mom picked up. After a minute of small talk, I got to the point. "Mom," I said, "I wanted to tell you that I'm seriously considering Islam as a way of life."

There was no pause, no hesitation on her part. "If that's where you feel God is leading you, you should follow your convictions," she said. I had been worried, since my parents were Jewish, that they might disapprove of the direction I was heading in spiritually. But she sounded positively enthused by the idea of my embracing this new religion.

When I finally landed in Venice, I was excited and overwhelmed to be an ocean away from the United States. I found a water taxi that bobbed along the waves, cutting a furrow in water toward the heart of Venice. I couldn't believe I was actually here.

We moved past lazily swaying boats tied to the tall wooden poles by the sides of the canals, past stone walkways, bridges, and buildings that looked like they had been ripped straight from a postcard. I finally got off in the Dorsoduro district and lugged my heavy bags past throngs of sweaty tourists and hungry pigeons. Eventually I arrived at Casa Artom, Wake Forest's palatial house on the Grand Canal.

I knew that my semester abroad would be a time of change, a time to learn about myself and the world from a vantage point I had never before enjoyed. But the coming changes would eventually take me places that I couldn't then imagine.

Within a couple of weeks of arriving in Venice, I e-mailed a Muslim group that al-Husein had told me about. Known as the Naqshbandis, they were a Sufi order that considered it vital to adhere to Prophet Muhammad's example. One of their distinguishing characteristics was that the men wore the garb of the Prophet, including flowing turbans. The group was located in the coastal city of Rimini, just a few hours away by train.

Jamaluddin Ballabio, who maintained the Naqshbandis' Italian Web page, invited me to come out and join them for a Thursday night *dhikr*. Although I had never heard of *dhikr*, I accepted the invitation. We had four-day school weeks that semester, and as soon as Thursday classes ended, I headed to the train station.

When I met Jamaluddin at his shop, a clothing retail store called Body & Soul, I found that he was a scholarly-looking Italian man who seemed to be in his late thirties or early forties. He wore spectacles and had a big, bushy beard. He told me the story of his conversion to Islam. He converted in India. He had been a Buddhist at the time, and was flying to India to see his lama, when he met a Muslim on the flight who held strong yet simple beliefs. Meeting that man caused Jamaluddin to embrace Islam before he returned home.

On hearing Jamaluddin's story, I had no doubt about how the past several months had illuminated a new spiritual path for me. I immediately asked, "How do I become Muslim?"

Jamaluddin said that I would need to repeat the phrase: *Ash shadu an laa ilaha illa Allah, wa ash shadu anna Muhammadar Rasulallah.* This Arabic phrase, known as the *shahadah,* or declaration of faith, means: I bear witness that there is no object of worship except Allah, and I bear witness that Muhammad is the Messenger of Allah. Jamaluddin said that the phrase had to be repeated in public, before two witnesses.

"I'd like to do that," I said. "Here. Today."

If Jamaluddin was surprised, he didn't let it show. "We will do it tonight, then."

I had read the Qur'an when I was in North Carolina but didn't have a copy at that moment. I told Jamaluddin that one of my concerns was finding a good English-language translation. He said that, unfortunately, they're hard to find in Italy.

After Jamaluddin closed the store, we drove to his apartment. Once there, he donned a green turban. Soon, some other Naqshbandi men, mainly Caucasian converts, arrived. Most of them sported bushy beards and turbans. Some wore Arabic-style robes.

Near the beginning of my semester in Venice, my Italian was lacking. The discussion was hard to follow. I wanted to understand all that was going on, wanted to be able to add to the conversation without someone translating for me. But the speech was too rapid. I felt like a stupid American, in a country where I couldn't speak the language proficiently, about to perform prayers for which I didn't even know the words. Then, Jamaluddin said in English that before we began dhikr, I would be converted to Islam.

Ash shadu an laa ilaha illa Allah, wa ash shadu anna Muhammadar Rasulallah.

I repeated each word after him while holding out my right pointer finger to signify the Oneness of God. Everybody in the room voiced each Arabic word as I did. There was a moment of silence, then one of the Naqshbandis handed me a beautiful white kufi. The kufi is an Islamic skullcap that, similar to the Jewish yarmulke, signifies that one is a believer. Over the course of the semester, I would come to see the kufi as an important symbol of my faith, a visual reminder of who I am and who I should not be.

We made *salat*, and I was better able to follow along now than I had been in Winston-Salem. After *salat* I found out what *dhikr* was. Jamaluddin dimmed the lights and we repeated verses from the Qur'an in a melodic chant. At first I wasn't confident enough to participate, but after a few minutes my voice joined the chorus. Jamaluddin would subtly alter the pace of the words and everybody followed his lead. We all contributed to this unique form of music in our own way, some of the men humming in the background while others chanted in Arabic.

Eventually we finished. The lights came back on. We hugged and talked about how beautiful the *dhikr* was. I learned then that *dhikr* is Arabic for remembrance of Allah. When performed out loud, as we did, it is known as "loud *dhikr.*" It can also be performed silently. One of the Muslims explained that *dhikr* is mentioned over a hundred times in the Qur'an. He said, "Through *dhikr* you can earn Allah's pleasure and stay away from the sins that come when He slips from your mind."

The next day, Jamaluddin and I drove to the countryside for *juma* prayers, the traditional Friday prayers. The services were held in the home of Abdu Salam Attar, a merchant of aromatherapy and perfumes. Before prayers, he splashed a small amount of musk perfume on all the worshippers' arms. Although I strained to understand the Italian-language sermon, I was content to be around so many other people who loved God as I did.

When we stood around talking after prayers, Abdu Salam asked if I had a Qur'an. When I said that I didn't, he walked to a bookcase and reached up to the top shelf. He pulled out an English-language translation of the Qur'an, a green hardbound volume inlaid with gold calligraphy. Abdu Salam kissed it and handed it to me.

"*Quanta costa?*" I asked, but he refused payment, explaining that this was part of Muslim hospitality. "*Grazie,*" I said. "*Grazie mille!*" I was genuinely thankful.

Later, when it was time to return to Venice, I asked Jamaluddin where I could buy a bus ticket to get back to the train station. He immediately handed me a ticket. I reached into my change purse and pulled out fifty thousand lire (about thirty dollars). It wasn't extravagant, but was enough to show my appreciation for his hospitality. But he, too, refused payment.

"Thank you so much," I said. "Thank you for treating me so well here."

"It is hospitality that all Muslims show," he replied. "It is what Allah wills."

I ruminated on the treatment I had received from people who barely knew me. "That's very profound," I said. We hugged and I left. I wore the kufi that they had given me all the way back to Venice.

Al-Husein was the first person I told of my conversion. I told him by e-mail and he phoned the next day to tell me how happy this made him.

For the rest of the semester, I proudly wore my kufi whenever I set foot outside Casa Artom. Other students would often find me in Casa Artom's main hallway, praying or making silent *dhikr* with my wooden prayer beads. Nobody harassed me about this.

I later received a short e-mail from al-Husein saying that he would spend winter break with me in Oregon. As was al-Husein's custom, he didn't ask. His e-mail simply informed me that he would spend most of December with me.

One evening, shortly after my conversion to Islam, I stood on Casa Artom's wood deck overlooking Venice's Grand Canal. Another student in Wake Forest's study-abroad program, Joy Vermillion, was also watching the gondolas make their way through the choppy waters.

Joy was a native North Carolinian, politically interested, with a beautiful singing voice and a distinctive laugh. She was a practicing Christian, and my conversion caught her interest. At the time, I was sensitive about people challenging my religious beliefs—but Joy's questions came off as honest inquiries rather than thinly veiled arguments.

In the course of our conversation, she asked, "Would you ever consider leaving Islam for another faith?"

She seemed curious rather than probing, but my answer was firm nonetheless. "No, I wouldn't. I don't think there's a *reason* that I would leave Islam, because I can find everything I need in this faith. I can have a mystical relationship with God. And if I'm looking for greater literalism, I can find that, too. There are plenty of directions that I can grow within Islam."

Later, when I became radicalized, I would think back to this conversation. I would feel that it epitomized all that I had wrong about my understanding of religion.

My parents loved al-Husein from the moment he arrived in Oregon, in mid-December. At his urging, my dad called him "Big Al." All four of us—me, al-Husein, and my parents—spent long hours around the kitchen table, talking about religion and politics while sipping yerba maté tea. We found little to disagree about. I wasn't the only one to notice the similarity between the beliefs I was raised with and al-Husein's brand of Sufism: al-Husein and my parents were struck by it as well.

I had come to appreciate Ashland more as I grew older. Part of the reason was that it seemed I could find anything I wanted there. Al-Husein's visit demonstrated that. Until he came to town, I didn't know that Ashland had a Muslim community. It was a town of only about fifteen thousand people, and was predominantly white. But one afternoon al-Husein and I were reading through the religion section of the local newspaper, and found a listing for the Qur'an Foundation, a local Islamic group.

We saw that they hosted juma prayers, and immediately vowed to attend. The services were in a house near the outskirts of town, past the municipal golf course. When we arrived, we found a small ranch house in the center of a sprawling lot. A metal trailer stood behind the house, along with a couple of cranes bearing the name of a local business, the Arborist. I spotted a couple of horses in a nearby field.

The property and the Arborist business belonged to Pete Seda, a short, wiry Iranian man who was about forty years old. He had black hair and a beard, and the look of a mischievous grade-schooler. I later learned that his dark skin often made locals mistake him for a Mexican.

All in all, Pete didn't make much of an impression on me during this visit. It was the last time that he would fail to make an impression.

I rang the doorbell. No one answered. Instead, a woman with a thick Persian accent shouted to us from behind the closed door. We couldn't tell what she was saying. "We're here for prayers!" al-Husein shouted back.

She told us to enter from the back. I was somewhat confused, but al-Husein—who had more experience with different Islamic practices—had a clue.

At the back of the house, we found a screen door that led to a cramped prayer room. White sheets that hung from the ceiling blocked our view of the other rooms. "The sheets separate the men and women," al-Husein whispered.

We were among the first to arrive. As other worshippers trickled in, I saw that there were a lot of Caucasian converts. This was clearly not the same as the mosque I had attended in one of Winston-Salem's black neighborhoods. As more Muslims came in, I took note of the lumberjack-style flannel, the work boots, the discussions of horseback riding and shooting. I thought of them as Muslim rednecks. Aside from bushy Islamic beards and the occasional kufi, these guys looked like hicks. I would later learn that most of them were outdoorsmen whose cultural context and theology made them unique: half redneck, half hippie, and one hundred percent Islamic fundamentalist.

Shortly before prayers, a hefty man named Abdullah showed up. He looked like a blind version of Willie Nelson, but far stockier. Abdullah used to be a truck driver, and his tattooed arms were testament to a well-lived past. He circled the room, bear-hugging his friends. Some of them he lifted into the air with his powerful arms.

You think you've seen everything, then Ashland throws you a curveball.

Aside from meeting my first Muslim rednecks, I also heard my first radical sermon that day. Hassan Zabady, a Saudi sheikh who lived in northern California, delivered the sermon to an audience of about twenty men (I never learned how many women had gathered in another part of the house). Sheikh Hassan was thin and slightly effeminate, with pale skin and a full beard. He spoke into a microphone. The microphone wouldn't have been necessary in the cramped room but for the congregation's strict sex segregation. A speaker in another room allowed the women to hear the sermon.

Sheikh Hassan spoke about the duty of *hijra*, or emigration. Historically, the *hijra* was when Prophet Muhammad and his followers migrated to Medina after facing severe persecution at the hands of Mecca's Quraysh tribe. Although the Islamic calendar begins with Muhammad's *hijra*, I had never given thought to the duty of emigration in modern times. I had assumed that because the *hijra* occurred fourteen hundred years ago, the Qur'anic verses mentioning it no longer applied to the lives of Muslims.

Sheikh Hassan's sermon argued otherwise. He said that Muslims now living in non-Muslim lands were required to move to Islamic countries because non-Islamic society is so inherently corrupt that it will destroy a believer's devotion to Islam. His style of argument was far different from what I had grown used to in my college classes. He didn't refute possible counterarguments. He didn't even acknowledge that another side existed.

Sheikh Hassan also didn't try to prove that the duty of *hijra* was a good idea from a secular perspective. Instead, he said only that it was a religious obligation. He read the relevant Qur'anic verses, referenced the *ahadith* (a *hadith* is one of Muhammad's sayings or traditions, distinct from the Qur'an; *ahadith* is the plural form of *hadith*), and that was it.

"The Holy Qur'an says, 'Verily, those who believed, and emigrated and strove hard and fought with their property and their lives in the Cause of Allah as well as those who gave asylum and help—these are

allies to one another. And as to those who believed but did not emigrate, you owe no duty of protection to them until they emigrate.' So as
Muslims we too must emigrate. We are living in a land ruled by the *kufar*
[infidels]. This is not the way of Muhammad," he said.

"Prophet Muhammad, *alayhi salaatu was salaam* [upon him be prayers
and peace], described the risks of living among the *kufar*. Our beloved
prophet said, 'Anybody who meets, gathers together, lives, and stays with
a *Mushrik*—a polytheist or disbeliever in the Oneness of Allah—and
agrees to his ways and opinions, and enjoys living with him, then he is
like the *Mushrik*.' So when you live among the *kufar*, and act like the
kufar, and like to live with the *kufar*, then brothers, you may become just
like the *kufar*. If you do not take the duty of *hijra* seriously, your faith is in
danger."

Sheikh Hassan used a tone of severe reprimand. He was so disdainful
of non-Muslims and the West that I wondered why he had moved here.

But I was also concerned. Since it was the first radical sermon I had
heard, I wasn't sure how to react. Worse, I wondered if he was right. I
hadn't before given any thought to whether there was a continuing duty
of *hijra*. What if there was?

I found myself glancing over at al-Husein through much of the sermon. I shot him quizzical looks, as though to ask *Should I take this stuff
seriously?* Al-Husein answered with a knowing, reassuring, smile: *Don't
let it bother you. There's nothing to this.*

Sheikh Hassan finished speaking and the congregation prayed. When
we were done, there was a question-and-answer session with the sheikh.

The first person to ask a question was a large red-haired man named
Charlie Jones. Charlie had both a muscular frame and a sizable gut. His
eyes were pale blue. Although he was starting to go bald, he had a large
beard, the hallmark of a serious Muslim. Charlie's speaking style reminded me of Eeyore, the perpetually depressed donkey who was friends

with Winnie the Pooh. He leaned forward with his head slightly bowed, speaking earnestly and with great sadness.

Charlie spoke into the microphone so that the women in the other part of the house could hear his question. There was no microphone for the women. If they had questions, they would have to write them down on a sheet of paper for Pete's son Yusuf, who was then around ten years old, to bring to the main prayer room. Today, they did not ask questions.

"I think if we go to the Muslim world, we need to go ashore ready to fight." Charlie nodded his head when he said this and his eyes widened. "Those governments don't practice true Islam. They go from house to house and take their citizens' guns away. Muhammad, peace be upon him, never took away the *Ummah*'s weapons." (The *Ummah* is the worldwide community of Muslims.)

A Muslim whose main concern about the corrupt Middle Eastern dictatorships was the lack of Second Amendment rights? I suppressed a chuckle, still amused at stumbling upon a congregation of Muslim rednecks.

Sheikh Hassan spoke softly in his response and looked away from Charlie. He said that while Middle Eastern governments weren't practicing true Islam, it was still better to live in the Middle East with other Muslims than to live in this *kafir* (infidel) society.

Just as Sheikh Hassan's style of argument was strange to me, so was the way that he answered questions. His answers were short, and came across as rebukes more than explanations. His message was: I am practicing true Islam, and you should be ashamed of your doubts.

As a new Muslim, his approach intimidated me. When I first converted to Islam, al-Husein had told me, "No other Muslim will accuse you of not being a Muslim." His point was that this faith is different from Christianity. We were both struck by how often Christians would accuse others who professed the same beliefs—like the Mormons or Jehovah's

Witnesses—of not being true Christians. The thought that other Muslims would accept me as a brother in faith even if we disagreed on some theological points was comforting.

But I didn't get that impression from Sheikh Hassan. He thought that his way was right and all those who disagreed were deviants, or worse.

Al-Husein didn't share my sense of intimidation. He took the microphone after Charlie and spoke into it with a slow, gravelly voice. "To me, the Muslims in the Middle East are bigger *kufar* than those in the U.S.," he said. "When I look at the Middle East, I see people who aren't practicing Islam even though they live in the Muslim world. I see people pushing for a version of *sharia* law that puts women in an inferior position. I see people who want to destroy personal freedoms. That is in itself a distortion of true Islam."

Sheikh Hassan turned to Dawood Rodgers, a beefy man who trained horses for a living, and asked him to explain. Dawood picked up the microphone, turned to al-Husein, and said, "Brother, I used to believe the way you did. I used to think that Middle Eastern Muslims had it all wrong, and that they were missing out on the true, progressive Islam." His voice oozed with sarcasm when he said the words *progressive Islam*. "But, brother, when I learned more about the faith I realized—"

Sheikh Hassan cut him off. He didn't want Dawood to explain why al-Husein was wrong. All he wanted was a simpler explanation of al-Husein's statement. Sheikh Hassan apparently didn't understand what al-Husein had said.

When the statement sank in, it kicked off an extended theological debate between Sheikh Hassan and al-Husein. The room was packed when they started, but the worshippers trickled out as the debate progressed until only a handful remained.

I found the debate mesmerizing. It was reassuring to see how comfortable al-Husein appeared to be while debating Sheikh Hassan. I was reminded of something else that al-Husein had told me about Islam:

qualifications were not as important as a person's ideas. Even a child could be right about a theological point, while an imam could be wrong. I noticed that Sheikh Hassan never actually answered al-Husein's arguments. Instead, he was satisfied with his assumption that he had found the true Islam, and that everybody who disagreed was delusional. His lack of respect for al-Husein's arguments was typified by an exchange where al-Husein brought up the Moroccan author Fatema Mernissi, who has cast doubt on the authenticity of certain *ahadith* that place women in a subordinate position. When al-Husein mentioned Mernissi, Sheikh Hassan said, "There are good, sound scholars who answer her arguments. You should read them so you can understand the problems with her."

I was struck by that reply: there are answers to her argument and you need to find them. If Sheikh Hassan couldn't articulate those answers, how did he know that Mernissi was wrong?

Sheikh Hassan ended up leaving before al-Husein and I did. Out of politeness, we walked him to the door. As he stepped outside, Sheikh Hassan waved his hand at the valley. The green peaks surrounding us had always epitomized peace and beauty to me, but to Sheikh Hassan they were an object of scorn. Trying to put in a final word, he said, "You'll be compromised if you stay in this *kafir* country. Just look at all these homosexuals."

It would not be the last time I met Sheikh Hassan, but the shock of these parting words never left me.

Despite Sheikh Hassan's hateful views and scornful tone, the debate was fairly civil. There was no yelling. Sheikh Hassan addressed al-Husein in his soft voice throughout, always looking away from us while he spoke.

And while Ashland's Muslims—or at least, those who seemed to comprise the Muslim community's inner circle—apparently agreed with

Sheikh Hassan, Dawood sat on the floor with us after the sheikh left. We drank heavily spiced mint tea together.

I told Dawood that I was having trouble perfecting my *salat*. The Islamic ritual prayers are difficult to master because they consist of a series of physical positions—standing, bowing, kneeling, prostrating—as well as prayers in Arabic. When I mentioned this, Dawood gave me a small saddle-stapled booklet detailing how to pray. It included illustrations showing the positions that the worshipper should take, along with transliterations of the Arabic prayers.

In the end, the exchange between al-Husein and Sheikh Hassan reinforced my view that the moderate interpretation of Islam had more intellectual force. If a learned sheikh couldn't answer the arguments of a college student, what hope did the radicals have?

Later in al-Husein's visit to the West Coast, we drove up to the state of Washington to visit some of my old friends. This was the only time that al-Husein and Mike Hollister would meet face-to-face.

Their meeting was less eventful than I thought it might be. There was some religious debate but no fireworks, no arguments that were clean kills for either side. I still liked Mike, but more than ever it seemed that the strong connection we once had was fizzling. I feared it would eventually be lost.

Al-Husein and I also visited another friend of mine from high school, a woman named Tami Garrard who lived in Port Angeles, Washington. While in Port Angeles, we went camping near a beach with Tami and some of her friends.

At one point during the camping trip, al-Husein and I were angry at each other. The passage of time makes me forget the reason for our fight, nor is it particularly important. Two people with personalities as strong as al-Husein's and mine are bound to clash from time to time. I was struck, though, by what happened after we fought.

We walked down the sandy beach for a few minutes. Eventually we found a piece of driftwood large enough for both of us to sit on. Al-Husein wordlessly pulled out his prayer beads, then started chanting Allah's name. Recognizing the same kind of loud *dhikr* that I had taken part in the night I became Muslim, I instantly joined. We chanted for more than twenty minutes, with al-Husein taking the lead in setting the words and pace. By the time we finished, I didn't feel any more anger toward al-Husein; all I felt was joy at the presence of the Almighty.

Al-Husein slowly got up from the driftwood. "Do you know what you learned today?" he asked.

"What?"

The fact that I was an only child gave special significance to al-Husein's next words. "You learned how to be a brother."

When I returned to Wake Forest in January 1998, I did so as a full-fledged campus activist. I realize now that, by taking me outside of myself, the beginnings of my activism had propelled me toward Islam. And on my return to campus, my Islamic faith drove my activism.

Al-Husein and I used the term *jihad* to describe our political activities. To us, this was the "greater jihad." The concept of a greater jihad came from a *hadith* in which Muhammad, on his return from a battle, said, "We are finished with the lesser jihad; now we are starting the greater jihad." The implication was clear: military fighting is less important than the battle against the evils within oneself. Later, when I became radicalized, I would scoff at the idea that a greater jihad even existed.

But at Wake Forest, al-Husein and I saw our activism as the greater jihad. It always amused us when another student took our use of the word *jihad* in the wrong way, thinking it meant terrorism or holy war. We would explain—patiently and somewhat condescendingly—that jihad was Arabic for "struggle," and we were engaged in a struggle for social justice.

My biggest idea for creating social change was coalition-building between Wake Forest's various minority student groups—groups like the Black Student Alliance, ASIA, the Gay-Straight Student Alliance, and the Islam Awareness Organization. (Knox's group, VOICE, turned out to be stillborn.) I thought these groups' common bond of being minorities at Wake Forest was enough for them to work together and become the most powerful political bloc on campus.

Although this coalition represented a patchwork of agendas, I tried to make sure that my activism was consistent with my faith. The area where this was most difficult was the work we did on behalf of gay students. Even as a progressive Sufi, I knew that Islam didn't exactly endorse homosexuality. So whenever someone questioned me about it, I'd appeal to a higher principle: "Regardless of whether I believe that homosexuality is a sin, gay students are entitled to human rights." If pressed, I'd admit that Islam held that homosexuality was wrong—but that didn't change the need to combat discrimination.

Al-Husein had a different take. I once heard him tell a woman student that homosexuality wasn't *haram* (forbidden) in Islam, but that the faith regarded it as something to be avoided. He explained that homosexuality should be avoided not because it's morally wrong, but because society is prejudiced against gays. People should avoid homosexuality so as not to subject themselves to such a stigma, al-Husein said.

I thought he was trying too hard to appeal to his audience. "Come on, al-Husein," I said, "doesn't your faith have a stronger position on homosexuality than that?"

To my surprise, something was stirring in me. A desire for a stronger version of Islam, a kind of theological clarity at odds with my liberal principles.

Shortly after returning to Wake Forest in January 1998, I met Amy.

I was helping to coach the debate team. On the way to the first tournament of the year, in Carrollton, Georgia, one of the new Wake Forest debaters caught my eye. Her full name was Amy Powell, a second-semester freshman. Amy had a rare beauty that was matched by a powerful intellect. She stood five feet four with blue eyes and long, light brown hair that fell halfway down her back. She wore a long-sleeved flannel shirt over her T-shirt, along with blue jeans and a black beret.

To get Amy's attention, I winked at her. She smiled in response, a smile that radiated warmth. We had a long talk on the van ride down to Carrollton, and over the next couple of days I asked some of the Wake Forest debaters about her: *Amy seems cool. What's she like? Is she dating anybody?* Happily, I learned that she was single—and seemed interested.

When the tournament ended, I made sure that Amy and I were put in the same van for the ride back to Winston-Salem. We sat next to each other in the backseat. Our conversation was halting, but the eye contact said everything. When I looked straight into her eyes, she gazed back unblinking and unhesitating. Eventually we stopped trying to talk. Our lips met in a long kiss that communicated far more than talking ever could.

Amy and I began dating shortly after our first kiss. She quickly became a constant presence in my life.

We learned that both of our names meant "beloved," and soon that was what Amy and I called each other: Beloved.

Amy was three years younger than I was, born in 1979. She grew up in eastern North Carolina, in a town that was about the size of Ashland called Elizabeth City. It was a rural town with an expansive waterfront, a short drive from the Outer Banks. Although Amy was raised Presbyterian, her parents weren't big churchgoers, and she was never baptized. Religion wasn't very important to her when we started dating; the fact that I was Muslim didn't faze her.

At the time, Amy didn't know what she wanted to do with her life. Both of her parents were doctors, and she thought about medical school. She also toyed with ideas like becoming a veterinarian, lawyer, professor, or journalist.

The aspect of Amy's personality that stood out most at the time was that she was incredibly low-key. This would take on increasing significance in the future.

Almost every night Amy would make the trek to my dorm on the north end of campus. There was much to share. I made Amy learn to love *The Simpsons*, and in return she tried to teach me calculus. She would stay up until all hours with me and al-Husein, listening to our ruminations.

Amy and I had dinner together almost every night, usually macaroni and cheese or some other simple dish that college kids often make. Sometimes we'd watch TV or a movie. Often we'd just do schoolwork. But even if that's all we did, I loved having her around—being able to chat with Amy, to lean over and kiss her. Soon it was hard to remember what things had been like before we were together.

Al-Husein and I went to Turkey over spring break in March 1998. He was still teaching me new things. This time around, I learned that I could get Wake Forest to fully fund a dream trip to the Islamic world. We received a grant to study Islamic Sufism in Istanbul. (During my semester abroad in Venice I traveled to North Africa on my own, but Wake Forest did not foot the bill.)

One night, we had just returned to our low-end hotel after prayers in an ornate mosque down the road and I was sitting on the hard, lumpy bed, writing in my journal. Although she was half a world away, I found myself thinking of Amy. I mentioned this to al-Husein.

He remained silent for a moment, then said in a soft voice, "Let me ask you something. Is she a comfort to you?"

"Is she a *comfort* to me?"

"Yes. Is she a comfort to you?" Al-Husein paused, realizing that his question wasn't sinking in. In an atypical effort to be understood, he said, "In a *hadith*, Prophet Muhammad said that wives should be a comfort to their husbands."

I thought for a short time. "Yes," I finally said. "Yes, I think she *is* a comfort to me."

Because of my religion, my passion for social justice, and my college debate background, the topic of my honors thesis came naturally. I wrote about the rhetorical differences between Louis Farrakhan's Nation of Islam and more traditional Muslim groups in appealing to the African-American community.

The mosque I attended in Winston-Salem was part of the Islamic ministry of W. D. Muhammad. W. D. Muhammad, the son of longtime Nation of Islam leader Elijah Muhammad, had led his followers from the Nation of Islam's old black-nationalist teachings toward traditional Islamic practice. As I researched for the thesis, I found my respect for him growing.

The Nation of Islam was founded by W. D. Fard (after whom W. D. Muhammad was named), a carpet salesman who lived in Detroit. Although W. D. Fard's teachings were steeped in Islamic themes, much of what he taught was actually deeply anti-Islamic, merely designed to appeal to what he thought blacks wanted to hear. The most well known of these teachings was that the black race was the world's original race, and that whites were a race of devils created by an evil scientist. But far more deviant from an Islamic viewpoint, Fard taught that he was God. This was contrary to the faith's strict monotheism.

Elijah Muhammad was Fard's star pupil. On leaving Detroit in 1934 for parts unknown, Fard left him in charge of the fledgling religious group. Under Elijah Muhammad's leadership, and with the help of national spokesman Malcolm X, the Nation of Islam grew into a powerful organization. At its height, it had eighty-seven temples scattered across the country. When Elijah Muhammad died in 1975, W. D. Muhammad inherited the leadership—even though many members thought that Louis Farrakhan would claim the top post.

W. D. Muhammad proved to be a religious man who was committed to true Islam. When he took the Nation of Islam's reins, he transformed it. He first initiated smaller reforms designed to bring the group's practices in line with those of the worldwide Muslim community, such as prayer five times a day and fasting during the lunar month of Ramadan rather than December. Eventually he also abandoned the group's racist teachings and its elevation of W. D. Fard. These changes angered Farrakhan and prompted him to create a splinter group, also called the Nation of Islam, devoted to the old black-nationalist theology.

Eventually W. D. Muhammad abandoned his group's organizational concept entirely. He told his followers to give up any labels that set them apart from the worldwide community of believers, and to think of themselves simply as Muslims. I was impressed that a man who could have gained so much power by fostering the Nation of Islam's old teachings voluntarily moved the group in a different direction. In doing so, W. D. Muhammad seemed motivated solely by his devotion to God.

I would later work with other Muslims who had a very different view of W. D. Muhammad. Despite his sacrifices, I would learn that he was viewed as a heretic, and even worse, in some circles. But at the time I wrote my honors thesis, I had no idea how hatred could spring from seemingly small doctrinal differences. And at the time, I had no idea that I would eventually come to see these small doctrinal differences as momentous.

Amy and I often hung out in al-Husein's dorm room. Amy intuitively recognized how important al-Husein was to me. She hadn't known me before I became Muslim, back when I felt isolated from the world. But she could tell that al-Husein was both a brother and a mentor to me.

Amy was quiet in general, and this was even more pronounced when we were around al-Husein. And who could blame her? Al-Husein and I would bandy about concepts related to a religion that was alien to her, and were enraptured by our own revolutionary political ideals. Amy was still a work in progress. As was once the case for me, she was still finding her own way politically, spiritually, and socially. I didn't push my political ideas on her, but always conveyed how important they were to me. One night I got an e-mail from Amy describing her political awakening. She wrote that she hadn't thought much about issues like discrimination and inequality before, but was coming to see their importance. Her e-mail said that she didn't want to have her head in the sand. I was so heartened after getting the e-mail that I called al-Husein and read it to him aloud.

Sometimes al-Husein could push a bit too far with Amy. She had a T-shirt that said, "Drink your coffee. There are people in India sleeping." Al-Husein did not see the humor in the shirt. "There are people doing a lot more than sleeping in India," he said. "There are people without houses, people living in abject poverty, people without food or running water."

Al-Husein didn't get the joke. It was a play on the line that American parents are known to say to their kids: "Eat your peas. There are people in Africa starving."

Despite that, it would be a long time before Amy wore that shirt again.

Mike Hollister's wedding was an intimate affair. I returned to Bellingham at the beginning of the summer of 1998 to be one of his groomsmen. Mike was marrying Amy Childers, whom I had met during my last visit. I still had a bad taste in my mouth from our first encounter. It seemed that all she could think about upon meeting me was that I wasn't Christian.

But when I touched down at Bellingham's airport, I found that she at least had a sense of humor. Amy and one of her bridesmaids waited in the airport with a fake limo driver's sign that said Daveed. It was a funny touch for an airport with only one gate.

I was Mike's only non-Christian groomsman, and the others let me know it. During my last visit to Bellingham, I had been interested in meeting and talking with Mike's Christian friends. I found the experience more grating now. Last time around, I was spiritually confused. This time, I had found my path. I was Muslim, and resented the fact that Mike's friends didn't appreciate that I was also a man of faith. Instead, they seemed intent on proving that their religion was better than mine.

I had a handful of religious debates with Mike's other groomsmen. The one that stood out most was with Tim Prussic, a somewhat pudgy man with sandy blond hair and a sharp wit. Tim was studying to go to seminary, and I would catch him thumbing through flash cards during spare moments, trying to learn biblical (koine) Greek.

In explaining my conversion to Islam to Tim, I touched on the "liar, lunatic, or Lord" argument with which I had once grappled: "Christianity never really appealed to me because I couldn't accept the idea that a man could be God."

"We don't really believe that a man became God, though," Tim replied. "It isn't a question of whether a man can turn into God. What you're saying is that you don't think God is able to turn himself into a man."

I didn't appreciate the interruption. I felt that I was trying to explain my deeply held beliefs to Tim, and he was just trying to score a debating point. I see our discussion differently today. Now I realize that Tim had touched on an area of genuine confusion on my part. He had taken my view of Jesus' divinity—that there was no way a man could become God—and turned it on its head.

But at the time, I was annoyed by Tim's obstinacy.

At the wedding, it was obvious how happy Mike and Amy made each other. And I found that I now enjoyed Amy much more than when I first met her. At the reception after the ceremony, I caught a few moments alone with Mike and Amy. Amy Hollister asked, "Will we be seeing you in another wedding that includes an Amy in the near future?"

I smiled. "Perhaps," I said.

I had been dating Amy Powell only since January, and had given no thought to marriage. But you never know how these things will turn out.

After being surrounded by fundamentalist Christians at Mike's wedding, I looked forward to being among Muslims again. On my first Friday back in Ashland, I went to *juma* prayers with the local congregation. Because al-Husein's debate with Sheikh Hassan had been so cordial, I felt no qualms about going back to worship there. The book that Dawood had given me on *salat* had helped, and I looked forward to showing Ashland's Muslims the progress I had made on my congregational prayers.

When I called ahead to verify the time and place of prayers, I was told that the services had moved to 3800 Highway 99 South, near the freeway exit at the south end of town.

I whistled as I drove toward the new location, impressed. Every house out there was its own little castle with an estate surrounding it—a row of McMansions. The new prayer building fit this mold. The cramped prayer room in the back of Pete Seda's house was a thing of the past. They had moved to a mansion-sized blue building perched on a hill. Horses, a donkey, and even a dromedary camel roamed the fields in front of it. As my car inched up the paved drive, I got an idea of just how big the property was. They were building a second access road to an area further up the hill, which was covered with blackberry bushes and other shrubs. Two bent palm trees near the fore of this second road brought a bit of the desert to Ashland.

As I got out of my car, I noticed clucking chickens scratching about a henhouse on the hill just past the main building.

When I walked in, the first thing I saw was a beautiful prayer room. It had a thick, blue carpet and its windows looked out on the fields surrounding us. Clearly, the group had more money than ever.

The *khutbah* that day was uneventful compared to my previous visit. I stayed after services were over, speaking with the other worshippers.

Pete Seda walked up to me. Though he didn't make much of an impression when I went to services in his house the previous December, I now wondered why. Pete, like al-Husein, was obviously gifted with extraordinary social skills.

Even though Pete had only met me once before, he greeted me as an old friend. "Bro, it's good to see you again," he said. "How do you like our new building?"

"It's great," I said. "Beautiful."

"Here, bro, let me show you around," Pete said, putting his arm around me. He first led me outside while rattling off the group's future plans one after another, like a veteran auctioneer. Pointing to the palm trees, he said that the group had bought an Arabian tent they were going to erect for a weekly event called "Arabian Nights." Non-Muslims would attend; the local Muslim community would serve them Arabic coffee and teach them about the Islamic faith and culture. Pete saw this as an opportunity for *dawah*, or Islamic evangelism.

Walking past the parking lot and pointing to the fields, Pete explained that the camel was also part of the group's *dawah*. It was named Mandub, "ambassador" in Arabic. And it proved to be a great ambassador, capable of melting the hearts of kids and adults at first sight.

Pete then gave me a tour of the main building. He had a plan for each room, sometimes several contradictory plans. When he showed me the enormous bathroom with its multiple sinks, he explained that he wanted to redesign it with benches and footbaths to make it easier for worshippers to make *wudu* (the pre-prayer ablutions). He wanted to re-carpet and redesign the downstairs area, where the women would pray.

Pete ended the tour in the office, which overlooked the drive leading up from Highway 99. It had a breathtaking view of the surrounding mountains. They were bucolic, with peaks and trees that looked like a bumpy green fur that you could run your fingers through.

It was no coincidence that Pete ended the tour in the office. He was a consummate salesman, and the tour had been one big sales pitch. The finale was explaining how the group managed to afford all of this. He said the congregation had just become affiliated with a Saudi Arabian charity called the Al Haramain Islamic Foundation. Al Haramain had given them a grant to buy the prayer building, which the locals called the Musalla.

At the time, I didn't know how active Al Haramain was in the United States, and didn't know whether it had other offices elsewhere in the country. It turns out that the group's U.S. headquarters was located in my hometown of Ashland, Oregon, and that this was in fact Al Haramain's only office in the United States at the time. (Al Haramain would later open another office in Springfield, Missouri, proudly declaring it the first mosque "in the heart of the Bible Belt.")

Pete had countless ideas for what he could accomplish in partnership with the Al Haramain Islamic Foundation. He was a visionary who had found a group to bankroll his vision. Among his dozen ideas for the future, the one that most captured my imagination was called the Medina Project. It was a plan to build an Islamic village here in the United States. The village would be run by *sharia* to the extent that U.S. law allowed. While they wouldn't have beheadings and amputations, the women would be veiled, pork would be banned, and so would alcohol.

"America is my home," Pete said. "I don't want to go overseas to practice Islam. I want to bring Islam here to America. The U.S. gives us freedoms as Muslims that we *couldn't imagine* in the Middle East. We need to take advantage of those freedoms."

I nodded. The difference between this vision and Sheikh Hassan's was not lost on me.

Pete then concluded his sales pitch. "Bro, with Al Haramain backing us, we're gonna do a lot. We're trying to hire another person for the office, and I think you're perfect." He rummaged around, then handed me a copy of an Islamic publication called *Al-Jumuah* magazine that featured their employment ad. It explained that there was a job opening in the Ashland office, and set the salary at $2,000 a month.

I told Pete that I would graduate from college in December (withdrawing from school when I was sick with Crohn's disease had set me back by a semester). I planned on going to law school in the fall, but was looking for something to do between college and law school.

"Bro, do you have a résumé?" Pete said. "Why don't you drop it off before you leave town?"

Pete brought me some of the trademark spiced mint tea that I tried the first time I encountered Ashland's Muslims. I liked the gesture; it was nice after a debate, or after talking business, to be able to slow the pace down, drink tea together, and turn to more personal matters.

Our brief talk after Pete had made his sales pitch convinced me that he was what we might call a character. He was completely controlled by his passions. Sometimes these passions were for the bizarre and destructive, but I thought at the time that when Pete was seized with passion for the right thing, he could be an amazing force for good. Since I was a newer Muslim, Pete—in his rambling way, changing topics before he could even finish a thought—told me why Islam was such a great religion. He talked about a documentary he'd seen on split-brain patients, those whose right brain and left brain are disconnected. He said that some of these patients found their left hand behaving in un-expected ways, as though it had its own malicious will. This, to him, confirmed the wisdom of Islam's preference for the right hand over the left.

But before Pete could drive home that point, he made an unexpected (but not uncharacteristic) turn to discussion of marriage in Islam. I found one of his remarks so humorous that I later told some friends about it. "The great thing about our religion," he said, "is that if you get tired of your wife, Allah will let you take on a second wife. You don't even have to divorce the first one."

I was amused rather than horrified to speak with such an outspoken fan of polygamous relationships. I didn't then realize how seriously he took this.

A few days later, I brought Pete my résumé.

I had known from the first time I encountered Ashland's Muslims and saw al-Husein debate with Sheikh Hassan that there was a name for

the kind of Islam practiced by the community's leaders: Wahhabism.
The Wahhabis are a Sunni sect founded by Muhammad ibn-Abdul
Wahhab, an eighteenth-century theologian who lived in what is now
Saudi Arabia. Abdul Wahhab was obsessed with returning Islam to the
puritanical norms that he thought were practiced in Prophet Muham-
mad's time. He had a severe and strict interpretation of the faith.

In accord with Abdul Wahhab's teachings, the Wahhabis have an
absolutist vision for Islam that holds that the Qur'an and Prophet
Muhammad's example (the Sunnah) are the only permissible guides for
the laws of a state and the conduct of an individual. They resent Muslims whose norms differ from theirs. They reject all Shias for starters,
and the Sufis are also particularly despised. The Sufis are mystical Muslims who aren't about religious absolutes. They tend to be more free-
form in interpreting the Qur'an, somewhat like Reform Jews' free-form
interpretation of the Bible. Despite the acrimony between the Wahhabis and the Sufis, I decided to apply for a job at Al Haramain because,
even if my views differed somewhat from those of my coworkers, it
seemed like a good opportunity to learn about Islam and to help advance
the faith. I could also live with my parents while in Ashland, saving on
rent and allowing me to spend more time with the people who meant so
much to me before beginning my "adult life."

When I gave Pete my résumé, I also showed him some of the work
I had done as a campus activist. I had produced a document called
"Agenda for Change," which listed our goals (such as making the school
adopt a hate-speech code and changing the core curriculum to require
students to take multicultural courses before graduation), as well as con-
crete steps for attaining the goals. I told Pete that I wanted to produce a
similar document that the local Muslim community could rally
around—except that our goals would be loftier, for instance, the creation of a functioning Islamic village.

At the end of the summer, I returned to Wake Forest to teach at its summer debate institute for high school students. Amy Powell was working there as an instructor, and also served as a resident adviser in one of the campus dorms. I had a somewhat more posh living space. I had the top floor of the Nia House (which, during the school year, was an African-American women's residence) to myself. Amy would usually come to the Nia House at night but return to the dorm before morning.

One night we were up late talking and fell asleep while cuddling. After a few hours Amy stirred. I saw the green glow from my alarm clock: 2:53 a.m. She needed to get back to the dorm. Amy leaned over and gave me a quick, tender kiss on the lips. She hesitated a second. "I love you," she said.

We had been dating about seven months. Although it was the first time either of us said those three words, I didn't hesitate. "I love you too, Amy," I said.

By the alarm's dim glow, I watched her walk out of the room, toward the stairs that would take her outside.

In the fall semester, it was back to the front lines of campus activism. A key question there was how to get people involved. The previous semester, before al-Husein graduated from Wake Forest and moved on to Harvard Divinity School, he and I both latched on to self-perception theory. Developed by Daryl J. Bem, self-perception is a psychological theory that holds that an individual only has about the same level of knowledge of his own behavior that another person could have. People's attitudes are developed by *observing* their behavior and then reasoning backward from it to determine what their attitudes must be. One implication of the theory is that if you can get someone to act in a certain way, eventually his beliefs will fall into line.

Applying this theory to campus activism, al-Husein and I thought that if we could get people involved, even in a minor way, they would start to define themselves as activists. If we got someone to sign a petition, that was a step. If someone showed up at a rally, that was a step. All the better if they'd actually write the petition or speak at the rally. Even in al-Husein's absence, I continued to think about and find new applications for this theory.

The interesting thing is that self-perception theory never crossed my mind when I thought about taking a job with Al Haramain. I knew as early as my first visit, when I heard Sheikh Hassan's sermon about the duty of emigrating to Muslim countries, that the group had a number of radical views with which I disagreed deeply. Yet I thought I could accept a job there, sample the group's beliefs, pick and choose from their positive ideas, and discard the rest.

I never considered that the methods al-Husein and I had gleaned from self-perception theory to try to shape people into campus activists could, in turn, be used to shape me.

Pete Seda e-mailed me that fall to let me know I had been selected for the position at Al Haramain. I was eager to channel my passion for activism into the world beyond the walls of Wake Forest. And now, my first opportunity to do so would come as part of a radical Wahhabi charity that funded al-Qaeda.

three

A FROWN AND AN AK-47

My first official duty as an Al Haramain employee was to speak to a high school class about Islam in December 1998. The presentation would take place at the Musalla, the prayer house near the south end of town.

Amy was visiting Ashland for her Christmas break, and she came to watch. I didn't consider the fact that my coworkers would think that even having a girlfriend was contrary to Islamic law.

Their views on relations between the sexes would become clear soon enough. But during this visit, nothing was said to me about Amy. In fact, Pete treated her with the same kind of suave charm that he used on anyone he found deeply distasteful. He even shook her hand upon meeting her, a theological concession that I didn't comprehend at the time.

Amy and I got to the Musalla half an hour before the high school class arrived. Pete handed me a sheet of paper. I smiled after reading it. The class had two teachers, one of whom I knew. Susan Thorngate stood out in my memories of childhood because of her willingness to put up with the antics of a bright but hyperactive kid. She had taught me both eighth-grade English and drama, but had moved from the middle school to the high school since then.

When Ms. Thorngate and her class showed up, she smiled broadly, doing her best to conceal her surprise at seeing a Jewish former student of hers now standing there wearing a kufi. "Daveed," she said, "*you're working here now?*"

I nodded. When I was at Wake Forest, I wore my kufi constantly, proud to showcase my Muslim identity. In Ashland, surrounded by people who had known me since before I turned five, I was somewhat shyer.

Ms. Thorngate moved forward as though to hug me, then hesitated. "I guess I probably shouldn't give you a hug in a place like this," she said in a low voice. I would have had no moral qualms about it, but she was right. I was just beginning to learn about Al Haramain's rules and restrictions, but already knew that hugging a woman would, to say the least, be frowned upon.

"Susan, I want you to meet my girlfriend, Amy," I said.

She was happy to see Amy. Her happiness was the kind that anybody who knew you when you were young has upon meeting an acquaintance you've made later in life. It was a happiness that comes of the opportunity to tell embarrassing stories.

Fortunately, the first tale she seized on was mild: my eighth-grade habit of wearing the same Guns N' Roses T-shirt to class day after day. She charitably added that I wasn't a slob, and I probably washed the shirt at the end of each day.

Thankfully, before she could start another tale, Pete intervened. Seeing that Ms. Thorngate and I knew each other, he said, "See what happens? You give us a few minutes with your students, and we go and convert them!"

Ms. Thorngate turned to me and said, in a tone that suggested she had given it some thought, "When I think about who you were back in middle school, I realize that you were probably always destined to be a Muslim."

Although I didn't know what she meant, I nodded thoughtfully.

Pete and the others led the class into the prayer room, where they would give the presentation. The other presenters were Dawood and a man I had just met, Dennis Geren. Dennis was another of Ashland's Caucasian converts to Islam. Having become Muslim several months ago, Dennis was a zealous novice. He sported a shaved head and long beard. The tattoo on his muscular arm was testament to another life before Islam. Dennis and the Eeyore-like Charlie Jones would be my office mates for the next nine months, all three of us working under Pete Seda's direction.

As the class entered the prayer room, Pete directed the boys to sit on the right side of the room, with the girls on the left. It seemed silly to make them do this, the kind of thing that could leave the class with a bad taste in their mouths. But I remembered from my last visit that the men generally prayed upstairs at *juma*, with the women downstairs. This group clearly had a very conservative approach to relations between the sexes.

Dawood opened the presentation. "These days, everybody is talking about multiculturalism. In higher education, in politics, in the media, multiculturalism is the new big thing. Well, in that light, you can think of this as . . . a cultural event." I understood the reason for Dawood's pause. He almost described this as a *multi*cultural event—but the students weren't learning about multiple cultures. Beyond that, I wasn't sure if Dawood approved of those other cultures that fell under the multicultural umbrella.

After that introduction, Pete took over. His salesmanship was in full force. At times he was quite funny, and he always came across as perfectly sincere.

Pete began by asking the students the first thing that came to mind when they heard the word *Islam*. After a couple of innocuous responses—*discipline, prayerfulness*—Pete said, "Come on, tell the truth. You're not gonna hurt my feelings."

Then he started getting the kind of answers he was looking for. *Terrorism. The burka. Oppression of women. Salman Rushdie.* The more negative the view of Islam, the wider Pete's smile became. These responses made his point: Islam has been erected as the new bogeyman.

Pete then said that he wanted to move past the media hype and show what Islam really is. Islam is a word indicating submission to God, he said, and it is derived from the same root word as *salaam*, the Arabic word for "peace." "So Islam means peace."

He then explained the basics of Islam. There was *tawheed*, Arabic for Islamic monotheism. "Islam has a pure, beautiful monotheism. We believe that there is one god and only one. We call our god Allah—that's Arabic for the word 'god.' In Islam, Allah is the unique and unchallenged lord of the universe. He's unique in his attributes, and worship should be reserved for Him alone."

Pete explained that Muhammad was the last in a long line of prophets that included Abraham, Moses, and Jesus. He explained that Muslims believe that the Qur'an is the literal word of Allah, revealed to Muhammad through the archangel Gabriel. And he described the five pillars of Islam: belief in the Oneness of God, the five daily prayers, almsgiving for the needy, fasting during Ramadan, and the pilgrimage to Mecca (hajj). At an intermission, Dennis Geren brought the students dates and tea.

After the break, the presentation turned from the religious to the sociopolitical. This was where Pete intended to knock down all the negative stereotypes about Islam that he had drawn out.

Pete started by addressing the students' concerns about so-called Islamic terrorism. He said, "Whenever you see a picture of a Muslim in the paper, they show you some guy with a frown on his face and an AK-47. People have these images of busloads of schoolchildren being blown up. But does anyone here remember what the word *Islam* means?"

A dark-skinned kid in shorts raised his hand. "Peace."

"Right." Pete smiled. "Because you were paying attention, you get a T-shirt as a prize." Dennis Geren brought the student a shirt. It had Al Haramain's logo on the front, along with the slogan Islam Means Peace. On the back, the shirt said Islam Rejects Terrorism.

"So Islam means peace, right? And terrorism isn't very peaceful, is it?" Pete said. "So this terrorism has nothing to do with Islam."

Dawood chimed in, "Look, everyone asks Muslims to justify that our religion doesn't support terrorism. But look what's happening around the world. Look at Kosovo, Bosnia, Chechnya, Palestine, the Philippines, Uzbekistan, Algeria, and Kashmir. People accuse Islam of being an aggressive religion, but when we look out at the world, we feel like we're being *pounded*."

Dawood's approach was typical of the rest of the presentation. My coworkers spent less and less time defending Islam against attacks. Instead, they went on the offensive. In every area where Islam had been criticized, they tried to show that *the West was worse*. It isn't the way I would have done the presentation, but they were passionate and persuasive, and it seemed to work.

When the presentation turned to women in Islam, Pete said, "A lot of people think Islam is chauvinistic because they look out at so-called Muslim countries and see women treated bad. But you gotta separate the true teachings of Prophet Muhammad, peace be upon him, from what these woman-haters are doing when they claim to act for Islam.

"The truth," Pete said, "is that Islam gave women rights they wouldn't have in the West for more than a thousand years, even gave them rights they *still don't have* in the West. It gives women the right to go to heaven. It gives them the right to earn wealth and own property. It lets women choose who they'll marry and keep their own last names. It gives women the right to seek a divorce."

Dennis Geren chimed in with a story about two men, a Westerner and a Muslim, walking down the street together. "They pass by a store that's selling TV sets, and there are all these TVs in the window display," he said. "One of the screens has a picture of a woman in a burka on it, and the Western man points and says, 'In my culture, we find that very offensive to women.' Then on another screen, here comes Pamela Sue Anderson"—he meant Pamela Anderson Lee, the buxom blonde *Baywatch* star—"in a skimpy little bikini, with her breasts flopping all around. The Muslim turns to the Westerner and says, 'In my culture, we find *that* very offensive to women.'"

The notion that the burka and soft porn could be equally offensive to female equality was not considered. The idea was presented as though one canceled out the other, as though it's impossible to be against both.

The presentation continued in this vein until the question-and-answer session. The student who had earned a T-shirt earlier asked the first question. He said he knew there were conservative customs regarding relations between men and women in Islam, and asked how you could find a spouse when you aren't allowed to date.

"The Islamic courtship process is different from Western courtship," Pete said. "In the West, you date a person here, date a person there. You're not thinking about spending your lives together. There's no deep connection between you, everything is physical. In Islamic courtship, you don't date. You're interested in a girl, right away you try to see if she's marriage material. You talk about religion, you talk about family, you talk about politics. You begin at a deeper level. We think this is *better* than the Western way of dating."

His answer made me realize that bringing Amy here may have been a mistake.

Another student asked about the Taliban, the fundamentalist group that had seized power in Afghanistan. They were known for forcing women to wear all-encompassing burkas; imposing harsh criminal punishments such as stonings, amputations, and public executions; slaughtering Shia Muslims; and harboring Osama bin Laden's al-Qaeda terrorist group. I had paid close attention to the Taliban during my last year at Wake Forest because they disgusted me. Since I thought the Taliban's rule was an unjustifiable distortion of Islam, this seemed like a softball question.

Dawood began to give the answer I expected. "You see a lot of things going on in the Muslim world," he said. His voice possessed the certainty of a true believer. "But you need to compare everything you see to Islam's true teachings to determine if this is really Islam, or if it's a distortion based on cultural practices."

Dennis Geren interrupted. "We have to remember that the Taliban fought against the Russians when they invaded Afghanistan, and the Russians brutalized the country. A lot of things have been said about the Taliban, and we have to resist Western media hype." (Of course, the Taliban didn't exist until five years after the Soviets left Afghanistan.)

Dawood didn't disagree. "Yes, let's all resist this Western media hype," he said, immediately pointing to another student.

Western media hype? I thought. The lack of women's rights, the slaughter of Shias, the complete suppression of freedoms—all of this was being written off as hype? But at the time, it seemed that nobody else noticed this. Not the teachers, not the students.

After the presentation, Amy and I headed back toward my home in my red Tercel. I told her that I was disturbed by Dennis Geren's answer. "I was with him for the first part of it," I said. "I agree that the Afghan mujahideen fought against the brutal Russian invasion. But what he should have said was that the Russians left behind a traumatized population that was willing to accept the Taliban's barbaric practices in exchange for some semblance of law and order."

After a few seconds, I added, "I'll have to talk to Dennis about that." Amy just nodded.

I continued my appraisal of the day. "Overall, I think the presentation was a success. I took a look at the evaluation forms that they passed out at the end, and all the students gave it high marks. I got to read some of the student comments on the forms, and most of them said that they learned a lot. More than a few said that Islam was a good religion, better than most other religions." Of course it was.

Years later, Susan Thorngate told me that many of the students had in fact been put off because they felt that the presenters were "majorly proselytizing." But at the time there was no indication of this, from either the student reaction or the evaluation forms.

"I thought Dawood and Pete were especially strong when they talked about terrorism and women in Islam," I said. "They sounded real forceful and persuasive on those subjects."

"You know what would make the section on women more persuasive?" Amy asked.

"What?"

"If there were at least one female presenter."

I remained silent. While Amy was clearly right, it felt like she was attacking the religious world that I had chosen to inhabit, and this made me uncomfortable.

There would be no female presenter the next time around. I would in fact see very few women over the next nine months, and would eventually, as my faith developed, view the absence of women as a *positive* thing.

four

DOGS BARKING

To my surprise, I found that the men with whom I had become Muslim were hated by the Muslims I now worked with.

I learned this while looking through our Web site at www.qf.org. QF stood for Qur'an Foundation, the Islamic charity that Pete had founded before he developed a relationship with Al Haramain. Al Haramain's head office in Saudi Arabia also had a Web site, but qf.org was our local site. One of the pages at qf.org featured a handful of links to other Islamic Web sites, and the first link I clicked on led me to the site of a man named Salim Morgan.

The top of Salim's Web page was normal enough, beginning with the inscription, "In the Name of Allah, the Benificent [sic], the Merciful." These words are known as the *basmallah*, and are commonly seen at the top of Muslim writings. They're meant to denote that the writing is dedicated to God. The *basmallah* was followed by an explanation that the Islamic section of Salim's Web site featured translations and articles on various Islamic subjects, as well as handouts and class notes from lectures and seminars that Salim had given.

When I scrolled down to the featured articles, I found that the first

one was titled "The Naqshabandia Tariqa [Path] Exposed." The itali-
cized explanation next to the link to that article said, "If you have been
confused by the schemes of Shaitaan [Satan] coming from this group or
know others who have been, READ THIS concise and informative
article NOW!"

I was taken aback by seeing that not only did Salim despise the
Naqshbandis, but that he felt strongly enough to make an attack on
them the lead link on his Web page. Scrolling down further, I saw a link
to an audio file ominously titled "Barking of Dogs." Beside the link,
Salim commented: "Hear some truly bizarre carrying-on which some
people call 'worship'. You won't believe your ears! I seek refuge in Allah
from all forms of bida and deviation." *Bida* was innovation in religion.
Salim's belief—one shared by my coworkers—was that any religious
practice that differed from those of Prophet Muhammad was unacceptable *bida*. *Bida* would at the very least earn Allah's anger, and could even
take you completely out of the Islamic faith.

By "truly bizarre carrying-on which some people call 'worship,'" I
realized that Salim was referring to loud *dhikr*, the religious chanting in
which I had taken part the night I became a Muslim. He was saying that
it was the same as the barking of dogs. And dogs are never items of affection in radical Islam.

One of Pete's sons, Yunus, entered the office while I was looking at
Salim's Web site. Yunus, who was just beginning high school, was skinny
and stood about five feet four—but looked like he could grow another
foot and a half overnight, probably gaining not a pound in the process.
Yunus's skin was much lighter than Pete's, his brown hair had a tint of
blond, and he spoke with a voice that was far too loud for our rather
small office.

Basically, Yunus displayed all the complexes and insecurities typical
of a young high school kid. His personality would go through wild
swings, from brash, arrogant, and dismissive to lonely and needy. I could

never get work done while he was in the office because he always demanded my attention.

Lacking any concept of personal space or privacy, Yunus walked up right behind me when he entered, craning his neck to see my computer screen. "Those guys are so weird," Yunus's booming voice said when he saw Salim's comments about the Naqshbandis. "I heard a tape where Idris Palmer goes around and interviews them. They're sitting around chanting." He did a mocking imitation of loud *dhikr*. (I was familiar with the name Idris Palmer; while working on my honors thesis on the Nation of Islam I read an emotional pamphlet that Palmer wrote attacking the group. I did not, at the time, realize that he and his writings would become a daily staple at the office.)

"I don't think he should compare their worship to the barking of dogs," I said.

I was sitting in the corner of the office farthest from the door, by the desktop computer. The office was supposed to hold three workers, and was fairly cramped for those purposes. There were two side doors. One led to a bathroom; the other led to a supply closet packed with thousands of Islamic books, booklets, and pamphlets. There was a CPR poster on one wall. To make the poster more Islamically appropriate, somebody had drawn beards on the illustrated figures demonstrating proper CPR technique, even on the female characters. The same person had also drawn sunglasses over their eyes, although it wasn't clear why the sunglasses made the illustrations more theologically acceptable.

I had two office mates, Charlie Jones and Dennis Geren. I had already noticed Charlie's frequent absences, although I didn't yet know why. Dennis was rarely gone, even after work hours had ended, since he lived in the Musalla. In return for the free housing, Dennis also did custodial chores and let Pete pay him a very low salary. Dawood and his wife and kids also lived in the building, in the downstairs area where the women would pray. They would soon leave for Saudi Arabia, since

Dawood didn't want to raise his kids in the infidel West. Perhaps Sheikh Hassan had gotten to him.

Today, Dennis wasn't in the office, but Charlie sat next to me, a few feet down the long wooden counter that made a 90-degree turn along the wall and served as a desk for all of us.

Hearing our exchange, Charlie turned and said, "We shouldn't refer to anybody as dogs. Prophet Muhammad, peace be upon him, said that you should be soft on the Muslims and hard on the kufar. We shouldn't go around calling other Muslims dogs." Charlie spoke softly, nodding emphatically as he spoke.

I knew that dogs were held in low regard in Islam. I learned this when al-Husein and I visited Turkey together. We spent a lot of time with Turkish Muslim groups irate about the forced march to seculariza- tion orchestrated by Kemal Atatürk, the father of modern Turkey. One night, as we were bemoaning Istanbul's spiritual emptiness, al-Husein pointed out a dog behind a fence by one of the mosques. He said that many Muslims find scenes such as that offensive. When I asked why, he told me about a hadith where the Prophet said that the angels refuse to enter a house with a dog in it. So I understood why Charlie said that you shouldn't refer to other Muslims as dogs. (Later I'd see firsthand that Islamic radicals' distaste for dogs ran far deeper than I suspected.)

Despite Charlie's statement, I suspected that he'd agree with Salim that the Naqshbandis were religious deviants. I suspected that his only objection was to actually calling them dogs. After only a few days on the job, I could already sense an environment where religious beliefs that differed from the norm were sniffed out and condemned, both publicly and privately. But I didn't ask Charlie his view of the Naqshbandis. I was just starting to settle in at Al Haramain, and didn't want to begin by drawing out areas of disagreement with my coworkers—especially not those areas of disagreement that could make me unpopular.

Instead, I kept browsing Salim Morgan's Web page, trying to tune Yunus out. I clicked on the "Naqshabandia Tariqa Exposed" link that first caught my eye. The Web page it led me to reprinted an anonymous pamphlet denouncing the Naqshbandis. The pamphlet stated: "Over the years many deviant movements have arisen in the Muslim world bent on corrupting the teachings of Islaam* and thereby mislead the Muslims." It said that the Naqshbandis were "one of the most common and dangerous" of these movements. Indeed, the Naqshbandis, "while wearing the cloak of Islaam, are striving to destroy it from within, in a vain attempt to extinguish the light of Islaam and divert the Muslims from the true religion."

The pamphleteer's main denunciation of the Naqshbandis was that they were guilty of *shirk:* that is, they had compromised their monotheism by associating partners with Allah. The example that most caught my attention involved Abu Yazid Bistami (d. 874) and Mansur al-Hallaj (d. 922). Both men were mystics who attempted to vanish into the object of their love, Allah. They were still revered in mystic Muslim circles because they had *succeeded,* reaching states of spiritual ecstasy where they no longer remembered themselves, but knew only Allah. In this state, Bistami famously declared, "I am the Truth"—as had al-Hallaj. In fact, it is often said that al-Hallaj was executed for these words when the religious authorities mistook his God-consciousness for a declaration of divinity.

Overlooking the nuances of the Sufi desire for the annihilation of self in service of God, the pamphlet declared that the Naqshbandis disregarded a core tenet of Islam, that Allah is the only truth. The book *The Naqshbandi Way* stated, "Whoever recites Bismillaah and the verses

---

*Some writers—primarily the Salafis—transliterate the word *Islam* with two *a*'s rather than one to signify that it has a long vowel in the middle.

Amana'r-Rasul until the end, even a single time will attain a high rank
and a great position. . . . He will get what the Prophets and Saints could
not get, and will arrive at the stage of Abu Yazid Al-Bistami, the Imam
of the order who said: 'I am the Truth (al-Haqq).'"

The pamphlet responded in a rage:

> The above statement "I am the Truth"—is a clear example of Shirk
> (association) in the aspect of the Names and Attributes of Allaah,
> since Al-Haqq in the definite form, is one of Allaah's Unique attrib-
> utes and is not shared by any created being or thing unless preceded
> by the prefix 'Abd meaning "Slave of" or "Servant of". (In fact the
> Mystic al-Hallaaj was publicly executed as an apostate for daring
> to openly claim divinity in his infamous pronouncement "Anal-
> Haqq—I am the Truth").

This was the first time I had seen another Muslim laud the execution
of al-Hallaj. Until then, I was always told that al-Hallaj's proclamation
was deeply misunderstood by the authorities who killed him. (Although
I would later learn that the real reasons behind al-Hallaj's execution are
likely more complex than the Sufi narrative holds, in this instance both
the Naqshbandis and their critic accepted the same set of facts.)

I glanced quickly through the rest of the pamphlet. I saw that the
Naqshbandis were condemned for believing that Allah was everywhere,
rather than being only above in the heavens; for believing that Muslims
and non-Muslims are equal; and for believing that there is hidden
knowledge within Islam.

I had nothing but good feelings toward the Muslims with whom I had
taken my *shahadah*. They were men of intense faith. When I spent time
with them in Italy, they seemed to strike a rare balance: rejecting Western civilization's materialism and licentiousness but remaining skeptical
of the extremes of fundamentalism. But I took two clear messages from

Salim Morgan's Web site. The first was that I was not to speak well of the men who were present at my *shahadah*. The second lesson was more general, but just as unmistakable: I needed to watch what I said.

I didn't realize it at the time, but this was one of the first steps in my indoctrination. When I was a campus activist at Wake Forest, I was always eager to speak against injustice, and often considered myself courageous when I did. But my approach at Al Haramain was the opposite. I recognized that disagreeing with prevailing religious sentiments could stigmatize me. My approach, starting with my first week on the job, was to avoid making waves, to try to understand where the others were coming from, and to emphasize our religious commonality rather than argue over differences.

But in December of 1998, thinking and believing like a Wahhabi seemed far removed from who I was. It may even have seemed inconceivable.

I was fascinated by how my coworkers started as average Caucasian high school students who grew up in liberal Ashland and eventually grew into Islamic fundamentalists. Although I would eventually come to know Dennis Geren the best, I learned a lot about Dawood and Charlie Jones early on.

At times Dawood's conservative views on Islam horrified me, but over time I came to look up to him as someone with a strong understanding of the faith, an understanding that was reflected in his practice. Like me, Dawood was an Ashland High School alum; he graduated in the early 1980s. His main passion in high school was football, and he still had the body of an athlete. Dawood once told me about his flippant attitude toward classes while in high school: he claimed that he told his teachers to let him know if his grade dipped below a C–. As long as he had at least a C–, he wouldn't give any thought to schoolwork.

Charlie had also graduated from Ashland High. I gathered that he and Dawood went to high school at the same time and had been friends. Charlie never went to college; he was ineligible for student loans because he refused to register for the Selective Service, which would make him eligible for the draft. He wouldn't register because he found America's past too sordid.

Charlie was an avid and impressive student of military history, and he often spoke about how he wished he could go to college, get a degree, and become a high school history teacher. But whenever he mentioned this, the specter of not registering for Selective Service returned. "Why do they have to stop me from going to college?" he would ask. "I leave the government alone. I don't wish it any harm. Why can't the government leave me alone?"

Often he would follow this up by talking about how disappointed he was in this country. "I would love to have lived in an honorable country," Charlie would say while nodding his head. "I wish I could be proud of my country and serve in the military. But when I read about the things that the government did to the Native Americans, when I read about how it stole their land and slaughtered them, I know that I can't be part of a military that did all that."

His bitterness was palpable. Charlie felt that if the U.S. government hadn't been such a disappointment, his life would be different. He could have been a soldier, a college graduate, a military historian. As his emotional problems grew, Charlie would cling more tightly to the idea that had the government not let him down, his life would be far better, his problems more manageable.

It was Pete who turned Charlie and Dawood to Islam. Charlie once told me that the two of them had met Pete when his car was broken down; I don't recall where they were, but it was one of southern Oregon's long and lonely roads. As Charlie and Dawood were driving along,

Pete came running from out of nowhere, trying to flag down their car. He needed help.

Charlie said that Pete was speaking quickly and they could barely understand him because of his thick accent. They thought at the time that he was Mexican. As with so many seemingly chance events in our lives, this encounter had profound consequences for Charlie and Dawood. Eventually they not only adopted Pete as a friend, but adopted his religion as well.

When I decided to clear away Al Haramain's six-month backlog of e-mail messages, I accidentally put myself on a collision course with more obscure Wahhabi beliefs.

I told Charlie that I wanted to get the office caught up on its correspondence. He nodded in his peculiar way. First he bobbed his head, then his blue eyes widened expressively, as though he had a hidden thought that he refused to share. Charlie then paused, pursed his lips, and bobbed his head again. When I later learned about Charlie's emotional problems, they cast his strange nods in a different light.

I spent the next day and a half answering our e-mail backlog. I spotted a message about W. D. Muhammad and read it with interest, since the reforms he had undertaken to bring his followers in line with mainstream Islam had figured prominently in my college honors thesis. Like the discussion of the Naqshbandis on Salim Morgan's Web site, the e-mail turned out to be a vitriolic attack that cast nuance to the wind.

The e-mail discussed the rise of pseudo-Islamic cults in the twentieth century, including the Nation of Islam. In doing so, it compared W. D. Muhammad to Louis Farrakhan and Rashad Khalifa, saying that all three were men who "have deceived many and are enjoying their present lives." (I found the assertion that Khalifa was enjoying his present life odd, since his controversial teachings got him killed by Muslim fundamentalists in 1990. His inclusion may have been a deliberate warning.)

The e-mail included more than a dozen quotes designed to show W. D. Muhammad's heresy. For starters, it claimed that W. D. Muhammad had publicly declared himself to be the manifestation of God:

> Yes, I myself am an Immaculate Conception. You say, "This man is crazy." No, I'm not crazy. . . . After we explain it to you, you'll know that I'm not crazy. The world has just been in darkness. I can truthfully say that My physical father was not My father. I have never had a physical father. . . . You say, "Who is your father?" Speaking in the language of the New Testament, My Father is God. . . . I am the Manifestation of God. . . . All praise is due to Allah.

By themselves, these words seemed crazy, potentially blasphemous. But one hallmark of African-American religious rhetoric was the extended metaphor—one that seems outlandish at first, but becomes clearly correct as the speaker fleshes it out. I assumed that the author of the e-mail was trying to make his readers take one of W. D. Muhammad's metaphorical statements literally. I was also amused that the e-mail capitalized the word *My* in W. D. Muhammad's statement to reinforce the impression that he was claiming divinity.

I was equally puzzled by the other quotes allegedly showing W. D. Muhammad's heresy. He once spoke against polygamy, stating: "The teaching of Muhammad and the teaching of the Qur'an is that 'one is better for you if you but knew.' No other Prophet did this for the polygamist mankind. It was Prophet Muhammad who worked against polygamy." What was wrong with saying that one wife is better than multiple wives?

W. D. Muhammad had also said that Christians didn't need to follow Islam: "I don't feel that all Christians have to have my religion to improve their lives. . . . I feel that some Christians are living very good lives. They have very good morals, they have a good sense of direction and I wouldn't want to disturb that for them." In the view of the e-mail's author, this offense was compounded by W. D. Muhammad's statement, "I have no problems with the Pope; I respect him and honor him."

The e-mail suggested that for these minor offenses, W. D. Muhammad was at best a heretic. Disturbed by the tone used in addressing a man who had been responsible for bringing so many former Nation of Islam members to true Islam, I asked Charlie Jones about it.

"The Prophet Muhammad, peace be upon him, said that there will be seventy-three divisions of Islam," Charlie said. "All these except one will be paths to the hellfire. You need to be very careful that your faith doesn't stray from the Straight Path." He paused, nodding. "If W. D. Muhammad is misleading other Muslims, he needs to be corrected."

"But it's so vitriolic. They're saying that W. D. Muhammad isn't even a Muslim because they disagree with some things he's said." I wasn't arguing the substance; I knew better than to defend his statements. The only option left was protesting the tone.

Charlie shrugged. It didn't disturb him.

Later I talked with Dawood about the attacks on W. D. Muhammad. He replied in a loud, unwavering voice. "W. D. Muhammad needs to be exposed. All I can say is that this guy let his daughter marry a Christian." Dawood laughed contemptuously, as though this fact took W. D. Muhammad to a place where no defense would dare to tread.

Although I was skeptical of the attacks on W. D. Muhammad, I had already learned to watch what I said, and to be cautious of praising or defending Muslims whom I had once admired.

Of all the people at Al Haramain, Pete was initially the one I felt most drawn to. Although I was learning to watch what I said in daily life at the office, Pete made me feel comfortable. His ability to do so was part of the remarkable social skills that I sensed soon after meeting him.

On the day that Pete convinced me to apply for a job at Al Haramain, he gestured at the rippling, tree-covered mountains that surrounded us. Unlike Sheikh Hassan, who saw homosexuals reflected in the hills, Pete was looking at the same mountains as me. "Why did we both come to Islam?" he had mused. "I could make so much more money if I weren't Muslim, if I just threw myself into business and didn't worry about how Allah was watching me. But, bro, something brought both of us to this faith, and there's a reason for that."

Although born into Iran's Shia Islam, Pete had converted to Sunni Islam somewhere along the way. I never learned exactly why Sunni Islam, and in particular Wahhabism, appealed to Pete. He had left Iran around the time of the revolution. In the early 1980s Pete was known as Falcon, a long-haired young man who was a committed environmental activist. His enthusiasm for the environment remained, reflected in his passion for his tree-care business. Pete once told my dad that he started to become serious about Islam when his mother was sick and he prayed to Allah to make her well again. Pete regarded her subsequent recovery as miraculous. After that, Pete said, he decided to take his religion more seriously.

I would find Pete increasingly difficult to figure out during my time at Al Haramain. He had an activist side that I could identify with, but there was another side as well. He was friends with the local rabbis; years later, when Pete's legal troubles came, a local rabbi would be his biggest defender. Pete had taken part in local meditation groups where people, including Jews and Muslims, would pray together for peace. But he would just as readily derisively refer to Rand McNally, which produced maps and atlases, as a "real *yahoodi* company"—that is, a sinister Jewish company. He would similarly refer to non-Muslims derogatorily as *kufar*, infidels, and make clear his belief in their inferiority. I would later see his eyes light up with belief when confronted with anti-Semitic conspiracy yarns.

Pete coupled a progressive activist impulse with a regressive anti-activist impulse. His own family was Shia, yet Al Haramain would distribute books at the Musalla with the provocative title *The Difference Between the Shee'ah and the Muslims*, along with booklets alleging that Shia Islam was part of a Jewish conspiracy to destroy the faith. Thing is, Pete seemed perfectly sincere at both ends. He seemed as sincere about interfaith dialogue as he did when he busied himself learning about Jewish conspiracies. He seemed sincere while speaking of Islam's tolerance and also while launching verbal assaults on non-Muslims.

Over the seven years since I first came to know Pete Seda, I've given a lot of thought to what he actually stood for. The answer isn't entirely clear. He may have been the ultimate con man. Or perhaps, in his fits of schizophrenic passion, he was sincere the entire time despite the apparent contradictions. This is one part of the puzzle that nobody has solved perfectly, even though there are now many strong views on the matter.

While Amy was in town for Christmas break, I shared all that I loved about Ashland with her. We hiked the trails above town, walked through Lithia Park hand in hand, went to my favorite restaurants. But she had to return to North Carolina a few short days after I began work. Before she left town, I broke up with her.

We were in my room, sitting on the bed. It was Amy's last night here.

For days, I had been asking myself where our relationship was going now that I had graduated from college and would be living three thousand miles from her. I didn't know if it could survive. Not only had all of my long-distance relationships failed, but each had caused great pain in the process. I ran the fingers of my right hand through Amy's long hair, leaned in, and kissed her gently on the lips. I loved Amy.

But I had to tackle this issue. I took a deep breath before speaking. "I love you, Amy," I said. "And you love me. But I'm worried about what will happen now that I've graduated from college. We're going to be three thousand miles apart."

Amy nodded, her eyes downcast. This had been on her mind, too.

I wasn't sure what to say. I had conflicting feelings, but my biggest fear was of a long-distance relationship where we felt bound to each other—but never saw each other, didn't know where we were headed, and where our interactions became increasingly tense as we struggled against the inevitable fate of such arrangements. "I've been in long-distance relationships before," I said, "and they're tough. They're tough because of all the time apart, because of the uncertainty. I'm worried that this won't work."

Amy spoke no words, but her expressive face said everything. She had the same worries, the same concerns. "I think the only way this'll work is if we know where we're headed," I said. "I think we either need to get engaged or break up."

I didn't know what I would say to Amy when we sat down to discuss this. And I still wasn't entirely sure where I was headed. Part of me wanted to propose to her right there. But we had been together for less than a year, and were both so young. That would be crazy—wouldn't it?

So we broke up. Afterward, we held each other in a long, tight, sad embrace. I could tell that Amy was devastated, and there was nothing I could say to make it better.

I felt the same way.

Early in my time on the job, Pete would often come by the office to chat with me. He would talk to me about work, then throw in some lessons about Islam and life. Pete was obviously trying to foster a mentor relationship with me. And I did see him as a bit of a mentor, but also as a bit of a clown.

I thought Pete's fascination with plural marriage fell on the clown side of the ledger. After work one day, Pete sat in the office with me, expounding about how wonderful it was that Islam allows you to have more than one wife. I had heard this before, so while I found the point amusing, it was somewhat less entertaining than the first time around.

Then Pete surprised me. "Let me tell you, though," he said, "it can be a real problem when you have a young wife and also wives who are older. The older wives will feel threatened by the young one and gang up on her."

"You have more than one wife?" I asked.

Pete smiled broadly. This was a point of pride for him. "I have two wives," he said. "I recently had a third wife from Persia. She was a Zoroastrian, they're a religious group that worships the sun. But since they only believe in one god, she was legal for me to marry under Islamic law." His smile broadened. When I didn't say anything, he continued the story. "But she was younger than my other two wives, and they'd always gang up against her. Eventually I had to divorce her because of them."

I didn't know how to respond. I had no idea that Pete was no mere advocate of plural marriage, but also a practitioner. I would later learn, from other members of the Muslim community, that the history of Pete's wives was even more sordid than he let on in this conversation.

I was told that his first wife was an American woman whom Pete had converted to Islam. She was the mother of Yunus and Yusuf. At some point she divorced Pete and returned to Christianity. Pete then married a woman from Morocco who left him after about a year, supposedly because she was horrified when Pete told her that he wanted four wives. After a brief marriage to a woman from Seattle, Pete went to Iran to marry a Persian woman—only he married a Russian immigrant before the trip to Iran. Pete's Persian wife was probably surprised when she landed in Ashland, only to find that another wife was already there. Sometime after that, Pete took on his young Zoroastrian wife.

Nor did things end there. After his other two wives managed to push the Zoroastrian away, Pete had the audacity to find her a new husband and hold the wedding in his house. The Russian left Pete soon thereafter, but Pete's Persian wife wouldn't have him to herself for long. Pete soon found another wife, a college student from a southern Oregon town called Grants Pass.

So Pete had no fewer than seven wives over the course of his life, at least four of whom were involved in a plural marriage.

But I didn't know any of this at the time. And, as was always the case with Pete, he quickly veered to another topic without any prompting.

As I continued to pore through Al Haramain's backlog of e-mail, I saw that Muslims and non-Muslims often wrote with questions about Islam. We should be ready to answer these questions quickly, I thought. We should try to become a recognized clearinghouse of information on Islam, one that people can turn to when they have inquiries.

One of the e-mail messages in the inbox said, "I'm a SOU [Southern Oregon University, a college located in Ashland] student and I'm writing a paper about infibulation. I know that this is practiced in a lot of Muslim countries, especially in Africa. Is infibulation required by Islam?"

Infibulation is a severe form of female genital mutilation that involves the removal of all or part of the clitoris, removal of all or part of the labia minora, and cutting of the labia majora. After the procedure, raw surfaces are created which are often stitched together to form a cover over the vagina, with only a small hole left where urine and menstrual blood can pour out.

The e-mail had been sent over a month ago, but hopefully the writer was still working on his paper. I relished the opportunity to educate non-

Muslims about how brutal things done in the name of Islam had no real connection to the faith.

I sent back an e-mail telling the writer that it was important to distinguish between true Islam and cultural practices. Female genital mutilation is not prescribed by the faith, and is in fact brutal. I included a quote from a human rights group's Web site that said that Muslim and Christian tribes in Africa practice female genital mutilation, but that the practice is rooted in culture rather than faith.

I got an e-mail from the writer a few hours later thanking me. I didn't give the exchange much thought until I came in to work a couple of days later and Dennis Geren had a grave look on his face. I addressed him with the traditional Muslim greeting: "*Assalaamu 'alaykum.*"

"*Wa alaykum salaam,*" Dennis said. "Bro, Dawood was not happy with your e-mail."

"What e-mail?"

"You sent out an e-mail about infibulation. Dawood was very upset. Pete thought it wasn't a big problem, just a mistake that you made because you're new and enthusiastic."

My mind raced back to the exchange. I was already on guard at work, knowing the kind of condemnations that "deviants" face. But I couldn't think of any problems with what I had written. "Well," I stammered, "what was wrong with it?"

"Basically, you and I aren't in a position to issue fatwas on our own. We shouldn't issue rulings about complex areas of Islamic law."

I gave a quizzical look but said nothing. *Removing a woman's vulva is a complex area of Islamic law?* I thought. But debating, I realized, would have been futile. Dennis had been told by Pete and Dawood—two men who had been serious Muslims far longer than either of us—that my e-mail shouldn't have been sent. He wasn't going to argue with them.

Dennis added, almost apologetically, "Isn't infibulation where they actually take out the whole vulva?"

"Yeah."

He cringed. "That's so disgusting."

But, of course, we were not to speak against it publicly.

Dennis's warning wasn't the last I would hear of that e-mail. Pete took me aside later that day. He made me feel more comfortable than Dennis had, as he was gentle and didn't seem reproachful. Instead, it seemed that his main goal was helping me to learn proper Islamic conduct.

I had signed my e-mail "Daveed Gartenstein-Ross, Al Haramain Islamic Foundation." Pete told me I shouldn't do that. "That way," he said, "if you send out an e-mail that says something crazy, it'll just have your name and not Al Haramain's."

I nodded. That, at least, made sense.

Then, Pete addressed the substance of the e-mail. "Bro," he said, "there are a bunch of sheikhs in Saudi Arabia just waiting to answer questions like that. We can send them a question and they'll sit around for a whole day discussing it. So if someone sends you a question about Islam in the future, you don't even have to try to answer it. We can take the question, send it to Saudi Arabia, and they'll get back to us with the right answer."

I was still puzzled that the prevailing view was that I shouldn't speak out on a subject like infibulation, which seemed glaringly obvious. But arguing, I knew, wouldn't have been productive. The objection to my e-mail—at least, the objection that had been relayed to me—was not that my coworkers believed in infibulation. Rather, it was that I wasn't qualified to issue an Islamic ruling.

Perhaps the best course is more study, I thought.

But I already sensed that no matter how much I studied, I'd never be qualified to issue these rulings in the eyes of my coworkers unless my interpretation of Islam squared with theirs. To them, being qualified to speak didn't just mean that you knew enough. It meant that you agreed with them.

As I studied more, I discovered more restrictions that I never knew existed. Ramadan had just begun, and one day I read a wire story about it in the local newspaper, the *Ashland Daily Tidings*. The story mentioned that during the fast, Muslims refrain from food, drink, sexual intercourse, and listening to music during the day.

I had never heard of this last restriction. When I got in to work I asked Dawood about it. "Practicing Muslims shouldn't listen to music at all," he said.

"What?" Immediately I regretted that I had asked the question.

"Yes," Dawood said. "The Prophet, peace be upon him, spoke about this issue directly. It has nothing to do with Ramadan. We shouldn't be listening to music, period."

I must have looked skeptical because Dawood came into the office half an hour later carrying a slim hardcover book, Muhammad bin Jamil Zino's *Islamic Guidelines for Individual and Social Reform*. This was the first time I saw the book, but it wouldn't be the last. Dawood had put a yellow tab on one of the pages. He handed the volume to me. "If you have doubts about the harms of music, you should read this. It explains the Islamic position."

I waited until Dawood left the office, then looked at the tabbed section:

ISLAMIC RULINGS ON MUSIC AND SONGS

1. Allah the Exalted says:

   "And of mankind is he who purchases idle discourse (like music, singing, etc.) to mislead (men) from the path of Allah without knowledge, and takes it by way of mockery." (31:6)

Many interpreters of the Qur'an said that the idle discourse in this verse means songs. Ibn Mas'ud also said that it is songs. Al-Hasan Al-Basri also said it means songs and music playing.

2. Allah the Exalted said addressing the Satan:

   "And befool them whom you can with your voice (songs, music and any other call for disobedience) . . ."

3. The Prophet said:

   "There shall be a portion of my nation who will consider adultery, silk (for men), wine and music permissible." (Bukhari and Abu Dawud).

   This means that some people would not consider adultery, wine, silk wearing and music unlawful though none of them has ever been made lawful. An instrument of music is an instrument which gives a tune to dancing—flute, violin, drums and bells etc. The Prophet said:

   "Bells are musical instruments of the Satan." (Muslim).

   The bells are abominable instruments which the Arabs used to play and hang on to the camel necks. This type of bell looked like that of the Christians. Bell sound can be replaced by the sound of the nightingale in the door-bells etc.

4. Imam As-Shafi'i in his Book of Rulings said: "Singing is an abominable amusement and whoever gives much importance is a fool and his testimony should be rejected".

My head swam when I read this. I read it a second time, then a third. As when I first heard Sheikh Hassan's *khutbah*, the unfamiliar style of argument overwhelmed me. I went back over the passage, trying to parse the evidence.

The first Qur'anic verse said: "And of mankind is he who purchases idle discourse (like music, singing, etc.) to mislead (men) from the path of Allah without knowledge, and takes it by way of mockery." At the time, I had little knowledge of Arabic. But the translation suggested that the Qur'an itself didn't say that music could mislead men from the path of Allah. If it had said this, the author wouldn't have put the statement in parentheses, and wouldn't have noted that many interpreters of the Qur'an believed that the phrase "idle discourse" meant songs.

I looked at the next verse: "And befool them whom you can with your voice (songs, music and any other call for disobedience) . . ." Again, "songs" was the author's addition rather than anything from the Qur'an.

I turned to the third proof, the *hadith* that read: "There shall be a portion of my nation who will consider adultery, silk (for men), wine and music permissible." This was trickier. I started to consider it—then abruptly stopped. What was the point? I couldn't debate with the book. And what would happen if I tried to debate with Dawood? He would say that I was wrong, and would refer me to the writings of one scholar after another who agreed with him. Just as Sheikh Hassan didn't engage al-Husein when they debated, Dawood was unlikely to engage me in an actual debate.

Dawood reentered the office a few minutes later. "Well, what do you think?" he asked.

I shrugged. "I didn't know about that before." I didn't say whether I would comply with this ruling. At the time, it seemed unfathomable that I would.

Every day during Ramadan we fasted until the sun's disk was hidden by the horizon. I would sit on the couch in the Musalla's living room, watching as the blue shade of twilight gradually covered the valley. It was a cold winter and there was usually a fire in the woodstove near the kitchen.

As dusk settled, most of Ashland's Muslims came to the Musalla to break their fast. We were often joined by Muslims from surrounding areas, like Klamath Falls and Northern California. After a day of refraining from food and drink, the first sustenance to enter our mouths would be buttermilk and dates from Saudi Arabia. I was told that a *hadith* said it was best to break the fast with dates.

My first sip of buttermilk would be slow. I'd let my taste buds absorb the sour yet nourishing taste before taking my first bite of date. All the Muslim men would sit on the floor together as the smell of wood smoke filled the room. The women were downstairs as usual, out of sight.

Sheikh Hassan visited us from California early in the Islamic holy month. He wore a white robe. I noticed the great deference the other Muslims had toward him, like he was royalty. After exchanging greetings with the others, Sheikh Hassan sat cross-legged near me, looking at the communal plate of food on the floor with a vague, aloof smile.

The treatment he received made clear that Sheikh Hassan wasn't used to being challenged, and I couldn't imagine that the debate with al-Husein had left a good taste in his mouth. So I didn't say anything to Sheikh Hassan when he sat down. A couple of other Muslims started talking to him; I didn't greet him, and he didn't greet me.

But then Pete drew me to Sheikh Hassan's attention. "*Ya sheikh,** look who's here," Pete said, pointing at me. "Daveed is working for us. He's become a Muslim now. Now he's on our side."

I smiled and nodded at the sheikh. My first thought was that Pete's

---

*"Ya" is literally the vocative for "O," as in "O sheikh." However, English speakers of Arabic use this as a term of endearment. Here, Pete's use of the phrase was meant to refer to Sheikh Hassan as "dear sheikh."

words were incorrect. It wasn't that I *became* a Muslim after my first encounter with Sheikh Hassan. I had been a Muslim then, as I was now. But I thought of how these guys viewed the Naqshbandis, how they viewed W. D. Muhammad—and I realized that they probably thought I *wasn't* Muslim when Sheikh Hassan first met me.

Sheikh Hassan smiled. He had a peculiar smile, one that simultaneously reflected humility in the face of the Almighty and a haughtiness toward us mere mortals. "I thought about you recently," he said in a soft voice.

I nodded. Although I didn't inquire about what Sheikh Hassan's thoughts had been, I had my guesses. But, as Pete had said, I was Muslim now and on Sheikh Hassan's side.

I received a small package from Amy in early January. After I pulled it out of the mailbox, I ran to my room and eagerly ripped it open. It had all the photos that Amy took while visiting me in Oregon. Before flipping through them, I grabbed the letter that Amy had written on lined notebook paper. Even though we were no longer together, I was anxious to read it. It reminded me of the anticipation I felt years ago, when my first girlfriend sent me my first love letter.

Amy's letter said:

Daveed—Beloved,

These are both rolls of film. And some wonderful memories. Some of these are quite good, like the ones of the duck pond near your house. All the pictures of us are cute. I like the one where we're on your bed and you're laughing. I've kept the negatives if there are any you may want a copy of. You can be quite photogenic.

I hope your work is going well. (I'm having the hardest time

making myself do debate work.) Take care of yourself—give your
parents my love. Bless you.

Love always,

Amy

I felt a glow when I finished reading. I carefully placed the letter in a
green shoe box by my bed where I kept all my valued correspondence.
The letter was sweet—a reminder of why I had loved Amy. Pausing a
second, I revised that thought. It was a reminder, I realized, of why I *still*
loved her.

On Pete's urging, I brought my dad to the Musalla as Ramadan began. I
was hesitant to bring him. When al-Husein had visited Ashland, we had
shared our beautiful, tolerant, and fundamentally liberal vision of Islam
with my parents. I knew how much it meant to them that our view of
God was so similar to theirs, and that we viewed them as fellow travelers
in faith. I knew that what my dad would see at the Musalla was far different than that. I feared that it would hurt him to see that I was working
for Muslims whose views were so at odds not only with al-Husein's, but
also his own.

When we drove back from the Musalla, my father seemed hesitant to
discuss his experience. It seemed that the encounter had indeed hurt
him in some small way. At first, all he said was that the people he had
met were "interesting." In my experience, my dad's use of the word
"interesting" is usually a code word for his having experienced a problem
with someone or something.

Operation Desert Fox had occurred just before Ramadan. The three-
day bombing campaign in Iraq had been ordered by President Clinton in
December 1998 in response to Saddam Hussein's refusal to comply with
UN Security Council resolutions calling for disarmament. When I asked

my father what he meant by the word *interesting*, he told me about a conversation he'd stumbled into about Operation Desert Fox. "They were
saying this was all Bill Clinton's fault, and that Saddam Hussein wasn't
part of the problem," my dad said, astonished.

I assured him that I didn't agree, but there wasn't much else I could
add. Best I could tell, this was a fairly representative view. I remembered
how I brought Amy to the Musalla shortly before she left town. Just as
Pete told me to bring my dad out, he had also insisted that I bring Amy
one night. She was not impressed. For one thing, her feminist instincts
rebelled against being forced to go downstairs with the women while I
was upstairs with the men. But she had also heard the women discussing
Operation Desert Fox, and said that their anger was focused solely on
the United States. One of the women did voice some mild criticism of
Saddam Hussein: she was upset that Saddam had cursed on television in
response to the strikes. "I'm pretty sure he's done worse things than
that!" Amy told me, with an incredulous laugh.

It would be a while before I dared bring my dad back to the Musalla.

A few nights after my dad's visit, I found Dawood continuing the
conversation about Operation Desert Fox, saying that the strikes
showed the United States to be an enemy of Islam. Someone tepidly
replied that the United States made sure the bombing ended before
Ramadan.

"Why?" Dawood said. "Because they *respect Islam*? Who are these
shaytans [Satans] trying to fool?"

So Clinton's nod toward Islam only drew laughter and jeers.

Later the conversation turned to the translation of the Qur'an that
Al Haramain distributed. Called the Noble Qur'an, it was translated by
a couple of Saudi scholars, Muhammad Muhsin Khan and Muhammad
Taqi-ud-Din Al-Hilali. They had decided to undertake a new translation because they felt that existing versions didn't properly reflect the
earliest interpretation of the faith.

The consensus in the room was that the Noble Qur'an translation was a masterpiece. It favored accuracy over flowery language, and thus included a large number of parenthetical statements meant to capture the precise meaning of the text. It also featured footnotes designed to explain the verses. Some other Qur'anic translations also had a large number of footnotes, but the Noble Qur'an's didn't feature the translators' own exegesis. Rather, they generally consisted of quotes from the *ahadith*, thus using the Prophet's example to explain God's word.

Dawood said, "There are some very good essays in that translation. There's a good essay on jihad in the back."

That comment stuck with me. Before I became Muslim, I was leery of the idea of jihad, afraid that it might impel believers to take up arms against non-Muslims. Before converting to Islam, I read widely on the subject and came away convinced that this was an extremist interpretation that neither reflected mainstream Islamic thought nor the best interpretation of the faith. As a campus activist at Wake Forest, I referred to my battle against racism and other forms of discrimination as a jihad in order to show that this was a broad concept that, at its heart, represented the fight against social injustice.

But I was now learning that my coworkers roundly rejected many of my preconceptions about the faith. I hadn't read the essay that Dawood referred to, but I intuitively knew that it rejected my mushy, liberal ideas. I intuitively knew that the essay wouldn't proclaim the struggle against racism to be a form of jihad. I was apprehensive about reading it because a clear pattern had already emerged in my short time at Al Haramain. I would venture again and again into theological areas unfamiliar to me with an offhand statement or remark. In response, my coworkers would reprimand me, tell me the proper Islamic view, and give me some material to read. I was never able to engage in debate because they thought my religious views were too rough to count. So

I'd read and digest the material they gave me, and would be left to stew over it.

Still, I was curious. My coworkers had firmly stated at the presentation to the high school class that Islam meant peace, that the religion rejected terrorism. What did the essay say about the matter?

When I got home that evening, I picked up my pocket-sized copy of the Noble Qur'an. I flipped to the back and found the essay: "The Call to Jihad (Holy Fighting for Allah's Cause) in the Qur'an." But all I read was the title. I closed the book without reading a further word. Not yet. I wasn't ready.

I justified this to myself by figuring that I could concentrate, for now, on finding points of commonality with my coworkers. We shared a religion, and that was the most important thing. I could talk to them about more basic issues, areas where we agreed. I figured that we could discuss and debate some of the vital issues of the day, like jihad, down the road.

But there was more. Although I wouldn't admit this at the time, not even to myself, seeing the reactions to the Naqshbandis and W. D. Muhammad gave me a taste of the vitriol that theological dissenters could expect. When I was a campus activist, I would scoff when people made personal attacks against me because of my efforts to combat discrimination. It didn't faze me. Now, though, I found this vitriol intimidating—and I didn't understand why there should be any difference.

five

"WHAT'S SHAKING, SHAKEY?"

A sheikh came to visit us during Ramadan. Born in Egypt but now an imam in South Carolina, Sheikh Muhammad Adly was a short man with a large gray beard that seemed to run the length of his body. I found him strange and off-putting, but the others appeared to revere him. Their deference toward him reminded me of the treatment that Sheikh Hassan received.

Early in Sheikh Adly's visit, Dennis Geren told me a story that illustrated this deference. "I was drinking Pepsi, and one of the other brothers was giving me flak about it," Dennis said. He didn't explain the reason for the flak: perhaps it was because Pepsi is unhealthy, or perhaps it was because the drink represents the infidel West. "I said, 'Well, Sheikh Adly drinks Pepsi, so as far as I'm concerned, it's practically Sunnah.'" That is, he was suggesting—playfully—that because Sheikh Adly drank Pepsi, one could almost consider it encouraged as part of the Prophet's example. The others immediately accepted this statement. Whether or not it was meant as a joke, Dennis's analogy made sense to them.

Sheikh Adly was visiting to teach classes on Islam and make a video detailing how to make *salat* properly. One day, after we'd shot the footage for the video, Pete told me that I should give the sheikh a ride to the home of Suzi Aufderheide, who was producing the video for us.

I immediately walked out to my car to make sure there weren't any random papers strewn about on the passenger seat. As I was walking toward the red Tercel, a dark-haired woman who looked to be in her late thirties greeted me. She wasn't wearing a *hijab,* the head scarf worn by Muslim women. I was surprised to see her. It took me a second to realize the reason for my surprise: it had been weeks since I'd had any real contact with a woman. And, to my dismay, I had begun to internalize the dress code of the Musalla. Her lack of *hijab* struck me as wrong.

The woman introduced herself as an elementary school teacher. She wanted to bring her class to the Musalla so they could learn about Islam, and asked who she could speak to about this. I told her that Pete Seda was the person to ask. Then I glimpsed Sheikh Adly out of the corner of my eye. He stood a short distance away, far enough that he wouldn't have to introduce himself but close enough to listen. After noticing him, I felt self-conscious.

When my brief conversation with the teacher ended, she stuck out her hand and said, "I appreciate the help. It was nice talking with you."

I hesitated, and let her stand there with her hand sticking out. Then I said, somewhat embarrassed, "No thanks." I felt uncomfortable shaking her hand with the sheikh watching.

She gave me a perturbed look. The awkwardness was my fault. Dennis Geren had prepared a semihumorous spiel that he'd use to explain to women why he wouldn't shake their hands. It included the line, "You probably shouldn't shake my hand, unless you want to marry me." I had never prepared such a speech—but "no thanks" clearly did not do the trick. The teacher turned and walked to her car without saying another word.

When Sheikh Adly got into my Tercel, he explained in a soft meandering voice that a lot of non-Muslims don't understand and don't like the rules that we Muslims follow. "That woman," he said, "she didn't understand when you didn't want to shake her hand."

I nodded.

Sheikh Adly and I hadn't talked much during his time at the Musalla. I had noticed that his resemblance to Sheikh Hassan didn't end with the deference paid to him. Sheikh Adly had the same kind of aloofness, the same kind of quiet hostility toward all that didn't comport with his ideas of how the world should be ordered. I hadn't been too interested in talking to him, since I sensed that my questions would be met with reproaches rather than dialogue.

But now it was just the two of us in my car. Sheikh Adly asked me a few basic, introductory questions. He wanted to know how I came to Islam; since I was young, he wanted to know my future plans. When I told him that I wanted to go to law school in the fall, he shook his head, astonished.

"You should not go to law school," he said. "If you go to law school, you will have to say that the Constitution is good."

I was surprised. What's wrong with the Constitution?

But that wasn't how I responded. My first inclination was not to defend the Constitution, but to question his facts. "I can study Islamic law when I go to law school," I said. "A lot of American law schools have good programs in Islamic law. I don't have to just study U.S. law for all three years."

Later I'd reflect on the fact that this was my first line of argument. Questioning Sheikh Adly's facts rather than defending the Constitution was my way of dealing with the emerging pattern where any religious opinion I had that differed from my colleagues resulted in incredulity, recommended reading designed to clear up my misconception, and lists of scholars who disagreed with me. Even if my mind wasn't changed, I could never argue the point. So it wasn't surprising that I didn't want to debate with Sheikh Adly about the Constitution.

He found my argument that I'd be able to study Islamic law unpersuasive. With a shrug he said, "If you go to law school, someone might try to make you say that the Constitution is good."

I didn't say anything in response, but put the car into gear and drove Sheikh Adly to the home of Suzi Aufderheide, who would edit the instructional video on making *salat*.

Suzi epitomized Ashland's hippie ethos. She was about the same age as my parents, with five sons and a daughter. Two of her sons had gone to high school with me. Her boys were tall, thin, and freckled, and they had different last names. One was named Zachary Zeus; the other was Morgan Starr. Although Zach and Morgan left Ashland after they graduated from high school, Suzi had three sons still in town. Two of them, Colin and Ian Riversong, were the same age as Pete's son Yusuf—eleven or twelve years old. Suzi's other son was Justin Shenandoah; the only reason she had given Colin and Ian the same last name was because they were twins.

Colin and Ian had been around when we filmed Sheikh Adly making *salat* for the instructional video, and they were captivated by having a real live sheikh in their presence. Suzi—in that follow-your-dreams spirit that characterizes Ashland—told them that they could become Muslim. And they did.

Their conversion wouldn't last. It was inevitable that two eleven-year-olds would turn away from a religious practice built around arcane, restrictive, and alien rules and customs. But for the next few weeks they would be an occasional presence in the Musalla.

From the moment we arrived at Suzi's house, I derived endless amusement from her interactions with Sheikh Adly. Unlike Ashland's Muslims, she wasn't awed by him. She wasn't disrespectful, but was playful, almost flirtatious. And although she meant no disrespect, I was sure that a man like Sheikh Adly felt deeply threatened by this.

"What's shaking, Shakey?" Suzi said when she opened the door for us.

If Sheikh Adly noticed this play on his honorific title, he didn't let on. He gave a slight nod of greeting, avoiding eye contact with her.

The sheikh and I immediately headed toward the studio in the back of Suzi's house, where he instructed Suzi on audio edits that he wanted. Suzi, who was blissfully unaware of the peculiar Islamic rules regulating conduct between the sexes, continued to tease Sheikh Adly during the editing process. She kept calling him Shakey.

Pete phoned halfway through the editing. He asked how things were going, but didn't wait to hear my response. "What are you doing right now?" he said.

"I'm here with Sheikh Adly. I'm just watching the editing process, and will continue to chaperone him."

"You didn't bring any of your work with you?" Pete said in a frantic voice.

"No, the work is back in the office."

Pete's voice became louder and faster. "Bro, you need to bring that with you when you go out for things like this. I can't have you just sitting around when you could be working. I need you to go back to the Musalla and get any work you can take with you so that you can keep busy."

"Okay, Pete."

I hung up the phone and told Sheikh Adly that Pete wanted me to go back to the Musalla to pick up some work. The round-trip would take about thirty minutes. Suddenly, Pete wasn't the only person who was upset.

Unlike Pete, Sheikh Adly didn't raise his voice. Instead, he lowered it to try to prevent Suzi from hearing. He said that he couldn't be in the same room with her. I instantly knew what he meant. There was a *hadith* where Muhammad said, "When a woman and man are alone, Satan is the third." Sheikh Adly thought it was *haram* to be alone in a room with a woman.

I called Pete. "Pete, Sheikh Adly doesn't want me to go. If I left, he'd be alone in a room with a woman, and he doesn't want that."

"What?" Pete asked. I expected him to instantly agree with the sheikh. I was surprised—and, I have to admit, pleased—that he seemed as dismayed as I was by Sheikh Adly's refusal to let me leave for the office. "Put me on the phone with Sheikh Adly," Pete said.

Sheikh Adly spoke quietly. Even though I was sitting across the room, I could sometimes hear Pete's excited voice through the receiver.

But they finally reached a compromise, which Sheikh Adly turned and explained to Suzi. One of her young sons was outside the room doing math homework. In a calm, polite voice, he asked her to leave the door to the studio open and make sure that her son stayed nearby. That was the solution to the Islamic legal problem: leave the door open and make sure an eleven-year-old kid was outside it.

The sheikh thanked Suzi quietly. He bowed his head slightly as he did, embarrassed that he had to make this request.

"It's okay, Shakey. To be honest, I take it as kind of a compliment that you think I'd want to jump your bones." She said the phrase "jump your bones" jokingly, but seemed almost regretful once the words left her mouth—as though, for the first time, she wondered if she had crossed a line.

The sheikh mumbled something. I didn't think he understood what "jump your bones" meant, but decided the best course was to get out of there quickly. I chuckled to myself as I headed out, shaking my head at Suzi's audacity.

But as I got back into my car, my thoughts turned to how Suzi had it wrong. She assumed that Sheikh Adly didn't want to be alone with her because he thought she was attracted to him. But in the end, it had nothing to do with that. Sheikh Adly probably didn't give a moment's thought to who Suzi was before deciding that being alone with her was improper. Suzi was irrelevant; the *hadith* pointed the way.

During Ramadan, I decided to grow a beard. While at Wake Forest I had worn a goatee, and that was the only facial hair I had when I started work at Al Haramain. But then I woke up late for three straight mornings. Because I had to hustle to work, I skipped shaving each time. In an office where the median beard length was six or seven inches, I figured nobody would mind that I had a little extra scruff.

Not only did they not mind, they were positively enthused. On the third day, Charlie Jones asked, "Are you growing a beard?"

The familiar pattern resurfaced. I hadn't given any thought to growing a beard before that, but figured that if I said no, I'd be treated to the now-standard routine of incredulity, assigned reading, and names of scholars I didn't know. "Yes," I said. "I'm growing a beard."

Charlie beamed, an anomalous expression for him.

But then something came up. Before I left Wake Forest, I was selected to the U.S. national debate team. I would be going on a brief tour of Britain, Ireland, and Portugal—competing in some tournaments, participating in public debates, giving lectures and workshops at schools and universities. Wake Forest had sent a press release to the local newspapers, and a reporter from the *Medford Mail Tribune*, Bill Varble, wanted to interview me. He wanted to meet in a coffee shop, where we could talk and his photographer could take some pictures.

The problem was that my beard wouldn't have grown in by the time we were to meet. My facial hair would be in a kind of nether-region where I wasn't clean-shaven but didn't really have a beard. The nether-region of facial hair that's desperately trying to be a beard but failing, and instead just looks like unkempt scruff.

The first person I told about the upcoming interview was Charlie, since I had promised him that I'd grow the beard. I told him that I planned on shaving before the interview so I'd look presentable for the photographer—but then quickly added that I'd *immediately* start growing the beard again once the interview was over. Charlie clucked his tongue disapprovingly. "Your only goal should be pleasing Allah," he said. "You're not trying to please cameramen or newspaper readers or anybody else—only Allah."

"I'll still have facial hair," I said. "It's not like I'm going to shave my goatee off or anything."

"But Allah gave you this hair on your face for a reason. Allah gave you hair on your *whole* face. Why would you shave it off? Was Allah's creation not good enough, so that you have to change it?"

I had no response. I didn't see how shaving the beard could be considered changing Allah's creation. But argument was futile. Charlie shook his head sadly, his eyes downcast. This was very serious for him.

So serious, in fact, that he told Dawood later that day. In the late afternoon, Dawood entered the office with two books for me. One was a pamphlet called *The Beard . . . Why?* The other book I had already seen. Dawood had put yellow tabs in a new section of Muhammad bin Jamil Zino's *Islamic Guidelines for Individual and Social Reform*.

Dawood probably realized how presumptuous this seemed because, for the first time, he spoke to me in something other than a booming, confident voice. With a soft, somewhat apologetic tone, he said, "Bro, I'm just trying to help you. Let me know if we're pushing too fast."

If I said he was pushing too fast, would that have been a wrong answer? "It's okay," I said. "I'm glad that you're helping to educate me about Islam."

I couldn't believe that shaving off my scruff had turned into such an ordeal. After looking through both books that Dawood had given me, I made up my mind. My decision wasn't swayed by religious argument, but by how silly the whole affair seemed.

I told Charlie, somewhat apologetically, that I would shave off the scruff. I made a point of promising that I'd immediately grow out my beard after that. He seemed disappointed, sadder than usual.

It was my first little rebellion. And like most rebellions, it was doomed to failure.

Sheikh Adly conducted a question-and-answer session almost every night, where people would ask theological questions and he'd render a verdict. That night, someone asked Sheikh Adly about the need for a beard.

Sheikh Adly said that having a beard was absolutely required. He quoted a *hadith*: "The Prophet, *alayhi salaatu was salaam*, cursed the men who intend to look like women." Shaving the beard, Sheikh Adly explained, makes a man look like a woman and so strips him of Allah's mercy. When he said this, I noticed some of the others—Charlie, Dawood, Dennis Geren, and Pete—glancing over at me, trying to see what effect the words would have.

I stuck around until half past nine that night. As I headed for the door, Dawood, Charlie Jones, and Pete took me aside. "I hope you'll consider Sheikh Adly's words before you decide to butcher all your facial hair," Dawood said.

Before I could respond, Pete began a rapid-fire interjection that was far more ambitious. "Bro, what you gotta do when you meet the reporter is wear your kufi and a *thobe* [a long, shirtlike dress worn by Saudi men, usually made of white cotton]. You'll look so much like a Muslim that the reporter can't ignore it even if he *wants* to." Pete saw this interview as an opportunity for *dawah*. What I didn't then realize was that these guys saw everything as a *dawah* opportunity.

"Pete," I said, "I don't even wear a *thobe* when I'm here in the Musalla. Why would I go to my interview in one?"

"At least wear your kufi, bro," Pete said. "You want that reporter to know you're a Muslim, and you want newspaper readers to read the story and say, 'Wow! If *this* guy's a Muslim, I can be a Muslim, too!'"

On the drive home, I decided that I wouldn't shave before the interview. As with most of our decisions in life, my choice wasn't based on any single factor. On the one hand, Charlie was right: my only goal was to please Allah, and not anybody else. But another factor, which I tried to downplay to myself, was the inevitable condemnation of my coworkers if I did shave off the scruff.

When I met *Mail Tribune* reporter Bill Varble in a coffee shop off C Street for the interview, he looked puzzled—but not as puzzled as his photographer, who had the unenviable task of making me look presentable for the newspaper. I wore khakis, a blue-and-white-checkered button-up shirt, a kufi, and a few days of scruff. In short, this was not what they expected when they heard that a local resident was a national debating champion who had been selected to represent the United States in a series of debates in Europe.

When the article came out, it featured two photos. My face didn't even appear in the main photo, which was just a shot of my hands gesturing to punctuate a point I made during the interview. My face did appear in a much smaller picture in the lower left-hand corner of the piece. And in that photo, it was shrouded by shadows.

One of the other worshippers who occasionally showed up at the Musalla was Mahmoud Shelton, a white convert with a long beard and turban—the garb and look of the Prophet. Mahmoud already stood out to me because he was a smart guy. He had earned an undergraduate degree in medieval studies from Stanford, which wasn't typical of the other worshippers at the Musalla. (He would later write a book called *Alchemy in Middle-Earth*, which analyzed the Islamic elements of *The Lord of the Rings*.) His appearance reminded me of the Naqshbandis with whom I had taken my *shahadah*.

I struck up a conversation with Mahmoud in the foyer by the front door. I told him briefly about how I had come to convert to Islam, and mentioned that I took my *shahadah* in Italy. "I know some Muslims in Italy," he replied with a sharp, inquisitive smile. "Who did you take your *shahadah* with?"

Normally a venture like this ("What Muslims do you know in Italy?") is a lark. But I named some names, and—sure enough—Mahmoud knew them. His smile broadened. "Those brothers are so full of life!" he exclaimed.

Dennis Geren was sitting within earshot. Mahmoud turned to him and said, "Apparently Daveed took his *shahadah* with some of the Muslims I know in Italy!"

"That's interesting," Dennis said. He didn't say anything negative, but neither did he say anything positive. To my surprise, I was actually embarrassed when Mahmoud mentioned that he knew the Muslims with whom I took my *shahadah*. I realized that I wasn't content to simply avoid saying positive things about the Naqshbandis. I didn't want Ashland's other Muslims to know the route I took to come to Islam.

Dennis left the room a few seconds later. When he was out of earshot, I said to Mahmoud, with a half-smile, "I thought you might be a Naqshbandi."

Mahmoud took a furtive look around to make sure nobody else was listening. "If I were you," he said in a low voice, "I wouldn't say that word too loudly around here."

I nodded. "Yeah, I had that part figured out."

"You obviously catch on quickly," he said.

"Well, it's good to know that you're friends with some of the brothers I took my *shahadah* with."

"Yeah," Mahmoud said, "it's good to see other Muslims here who are a bit more . . . open-minded about some of these issues."

"We should get together sometime and talk a bit more."

"Yeah, we could grab coffee, talk about Islam . . . make loud *dhikr*."

Mahmoud finished his sentence with a mischievous smile. Even bringing it up was a minor act of rebellion.

I nodded noncommittally. *Was loud* dhikr *really an act of* bida? I wondered. Already, just a month into my tenure at Al Haramain, I wanted
nothing to do with forms of worship that were theologically questionable. Although I liked Mahmoud and wanted to talk with him more, I
wanted no part in the loud *dhikr* for which he had such an affection.

I thought back to when I had chided al-Husein for telling another
Wake Forest student that homosexuality wasn't forbidden in Islam, just
something to be avoided so as not to subject yourself to society's stigmas.
At the time, I was surprised to find myself longing for a strong version of
Islam that clashed with my liberal principles. Was I starting to find this
stronger version of the faith?

I missed Amy.

I must have reread the letter that she sent me along with the photographs of her December trip about a dozen times. And I'd often go
through my old Wake Forest e-mail account, reading through messages
that Amy had sent months ago. She wasn't a flowery writer, but had her
style. It was obvious from reading her e-mail messages how much Amy
loved me. I loved her, too, deeply.

We spoke often. Even our phone etiquette suggested that this
breakup wouldn't last. We'd call each other Beloved on the phone, the
nickname we'd long had for each other because of our names' shared
meaning. Sometimes we'd end phone calls with an "I love you." And
while there's plenty of platonic love in the world, this wasn't it.

When I looked at Dennis Geren, I saw the man whom other members
of Al Haramain's inner circle wanted me to develop into. Dennis was

older than me and hadn't graduated from college—but, unlike me, he readily accepted the theological teachings that were passed along to him. Dennis had been Muslim for less than a year, less time than I had been in the faith. But he was regarded as more theologically mature because he gleefully embraced the conservative teachings of which I was skeptical, and resented Muslims who differed from him.

Daily life in the office only reinforced Dennis's extremism. Part of the reason was that most everyone else—or at least, the others who were outspoken—shared Dennis's radical outlook. Beyond that, he read a constant stream of vituperative incoming e-mail purporting to show the oppression visited upon Muslims throughout the world. Much of this came from Idris Palmer, the man whose anti–Nation of Islam pamphlet I had encountered while working on my college honors thesis, and whom Yunus had mentioned to me when we were looking at Salim Morgan's anti-Naqshbandi Web pages.

Idris was the executive director of the Washington, D.C.-based Society for Adherence to the Sunnah, an organization that shared Al Haramain's desire to promote a "pure" vision of Islam. Idris's e-mail covered a wide range of issues, but virtually every subject that he e-mailed about seemed to make him livid. His topics ranged from the mistreatment of Muslims in Algeria, to the Israeli-Palestinian conflict, to the Nation of Islam, to the moderate sheikh Hisham Kabbani accusing other Muslims of radicalism, to the court decision holding that the Boy Scouts had to accept gay scoutmasters, to the mufti of France's distortions of Islam.

Idris's e-mail on this last point was particularly interesting. There was an incident at a junior high school in Flers, France, where a twelve-year-old girl had been told to remove her *hijab*. When she refused, teachers at her school went on strike. Idris forwarded an article about this to his e-mail distribution list, along with a note that went into further detail. Dennis Geren printed out Idris's e-mail and read it to me. "'The girls and their families said they were merely observing the

Moslem religion but the French government and many teachers argued the scarves, as symbols of Islamic fundamentalism and the repression of women, were preventing their wearers from becoming integrated into French society,'" Dennis read from the Reuters news story.

He then began to read Idris's words without noting where the article ended and Idris's writing began: "'Indeed, the picture of Islam in France is quite ugly. France was directly responsible for fighting Islam in North Africa for one hundred and thirty-seven years, and the French have never gotten over their defeat at the hands of the Muslims, and have hated Muslims ever since. Especially after hundreds of thousands of French missionaries adopted Islam. . . .'"

"The article says *that?*" I interrupted.

"It's written here," Dennis said, showing me the printout.

"That's not the article," I said. "That's Idris Palmer's *commentary* on the article."

Dennis shrugged. To him, Idris Palmer was no less objective than the Reuters news service. If anything, he probably thought Idris was a better source of information.

I took the printout from Dennis and read it. Idris was vexed that Muslim schoolgirls who wanted to wear *hijab* to class were opposed not just by their secular schools, but he claimed that they were also opposed by Dalil Boubakeur, the mufti of France. (A mufti is an Islamic scholar who interprets *sharia* law.) The e-mail was typical of Idris's writing style and tone:

> Some time ago I visited Dalil Boubakeur's Paris central "mosquee". His office is guarded by a secretary without hijab and by several armed French police 24 hours a day. He is well known in Paris for promoting what is called, "French Islam" (which equates to "no Islam"). His rulings over the years have caused major problems for any Muslim who wants to assert his or her identity in France. His

"fatwas" enjoy the backing of the French government (which recognizes him as the official "mufti"), and many are directly aimed at women. For instance, he made a "ruling" in 1995 that hijab is incompatible with French lifestyle and is thus haram. This came at a time when several Muslim sisters had been expelled from school because they chose to wear hijab. He also informed Muslim fathers that if they want their daughters to be respected in France, they should prepare them to marry kufar.

In fact, I know a brother who went to the Paris central masjid [mosque] when he was in high school, and one day noticed a young lady in the masjid without hijab. The brother went to the front office and notified the director who told him, "if you want a date with her, just go and ask her." It is not uncommon to see a bar located only one block from the mosque, full of Muslim men drinking booze on Jumuah.

Besides, it is common knowledge that the Paris mosque is not only the functionary of the French government but it is the extended arm of the Algerian anti-Islamic regime. This is the same Algerian regime which was exposed last year as being directly responsible for the massacres they have blamed on "fundamentalists" since 1992.*

Some of the imagery that Idris conjured sounded far-fetched. His statement about bars packed with Muslim men getting drunk on *juma* seemed to be breathless hyperbole. So did the scene with the man who was trying to complain about a *hijab*-less woman in the mosque, only to be told that he could ask her on a date. An image flashed through my

---

*I was able to obtain the exact text of this e-mail because Palmer mass distributed it, and it was posted on an Islamic Web site. As of this writing, the e-mail can still be seen at http://members.tripod.com/jummahcrew/fr.htm.

mind of a meddling high school kid scampering to the mosque leadership to report a Muslim sister for improper attire.

To Idris, every news story he distributed showed the conspiracy to physically subjugate Islam and to undercut the moral principles on which it stood. Just as Idris was angered by every article that he distributed, so was Dennis. And even though Dennis and I had access to the same e-mail accounts and both got Idris's messages, he would rant to me about them anyway. Dennis was a man who needed to emote.

I saw Dennis as a human parrot. He'd read an e-mail that was supposed to make him angry and he'd be angry. An imam would tell him about a fine point of Islamic law and Dennis would instantly agree (provided that the imam's view was sufficiently conservative). He'd read a fatwa in one of Al Haramain's books and would instantly accept it.

Despite this, I was well aware of our relative positions in the local Muslim community. Dennis was viewed as more theologically mature because he accepted those aspects of Wahhabi theology of which I was still skeptical.

I was in the uncomfortable position at work of disagreeing with the prevailing political and theological sentiments, but lacking the confidence to challenge them. But if this was true for me, the feeling was no doubt much greater for many of the non-Muslims who visited the Musalla.

A local reporter, Traci Buck of the *Ashland Daily Tidings*, visited near the end of Ramadan to write a "local Muslims celebrate Ramadan" article. She was a very pretty young woman. After she left, Charlie Jones commented on her tight sweater. It was the style of comment that I would become used to during my time at Al Haramain. The point was not simply to objectify her, but to make clear that you *couldn't help* objectifying her since she had chosen to dress inappropriately.

But while she was in the Musalla, Traci got more than she bargained for. I was ready for a typical, and no doubt boring, interview: some information about Islam, some background on Ramadan, some complaints about how our faith was misunderstood. But Dennis Geren didn't have the standard script in mind.

When Traci arrived, she wanted to shake our hands. Not wanting her to feel uncomfortable, I did shake hands with her. But Dennis refused. "You probably shouldn't shake my hand," he said, "unless you want to marry me."

As the interview began, Dennis sat in a chair in a corner of the office. Looking at Traci with an unblinking gaze, he reeled off a series of political statements dressed up as questions. "Muslims are getting battered throughout the world," he said. "Look at Algeria. They blame all the violence on Muslim 'fundamentalists.' But there are videotapes showing the men who've been going around slaughtering villagers. These guys are wearing headbands that say, There is no God. Is this the kind of thing a Muslim 'fundamentalist' would wear? Or have the government troops been doing this and trying to blame it all on the Muslims?"

Traci was speechless. She had probably never heard of the Algerian civil war, and had no idea what Dennis was talking about—but his anger was unmistakable. "In France, they're making schoolgirls take off their *hijabs*. There are twelve-year-old girls who just want to wear their head scarves to class, and teachers are going on strike to make them leave their *hijabs* at home! Is this the freedom of religion that I hear so much about in the West? Is this an example of the human rights that people keep talking about?" Dennis laughed contemptuously.

I couldn't stop Dennis. The best I could do was wait until Traci looked frantically around the room, trying to find someone who inhabited the same universe as her.

When she made eye contact with me, I smiled broadly and spoke in a calm, soft voice about the religious aspects of Ramadan. When all was said and done, only my remarks made it into the paper. The reporter was looking for a stock story line—Ramadan is a time of spiritual purification for local Muslims, adherents of a misunderstood religion—and I gave it to her. There was no mention of Dennis's rant in the article.

And so, as I often did myself, the reporter chose not to acknowledge that a real clash of values existed here. But for me, this clash of values would become increasingly difficult to ignore.

At the end of January, it was time for my first paycheck. It was dark outside, nobody else was in the office, and Pete was filling out the check. When he showed it to me, I saw that the memo line said "computer."

I didn't know what to say. My very first job after college, and Pete intended to pay me under the table.

Going into salesman mode, Pete said, "Bro, if we say we gave you this check because you sold us a computer, you won't have to pay taxes on it. Can you stick to that?"

This isn't what I wanted, but I worried about what would happen if I refused. Would I be fired? I needed the money. "Yeah," I said. "Yeah, I can stick with that."

Pete leaned forward, jabbing his finger in the air for emphasis. "Are you ready to get on the stand and testify and tell the court that we paid you over two thousand dollars for an old computer?"

I didn't realize it was this serious. "Yeah," I said, uncertain.

Pete smiled and slapped me on the back. "We'll just say you were real persuasive," he said, chortling. "A champion debater, you got us to give you a real good price on that old computer."

This moment would take on more significance years down the road.

six

HAWK

After three months' working for Al Haramain, I had begun to believe in new rules, restrictions, and moral injunctions that I never could have accepted as a campus activist. I became more amenable to the idea that *sharia*, or Islamic law, was the best way to govern a society. Weren't God's decrees superior to the shifting sands of modern morality? And with that, many of my old liberal assumptions came crashing down. Why shouldn't the state ban homosexuality? Why shouldn't the state enforce the modesty of women? For the first time, I began to take these questions seriously.

But sometimes the ideas foisted upon me were beyond anything I was ready to accept. Many of the ideas that pushed my boundaries came from Dennis Geren. Dennis's personality was an interesting mix of anger, alienation, and unexpected compassion.

Dennis was in his midthirties. He had served in the navy as a younger man, and seemed to have led a shiftless life after that. After deciding to hike the Pacific Crest Trail, a 2,650-mile-long trail that runs from the U.S.-Mexico border to the Canadian border, he discovered Ashland. Like my parents, he instantly fell in love with the town. And like my parents, he decided to stay.

Dennis's first job in Ashland, selling vacuum cleaners door-to-door, took him to Charlie Jones's apartment. Once invited inside, Dennis was intrigued by the Qur'anic calligraphy on a poster on the wall, and by the sight of Charlie's wife in a *hijab*. They ended up in a long conversation, and Charlie gave Dennis a Qur'an. Soon after reading it, Dennis converted.

Perhaps because Dennis was a new Muslim, he was generally easier than the others to talk with and debate on the theological issues with which I was wrestling. We spent countless hours in intense religious discussion.

While Pete had once been known as Falcon, Dennis took after a different bird of prey. Charlie had given Dennis the nickname Hawk because of his hawkish views. The nickname fit.

Dennis could have a pleasant demeanor. He was modest and self-effacing, and genuinely cared about others. One day, from the office window he glimpsed a car pulling onto the gravelly shoulder just off Highway 99, seemingly with mechanical problems. Thinking the people in the car might need help, Dennis immediately told me to head down there and see what was going on. We weren't that far from town, and most people would probably have left them alone. I was struck by this gesture. In part, I was struck because it displayed such an altruistic side of Dennis. But I was also struck because Dennis usually had so much anger toward the *kufar*, launching scathing verbal attacks on non-Muslims and placing the blame for most of the world's problems on their shoulders— yet here he was concerned about whether these same non-Muslims needed help getting their car to a mechanic.

The angry side of Dennis was on display more frequently than the compassionate side. One thing that made him angry was current events. While I was often skeptical of Idris Palmer's e-mail purporting to detail injustices inflicted on Muslims half a world away, Dennis's first reaction was not skepticism but anger. It wasn't just that he was certain that the injustices described in these e-mail messages had really occurred; it was as though they were happening before his eyes.

Another thing that made him angry was fellow Muslims who he believed were distorting Islam. Sometimes he'd get angry because they were too liberal; other times deviant practices and beliefs caught his ire. We both thought that Louis Farrakhan's Nation of Islam had little in common with real Islam—but I was never able to muster the anger toward them that Dennis did.

To me, one of the pamphlets that Al Haramain distributed perfectly encapsulated Dennis's vituperative attitude toward the Nation of Islam. Appropriately enough, Idris Palmer wrote it. The title was *The Nation of Islam Exposed.*

The pamphlet argued, in heated language, that Farrakhan wasn't a Muslim and the Nation of Islam's doctrine was not Islam:

> [I]t is an error to oversimplify the issue by denouncing Farrakhan's racist diatribes while playing down Farrakhan's God-is-a-man and Prophet-after-Muhammad beliefs. Racism has very little to do with the issue. Sure, racism is contrary to Islamic principles and Islam rejects it. However, the deviation of Elijah Muhammad and Louis Farrakhan are [sic] MUCH more serious than racism. It is the sin which Allah DOES NOT forgive. If Farrakhan would leave his man-is-god and prophet-after-Muhammad beliefs, but was still a raving racist, he would be much better off than the other way around! Let me say very clearly, that there is NO ideology on the face of this earth which could be farther from Islam than that of Louis Far-rakhan. *NONE!*

I wouldn't have used the same heated language, but agreed with the substance of his argument. There were two key tenets in the *shahadah,* the declaration of faith that makes one a Muslim: there is no god but

Allah, and Muhammad is His Messenger. The Nation of Islam fell short
on both counts. They didn't believe that there was no god but Allah:
they held that God had lived on this earth in the person of W. D. Fard.
And while the Nation of Islam believed that Muhammad was a prophet,
he had specifically claimed to be Allah's *final* prophet. Believing that
Elijah Muhammad was also a prophet thus seemed to violate the second
part of the *shahadah*.

Al-Husein and I disagreed in our approach to the Nation of Islam.
Whenever we discussed them, I'd criticize their theology as un-Islamic.
But al-Husein saw a deeper, political purpose behind the group. Once, in
college, we were driving back from a community event in downtown
Winston-Salem that dealt with racism. Another Wake Forest student in
the car asked about the Nation of Islam. As I was explaining how its the-
ology took it outside the fold of Islam, al-Husein politely interrupted.
"Don't you think it's really all about opposing racism?"

"That *is* a large part of what the group is all about," I said. "But they
also claim to be Muslim, and there's an objective standard you can use to
see if they are."

When I finished writing my honors thesis, I sent it to al-Husein, who
went to Harvard Divinity School after Wake Forest. Because this had
been a small point of contention between us, I was interested to see his
reaction. The thesis went into detail about why the Nation of Islam
wasn't actually Muslim, but also acknowledged that the group's appeal
lay in its willingness to take a stand against racism in America. The thesis urged more traditional Muslim groups to take a similar stand.

After reading it, al-Husein sent back an e-mail that began with the
word *"alhamdulillah,"* Arabic for "all praises due to God." (It is a word
that Muslims use when they receive compliments or accomplish something of significance. It is a word of modesty: this is not *my* accomplishment, but rather God has allowed me to do it.) While the thesis took a

definitive stand about the Nation of Islam's heterodox theology, al-Husein praised it for being compassionate at the same time. He added in the e-mail that he wasn't sympathetic with the approach of Idris Palmer's pamphlet because Palmer lacked any empathy for the Nation of Islam and its adherents. Al-Husein's praise, at the time, made me feel a glow.

The difference between my honors thesis approach and that of Idris Palmer's pamphlet left me with mixed feelings about Dennis Geren's rants about the Nation of Islam. They were certainly a pleasant change from his rants about, say, Algeria—where he blamed the Algerian government for all the violence in that country, completely absolving Islamic terror groups of any responsibility. Here, at least we agreed that the Nation of Islam had a non-Islamic theology. But the depth of his anger puzzled me.

The news had just come out that Farrakhan was diagnosed with prostate cancer. Idris Palmer had distributed an e-mail addressing how Muslims should respond if Farrakhan died. The answer: there was a series of supplications we could use to thank Allah for Farrakhan's death.

Dennis was amused by Farrakhan's illness. Clearly about to enter rant mode, he asked with a laugh, "If Farrakhan really is a god, why doesn't he just heal himself?"

Dennis was mixing up the teachings of the Nation of Islam with those of the Five Percent Nation offshoot, which held that every black man was his own god. He often made this mistake. "He doesn't claim to be a god," I said. I wasn't trying to stick up for Farrakhan, just correct a factual error. "He believes that God appeared as a man, but as far as I know he never claimed to be God."

"That's right," Dennis said. "God appeared as W. D. Fart." Dennis then made a farting noise.

"You know," I said, "I wrote my college honors thesis about the Nation of Islam. Their theology is a lot stranger than you even realize."

Dennis's eyes widened. "Really?"

"Yeah. They believe that mountains were created when black scientists used drill bombs to create explosions beneath the earth's surface. The drill-bomb explosions caused the mountains to form." Dennis laughed. "And the end of the world will come when the black scientists return and rain down drill bombs that destroy civilization. Before they do, the mother ship will come down and pick up all the black Muslims who don't weigh more than one hundred fifty pounds, ushering them to safety."

Dennis was almost giddy at the thought of more ammunition to use against the Nation of Islam. I told him that I'd bring him a copy of the thesis. Inwardly though, I hoped the thesis might help Dennis understand why people were attracted to the Nation of Islam; I hoped it would make him feel less hatred toward them. Clearly, the idea that my differences with my coworkers could be ironed out through dialogue hadn't left me.

Later that week, I brought copies of the thesis for Dennis and Charlie. It was eighty-four pages long, providing a detailed explanation of the group's history and theology, its appeal to the black community, and the attempts of more orthodox Muslim groups to appeal to African-Americans. (I homed in on W. D. Muhammad as a more orthodox alternative to the Nation of Islam—an obvious choice since W. D. Muhammad had originally been given the Nation's top leadership post but decided to bring his followers to more traditional Islam.)

Dennis was excited to get the thesis, but I could tell right away that his expectations were off. "This is great," Dennis said to Charlie. "Daveed wrote a paper that really exposes the Nation of Islam." But it was far more than an exposé.

The next day, I saw that Dennis had put the honors thesis aside after reading only twelve pages. He looked angrier than usual. "You're putting

W. D. *Muhammad* forward as the orthodox alternative to the Nation of Islam?" Dennis snorted. "There's no way that W. D. Muhammad is an *orthodox* Muslim."

"You understand why I call him that, don't you?" I asked.

A couple of footnotes in the paper made clear that it used a loose definition of Orthodox Muslim. The main theological distinction that the paper drew was between the Nation of Islam and other groups that professed a more traditional view of Islam. The paper wasn't attempting to resolve theological controversies beyond that, nor was Orthodox Muslim used as a term of praise.

As I began to explain this, Charlie cut in. He shook his head woefully as he spoke. It seemed that my referring to W. D. Muhammad as an orthodox Muslim saddened him. "We shouldn't refer to these guys as orthodox Muslims," he said. "That's praise they don't deserve. Maybe they're Muslims, but *orthodox* Muslims? They aren't that."

He stared out the window as he continued. "Why do these guys even call themselves Muslims?" he asked, his thoughts now turning from W. D. Muhammad to Farrakhan's Nation of Islam. "I'd be fine if they just called themselves Black Nazis. But why Muslims? Why are they trying to claim *my* religion?"

A few days later, Dennis showed me a photocopy of a Nation of Islam pamphlet that we had on file. A Muslim prisoner had sent it to us.

Al Haramain's prison *dawah* program had become quite popular. The group was well known among prisoners for distributing Islamic literature, occasionally in the form of handsome hardcover volumes. There was a somewhat sophisticated system for doing this. When prisoners wrote requesting literature, they were sent a questionnaire designed to evaluate their Islamic knowledge. It asked a number of questions, ranging from the simple—Who is Allah (swt)?* Who is Jesus (pbuh)?**—to the obscure—What are the ten *sunan al-fitra?* After a prisoner filled out the questionnaire, his answers were graded. Those who performed better would get more advanced books. As a result of the program's popularity, prisoners often sent us long letters. (The disturbing frequency with which we received ten-page letters from prisoners borne out of their boredom produced the only pun that I ever heard Pete make: he called the prisoners a "captive audience.") Sometimes these letters contained interesting items they had come across in prison, such as the Nation of Islam pamphlet that Dennis now clutched in his hand.

The pamphlet tried to justify the Nation of Islam's bizarre theology. The arguments were so bad that they were embarrassing. Almost every Qur'anic quote was clearly out of context. Particularly amusing was the claim (intended to justify the Nation of Islam's racism) that Prophet Muhammad had been a black man, and this fact had been covered up for centuries. The claim was accompanied by a picture purporting to show that Muhammad had been black. Aside from the fact that pictures of the Prophet were *haram*, that "proof" was humorous because the pamphlet was a low-quality photocopy. The picture didn't look like a person, just a splotch of black ink.

After having a good laugh about the pamphlet, I wanted to move the conversation from ridiculing others to the deeper issues that Dennis might be overlooking. I said that racism is a real problem, and even though we sharply disagreed with the Nation of Islam's theology, we had to be sympathetic and compassionate about why people are drawn to it.

---

*The parenthetical "swt" stands for "*subhana wa ta'ala,*" which means "may He be glorified and exalted." It is a statement of worship that often follows Allah's name.
**The parenthetical "pbuh" stands for "peace be upon him." Muslims generally use this phrase after saying the name of a prophet.

"Compassionate?" Dennis asked. "For those people who are part of the Nation of Islam and believe in black gods and W. D. Fart"—again, he made a farting noise—"you should just hand them this pamphlet and Idris Palmer's pamphlet and let them choose. And if they choose Farrakhan's cult, with its mother ship and W. D. Fart"—a farting noise— "then you'd punish them the way heretics have always been punished."

"Punish them?"

"Yeah, let them choose true Islam or cut off their heads."

Daveed, if I were you I'd take your necklace off right now."

I bought the necklace in Chicago the previous February. Since then, I had worn it every day for almost a year. I wanted a physical reminder of my faith—similar to how my kufi served as a visible reminder, only less conspicuous—so I bought a string necklace with a metal star-and-crescent symbol on it. And now Dennis Geren was telling me to remove it.

"Why?"

"Last night, Yunus asked Sheikh Adly if it was okay for men to wear necklaces. Sheikh Adly said that men are not to wear necklaces under any circumstances. He said that necklaces are women's clothing, and men shouldn't wear women's clothing."

I looked down at the necklace. Another day on the job. New and exciting points of Islamic law to discover.

Dennis shrugged. His tone was apologetic. Far from being one of his hawkish moments, Dennis seemed as bewildered by Sheikh Adly's pronouncement as I was. "I figured I was doing you a favor," he said, "by telling you about it before Yunus could get to you."

I thought of Yunus and his arrogant young man's way of speaking. Dennis was indeed doing me a favor. I slowly took the necklace off, crumpled it up, and shoved it into my pocket. I never wore it again.

When the Kosovo war began in 1999, Pete walked into the office on one of the rare days that Charlie, the Hawk, and I were all there. He pressed his lips together as though deep in thought, nodded his head, and said, "You know, I think I'm for what the U.S. is doing in Kosovo. They're actually going in to save Muslims."

Yugoslav president Slobodan Milošević's crackdown on the ethnic Albanian majority in the province of Kosovo, who were predominantly Muslim, precipitated the war. Many observers feared that the Serbian forces led by Milošević were undertaking a campaign of "ethnic cleansing" against the ethnic Albanians. This concern led the international community to try to broker a deal to end the crisis early in 1999. When Milošević rejected the deal, U.S.-led NATO forces initiated air strikes against targets in Kosovo and Serbia in March 1999 to try to protect the ethnic Albanian population.

When Pete said that he was for the Kosovo war, the rest of us agreed with him. It was probably the last time that all four of us would back the United States in one of its military engagements, and soon the others' take on the war would change. Probably the biggest factor in turning Pete, Charlie, and Dennis against the Kosovo war was a torrent of e-mail that Idris Palmer distributed featuring articles from the left-wing British press. Some of these articles argued that the air war had only accelerated the Serbs' slaughter of the ethnic Albanians; others argued (absurdly) that the Kosovo war was in fact a "war for oil."

So after Pete, in his infinite fickleness, turned against the Kosovo war, he decided that he was single-handedly going to end it. Pete was one part activist, one part visionary, and one part con man. He would always come up with big, world-changing ideas that would inspire our benefactors in Saudi Arabia and convince them to devote tens of thousands of dollars. But the ideas never panned out the way Pete intended.

He came to the office in the middle of one of his workdays and explained his plan. He wanted to put together a convoy of trucks, manned by private citizens and loaded with humanitarian supplies, that would enter Yugoslavia. Pete believed that when the convoy entered the country to distribute supplies, it would send a powerful signal: the bombing campaign had to end.

Pete dictated a two-page letter to me that we sent to Dradana Ivanovich, the Yugoslav ambassador. In the letter, Pete framed the Serbs' situation in much the same way as he often framed the plight of the world's Muslims: "America's vast military industrial complex needs to create an enemy to justify the billions of dollars spent every year to build up our vast arsenal, and the Western media has aided them in constructing the Serbians as the new threat to the West. I believe that the Serbians are good people, and that innocent men, women, and children are being killed every day during this senseless bombing campaign."

Pete paused after dictating this, and said, "See, I left that vague. When they read that innocent men, women, and children are being killed, they'll think that I'm talking about the Serbs. But really, bro, the innocent men, women, and children are the Muslims."

The letter went on to explain Pete's peace convoy plan:

> I wish to break the ice and help bring peace to the region by leading a convoy of relief trucks into the Yugoslav Federation as a statement that the hostilities directed toward the Federation should cease. . . .
>
> The trucks will have flashing lights on them, so that if NATO's warplanes bomb them the world can see that NATO knew who it was hitting. I will drive the lead truck as a private citizen. The convoy will bring food and medical supplies for relief of the suffering citizens of the Yugoslav Federation, and the breaking of ice will also be a symbol that it is time to push the peace process forward.

I would like to lead the convoy from Albania, because the center of hostility is perceived in the West as a conflict between Albania and the Yugoslav Federation. We would like to get as much press coverage as possible, to protect ourselves from NATO's bombing and to dramatize the need for peace on the world stage. We will have no more than two drivers per vehicle, and each vehicle will hold food, medical supplies, and good will for all humankind.

Of course, Pete's idea was doomed from the start. If the Serbs ever gave serious thought to this proposal, they would certainly do a background check on Pete and the Al Haramain Islamic Foundation. What they would find would doubtless convince them that Pete's scheme was far more trouble than it could possibly be worth.

My favorite person in Ashland's Muslim community was Abdi Guled. He was a tall Somali, standing six feet eight with a six feet ten wingspan. I was told that he used to play basketball for Somalia's national team and was a hero in that country. If Somalia hadn't deteriorated into lawlessness, he could perhaps be its president or hold some similarly powerful position.

Abdi was beloved in Ashland, with good reason. He was more full of life than anybody I had met. Even his broad smile reflected the love he had for others, black or white, Muslim or non. He also had a mellifluous accent and punctuated his speech with words that most people didn't understand, but that sounded endearing.

Abdi's wife, Mary Foster, was also a wonderful person. I had known her for years, as her son was a friend of mine in elementary school. (Actually, he used to beat me up back then, but the distinction between friend and bully sometimes erodes over time.) She and Abdi loved to travel together, and would sometimes show me videotapes of the exotic locales they had visited.

One day when we were standing around near the main room in the Musalla, Dennis Geren held both of his hands in front of him and pretended to shoot at cars that were driving by on I-5. Seeing this, Abdi said with a smile, "No, *baba*, peace! You shouldn't do that!"

"But, Abdi," Dennis said with a smirk, "they're *kufar!*"

"Peace, *baba*, peace," Abdi repeated. And so he put the Hawk in his place with three words and an infectious grin.

One reason that Dennis and I frequently ended up debating was because he had somehow gotten the idea that the most persuasive way of speaking was framing his comments as questions. When you ask questions, he reasoned, it seems that you're demanding an answer of the listener. So when Dennis ranted about Algeria, he'd rattle off a fiery series of questions: "They cancel the elections in Algeria and leave the Muslims to be slaughtered by the Algerian army. Is this justice? Is this the human rights I always hear them talking about? Do you stop 'terrorists' by sweeping through Algerian villages and slaughtering babies?"

The problem for Dennis was that each question *did* seem to demand an answer, particularly because his understanding of the international situations about which he had such strong opinions tended to be off base. After I'd let Dennis's first three or four questions go by, I'd eventually feel compelled to engage him. We'd then enter into wide-ranging debates in which Dennis tried to recount every evil inflicted by the Western world in the past five centuries, and would make me defend them all. Given my roots as a campus radical, I wasn't always happy with this role.

One day we were arguing about the Taliban. Ever since I became

Muslim, I had thought it obvious that the Taliban's brutal rule was contrary to true Islamic principles. I thought it obvious that my religion wouldn't countenance a dictatorial regime that treated its women like cattle and viewed free intellectual inquiry as a disease.

I remembered how Dennis had defended the Taliban when we made our presentation to Ms. Thorngate's class. I assumed then that he didn't understand the full brutality of their rule, and that I could change his mind. But it was I who was in for a surprise.

"Dawood spoke to a man," Dennis said, "who's actually *been* to Afghanistan. He said that they were practicing true Islam there, and everything was beautiful."

"Dennis," I said, "seriously. The country's most popular form of entertainment is public executions. Women can't get an education, and can barely get health care because of the ridiculous sex segregation. Those guys are running one of the worst governments in the world."

"That's not what Dawood's friend says. And, Daveed, the guy is a *brother*."

I shrugged. So the guy who said that everything was beautiful in Afghanistan was Muslim. Did that make him infallible?

Dawood walked into the office. I wanted to end the conversation. Dawood was more than a decade older than me, and became Muslim many years ago. He spoke with the unwavering certainty of a true believer, and was the kind of person who I felt uncomfortable engaging in argument.

But Dennis saw Dawood's entrance as a way to settle our dispute. He asked Dawood, "Didn't you tell me that a brother who came through here had been to Afghanistan and said that all the Western media stories were distorted?"

"Oh, yes," Dawood said. "He said they were practicing the truest form of Islam he's seen. He said that the whole country would fall apart if they didn't have *sharia* law, and what they're doing there is beautiful."

The look Dennis gave me was that of the bright pupil whose teacher said he had answered a classroom question correctly. It was as though the account of some guy I had never met meant more than hundreds of well-documented newspaper stories.

While trying to make his dream of a peace convoy into Yugoslavia a reality, Pete also pursued another ambitious project that would never come to fruition.

As the Kosovo war progressed, a stream of ethnic Albanian refugees entered the United States. Pete wanted Al Haramain to do something to help them. Although the refugees had a variety of needs, it was their religious needs that Pete cared about most. The proposal for the head office in Saudi Arabia that Pete had me type for him described their religious situation in breathless terms:

> As you know, Brothers, many years of Communist rule success-
> fully eradicated knowledge of Islam in the majority of Albanians who
> had lived in Kosova.* Reliable sources have informed us that the hor-
> ror stories we all hear about their lack of Islamic knowledge are true.
> Fifty-year-old Albanian men do not even know how to make *wudu*,
> many Albanians do not know what to say when making *salat*, and
> even fewer know what the Arabic words mean. And now they are
> amongst the Christian missionaries and temptations of the West.
>
> Christian missionaries are hard at work and well funded in the
> United States, trying to make the Kosovar Albanians disbelieve in
> the Oneness of Allah. The refugees' translators are not even Muslim,
> making it even more difficult for them to maintain their faith.

---

*This spelling of Kosovo was no error on our part. Some of the leading Islamic groups involved in assisting the ethnic Albanians insisted that Kosovo should be spelled with an *a*, since that is how the Kosovars spelled it.

Pete's solution to this problem was, like most of his ideas, ambitious. He wanted to immediately print business cards in the Albanian language so the refugees could contact the Ashland office. He wanted to create an 800 number for a 24-hour emergency help line manned by two new full-time employees who spoke Albanian. He wanted the Ashland office to be established as the State Department's Islamic organizational contact, so we would be informed whenever more refugees arrived in order to reach out to them. Pete wanted to get Islamic literature in the Albanian language from Saudi Arabia that could be distributed to the refugees. But that wasn't all; he also had long-term plans, such as creating a newsletter in the Albanian language that could grab their attention because of its political and cultural content—but the newsletter would eventually be used to introduce them to correct Islamic practices.

The head office in Riyadh bought into Pete's vision. They sent us about $50,000. But what came of that money? We received two large boxes of Islamic booklets in the Albanian language. These booklets contained translations of the first sura of the Qur'an (which was a mere seven verses long) and a portion of the second sura. Some of these booklets were distributed to Albanian cultural and Islamic centers throughout the country. Seven thousand business cards were printed. Some of the cards were sent out along with the Islamic booklets, while Pete personally distributed other cards on a trip to Fort Dix in New Jersey, where many of the refugees were stationed. We did create an 800 number for refugees, but never had an Albanian speaker to man it. And I did the paperwork necessary to get Al Haramain put on the State Department's list of organizations involved in refugee placement—but the paperwork was never sent in.

That's what the Riyadh office got for its $50,000. But they were so flush with cash that they might have never realized the total and complete waste of their money.

And, at the very least, it was a better use of cash than some of Al Haramain's future endeavors would prove to be.

It was dusk and I sat on the deck behind my house. Holding a cordless phone in one hand, I slowly punched in the Boston telephone number. I was calling al-Husein.

To me, religion was both a relationship with God and also a relationship with a community of believers. I thought back to how al-Husein had helped to draw me out of myself at Wake Forest. Through al-Husein, I was able not only to learn about Islam, but to reach a greater level of engagement with other people. But I was separated from Wake Forest and al-Husein not only by thousands of miles, but also by time. There had been a fleeting moment of community, a fleeting moment in Winston-Salem where my Islam fueled my activism and my activism fueled my Islam. But was that all illusory? Had I misunderstood the nature of Islam, the nature of my Muslim brothers and sisters?

I was again beginning to feel isolated. It was from these phone calls with al-Husein that I drew my sense of community, able to reconnect with the progressive vision of Islam that I had stumbled upon more than a year ago.

"*Assalaamu 'alaykum.*" Al-Husein answered his phone with the traditional Muslim greeting.

"Who the heck is Sam Alaykum?" I joked. It was typical for us to play off the image of the ignorant Westerner who can't understand Islamic concepts; here, the joke was someone mistaking the Islamic greeting for the other party saying his name.

"Bro!" al-Husein said. "Good to hear from you!"

"How have you been, brother?" I said. And thus began one of our many wide-ranging conversations. I had closed myself off more at the office, knowing that anything I put forward could be subject to attack, reprimand, and a reading assignment. My conversations with al-Husein were more of an anarchic free flow of ideas. The topics we discussed would bounce from Islam to class and race to foreign policy to social justice to progressive politics to the shortcomings of the radical view of the faith.

I filled al-Husein in on some of the interesting Islamic rulings that had been directed at me over the past few months. "So I was reading a newspaper article during Ramadan," I told him, "and it said that Muslims aren't supposed to eat, drink, have sexual intercourse, or listen to music during the day."

"Not supposed to listen to music during Ramadan? I've never heard that."

"Neither had I, so when I got into work I asked about it. Get this, right away I'm told that Muslims shouldn't listen to music *at all*. So one of the guys comes in with a book that has a complete fatwa on the matter. He wanted me to stop listening to music altogether!"

"I'm familiar with brothers who make that argument," al-Husein said. "But look at the Muslims who incorporate music into their faith. These are guys who have nothing. They don't have electricity, they don't have running water, they're trying to scrape up enough money to feed their families. I say let them have their music."

I saw a logical flaw in al-Husein's argument. Neither he nor I lived in desperate poverty; there should be no religious sliding scale that allowed *us* to commit acts that would otherwise be *haram*. But I didn't mention it. I was just happy to have some support for a more liberal interpretation.

I didn't even notice as two hours of conversation flew by. After talking with al-Husein, the difference was even more pronounced the next morning when I got into work and again had to face Dennis Geren. He had just taken in his morning ration of Idris Palmer e-mail, so had a fresh batch of talking points. *Here we go again.*

When Amy and I had worked at Wake Forest's summer debate camp last summer, there had been something unsaid between us. Amy was the first to broach it when, for the first time, she told me that she loved me. This time, I was the first to broach something else that had been unsaid.

Near the end of one of our phone calls, I said, "Amy, do you think we made a mistake in breaking up?"

There was a long pause. It wasn't an awkward silence. She was giving serious thought to what I had asked. "We may have," she said.

"Amy," I said, "I love you." Then I told her everything: how conflicted I felt when we decided to stop seeing each other back in December, how much I missed her, how I'd reread her letter and old e-mail messages several times, how I knew that I still loved her.

"I wish," I said, "that we weren't doing this over the phone. It would be more appropriate if I were down on one knee in front of you with a sparkling ring in hand."

I felt Amy smile on the other end of the phone. She said that she needed time to think about it. I told her to take all the time she needed. I didn't feel nervous or anxious. I simply knew that she was the one.

Despite Mount Dennis's tendency to erupt, I at least felt comfortable talking to him about our differences of opinion. Perhaps it was Dennis's good side—the fact that, despite his anger, he was a man of manners and compassion. Perhaps it was that Dennis was, like me, young in his faith. Perhaps it was that Dennis recognized his own extremes. Whatever it was, I felt more comfortable debating against Dennis than I did with the others at Al Haramain.

I realized that I now lacked confidence in my understanding of Islam. A year ago, I had such certainty in the moderate vision of the faith that al-Husein trumpeted to me. The problem was that I had always believed that extremists distorted the faith out of ignorance, or for their own political gain. Now I was surrounded by people with extremist views, and there was no obvious flaw in their interpretation. I could quibble with their evidence on some points, but where was their approach to the faith wrong? I couldn't find the silver-bullet argument that would slay their approach with a single shot.

Despite this, I continued to believe in progressive Islam. What I needed to do, I realized, was gain enough confidence in my knowledge of the faith and in my standing in the community that I could engage these issues openly. I redoubled my efforts at theological study, poring over the Qur'an, the *ahadith*, and theological treatises. As I learned more, my conversations with al-Husein continued to be my main outlet for ideas.

Little did I know that my studies would actually lead me to the legalistic interpretation of Islam that I then regarded as extreme, to a theology rooted in rules divorced from morality. And little did I know that al-Husein himself would help usher me down this path.

I spoke with Amy again a few days later. This time she had made up her mind.

Yes was her answer: Yes, she would marry me.

I felt an indescribable glow. This was the woman I loved, and now we would spend our lives together. We were already talking about having Amy come out for the summer, about shopping for a ring. I wasn't sure if I had ever felt as happy and complete.

Eventually this glow would fade as the religious changes I went through fundamentally altered the way I saw the world, altered things as central as my relationship with my parents or the woman I loved. But that would come later. For now, I felt nothing but pure, unmistakable joy.

seven

SALAFI

On a crisp night, the Gold's Gym in the shopping center off Siskiyou Boulevard provided the one spark of light in a row of closed stores. A woman stood on the sidewalk outside the large plate-glass windows looking into the exercise rooms and waving at me.

Her name was Kristy Hennan. She was a year behind me at Ashland High School, but I never really knew her until she began classes at my alma mater, Wake Forest. She was a tall, dark-haired woman with a robust sense of humor who was oddly shy at the same time. She had been passing by the gym and had seen me inside.

I walked outside hesitantly. Kristy and I had been friends at Wake Forest, and it had been a few months since we'd had a chance to hang out. Normally I'd be delighted to see Kristy, but a lot had changed over the last few months. Back at Wake Forest, nobody was looking over my shoulder to make sure that my interactions with women fell strictly within the bounds of Islamic law. Now, as I slowly walked to the gym door, I could feel Charlie Jones's and Dennis Geren's eyes following me, studying me in an effort to discern microscopic flaws.

For the past few weeks, I had been working out with Charlie and Dennis. But it wasn't your usual workout regime. Dennis had reprimanded me during my initial trip to the gym. He looked down at my gym shorts, then said in a stern voice, "Shorts should be *below* the knees." I couldn't believe he was commenting on my shorts. Suddenly my entire devotion to Islam turned on whether my clothing was long enough while I was exercising.

I muttered that I was just wearing shorts while I was in the gym, and wouldn't be venturing outside in them. I realized that this distinction would make no difference to Dennis. If I wore shorts again, I would be reprimanded again. Naturally, the next time I went to the gym with Dennis and Charlie, I wore sweatpants.

Then, there was Charlie's unique manner when we worked out together. Charlie was a strong guy. He had the same routine each time he threw up a set on the bench press. First he'd say the *basmallah* quietly: *Bismillah ar-Rahman ar-Raheem*, Arabic for "in the name of Allah, the Compassionate, the Merciful." Then, on finishing the set, he'd say, "*Alhamdulillah*. A drop of sperm can do this. I was once a drop of sperm, yet Allah could make me grow to do this." And he would nod his head emphatically, his eyes wide.

Charlie and Dennis watched me walk into the darkness outside and talk to this woman they didn't know. This alone was probably improper in their eyes.

After some awkward small talk where my mind wasn't on Kristy, but on how our conversation would be perceived by the others, she said that she was glad to see me but had to go. So her demand was natural enough. "Daveed, come here and give me a kiss." It wasn't a sexual or romantic demand, just the kind of thing that's normal between friends of the opposite sex.

I hesitated. I thought of the teacher whose hand I had refused to shake when I was with Sheikh Adly. I thought of Charlie and Dennis staring at me from inside the gym. I thought of Dennis correcting me when my shorts had come up above the knees. I smiled at Kristy, then said no.

Kristy knew me better than the teacher whose hand I had refused to shake, and didn't take offense. She assumed that my refusal had to do with Amy, my now-fiancée. This was wrong. It was about what two men she didn't know (and who she almost certainly wouldn't like) would think about what a peck on the cheek said about me as a Muslim.

"That's okay. Give me a hug, anyway." Her tone of voice was disappointed and somewhat surprised, but also understanding.

Kristy put her arms around me and I hugged her rather lamely, putting my right hand softly on her back. I never thought I would feel internal conflict over something as routine, something as small as a hug. But here, hugging a woman involved a significant moral and religious struggle.

For some women, a hug or a kiss on the check is no different from shaking hands. But to me, even shaking hands would have been out of bounds.

I wasn't the only one grappling with a more conservative, rules-based practice of Islam. One day I got a somewhat cryptic e-mail from al-Husein. He told me that he had just experienced a miracle, and couldn't wait to tell me about it.

Al-Husein had continued to be my one real outlet for religious discussion. At work, I would often be hit by conservative ideas that seemed ridiculous, but about which I judged debate to be futile. On those days, I couldn't wait to call al-Husein and get his perspective. I looked forward to these conversations the way I used to look forward to our walks on the quad.

I had become more serious, more rules-based in my practice of Islam than al-Husein. Yet I found him to be a fount of perspective on how not to lose sight of the *spirit* of the faith even while observing the forms of practice more closely.

I didn't know what to expect when al-Husein told me that he'd experienced a miracle. I called him when I got home from work.

"*Assalaamu 'alaykum.*" As always, he answered the phone with the traditional Islamic greeting.

"*Wa alaykum assalaam,* bro. So, tell me about this miracle."

He had been visiting one of Boston's mosques, he said, and after prayers a bunch of the worshippers stood up and started shouting off time periods. "Twenty days!" one of them shouted.

"Two weeks!" Another rose to his feet.

"Five days!" said a third.

Al-Husein said skeptically to a man sitting beside him, "This isn't some kind of Sufi thing, is it? Because I've tried that before and I'm not into it." The man assured him that this was not, and said that al-Husein had to experience it. So al-Husein stood up and said, "Three days!" (Al-Husein didn't know this at the time, but when these men shouted out these time periods, they were committing to leave home for that period and go on a mission trip for the Tablighi Jamaat, an Islamic missionary group.)

As al-Husein told his story, I silently took note of that question: "This isn't some kind of Sufi thing, is it? Because I've tried that before and I'm not into it." I hadn't heard al-Husein criticize Sufism before. When he helped teach me about Islam, it was through the lens of Sufism. So why did al-Husein brush Sufism aside as something that he'd already tried? I thought back to what al-Husein had told me a few weeks before about his experience running for office in the Harvard Islamic Society (HIS).

Elections and offices were clearly important to al-Husein. Given the political force he had been at Wake Forest, it was only natural that al-Husein would run for office in HIS.

But the HIS election meeting was not what al-Husein expected. He had never seen anything like it. When it was time to vote for each office, the various candidates left the room and stood in the hallway. The Muslims who remained would discuss them. But they didn't discuss the candidates' qualifications, as al-Husein had expected. Instead, the discussions focused solely on their *faith*.

This made al-Husein unexpectedly nervous. All his life, al-Husein had been judged on his secular qualifications, and they were never found wanting. But now he would be judged by different criteria, and for the first time he didn't know what the others would say.

When his office came up, al-Husein stood outside in the hallway while HIS's other Muslims debated about him. Even though he was running unopposed, he had to stew out there for fifteen long minutes while they considered his candidacy. Ultimately, they decided to give him the office. But for those fifteen minutes, he wasn't sure that they would. At the time, weeks before he experienced his miracle, al-Husein had told me that this was a wake-up call. "I need to start taking my Islam more seriously," he said.

It seemed strange to me that you would alter the practice of your faith because of *what others might say*. That is, it seemed strange until I thought of my own situation. Wasn't this what I was doing at Al Haramain?

Al-Husein continued the story about his miracle, describing a speaker in the mosque who addressed those who are born into Islam but don't understand or practice their religion. He spoke of Muslims who had strayed from their faith and needed to rediscover it. To al-Husein, it was as though this man were speaking to him. I knew that I had been craving greater theological certainty; so was al-Husein. And now it was explained in a way that fit his situation.

The speaker, al-Husein learned, was from an Islamic missionary group known as the Tablighi Jamaat, which was founded in Mewat, India, in 1927. Their *dawah* isn't focused on non-Muslims, but rather on nominal Muslims, those who claim the faith but don't really practice it.

The Tablighis encouraged al-Husein to spend the night in the mosque with them. That night, al-Husein experienced his miracle. It was unclear to me precisely what happened, but al-Husein said that his practice of Islam was transformed. Where he once wasn't serious about the faith, he was serious now. Where he once might have made theologically questionable arguments, al-Husein now thought he saw the true path that Allah wanted him to follow.

I was complimentary and encouraging. "That's great, brother," I said. "I'm glad that you were touched in that way. Keep me in your prayers, bro, and pray that Allah does the same for me."

I didn't want to say how nervous al-Husein's "miracle" made me. I had a feeling that I would be losing a dear friend—losing my best friend—to radical Islam. Al-Husein was the one who had brought me into Islam, but now my sense of the faith was changing. I was making a shift, hesitatingly but surely, toward a more conservative understanding of the religion. I felt rationally compelled to move in this direction, but emotionally my liberal ideals screamed out against it. I felt guilty that I might not be moving to a more conservative practice steadily or quickly enough, and al-Husein had been the one sounding board for what I was going through inside. (Since Amy was not a Muslim, I didn't think she could comprehend my struggles.) If I lost al-Husein to the radicals, I would lose the one person I regarded as a genuine ally in my quest for a moderate and progressive Islam.

I doubted al-Husein's motives. It seemed that, in actuality, his experience with the election coupled with the peer pressure he was experiencing from more conservative Muslims at Harvard was enough to bend something as fundamental as his religious beliefs. But I wondered if the same thing was also happening to me.

One day I was trying to get caught up on our reports for the head office in Saudi Arabia. That afternoon, when Pete entered the office, I handed him a stack of long-overdue reports. These had originally been Charlie's responsibility, but these days his productivity had diminished to almost nothing. He would be absent from the office for weeks at a time.

Pete flipped through the reports and eventually seized on the bottom of the stack, the December 1998 report. Among other things, it went into detail about the presentation to the high school class that I had participated in on my first day with Al Haramain. Pete shook his head. "Bro," he said, "you gotta give this as small a write-up as possible. The head office is pretty angry."

"Why are they angry?" I had come to hate asking questions like this.

"They were mad about all the male and female students being in the prayer room at the same time. We even sat them apart . . . so that we could stomach having them there." Pete said that some photos of the event had gotten back to the head office, and they were offended at the images of *hijab*-less women in the same room as male students.

In December, I thought it was strange to separate the students by sex. Now I learned that even that was not enough. As I revised the December report, I couldn't wait to hear al-Husein's thoughts.

When I spoke with al-Husein that night, I realized that I was indeed losing him as an ally. When I recounted the conflict with the head office over the high school presentation, his reaction was telling.

Or rather, his lack of reaction. This was the kind of conservative religious thinking that al-Husein and I used to mock. While I recounted the incident with all the amusement and bewilderment that had typified these conversations in the past, al-Husein responded with a pregnant silence. He didn't debate me, but neither did he agree. He said nothing.

I knew al-Husein and his silences well enough to know what it meant here. He was new to conservative Islamic thinking, but probably felt internally conflicted about the matter—and my flip dismissal of the head office's concerns likely made him uncomfortable.

Over the next few weeks, I became increasingly guarded in my conversations with al-Husein. We still spoke once or twice a week, but I felt that now I not only had to watch what I said at work, but also around al-Husein.

In our life before the Tablighis, I would sometimes call al-Husein out for making theological arguments that didn't reflect proper Islamic principles—such as when I heard him tell a woman student at Wake Forest that Muslims were only urged to avoid homosexuality because they shouldn't subject themselves to the prejudice against gays. Now he was overcompensating. Al-Husein seemed to believe that his search for social justice was itself the cause of his theological transgressions. So he simply abandoned it.

One figure at the center of al-Husein's spiritual transformation was named Brother Taha. I never knew Brother Taha's last name, but he was another Muslim whom al-Husein had met through the Harvard Islamic Society. I first heard the name Brother Taha from al-Husein about a month before he spent the night with the Tablighis. Al-Husein had mentioned that there was a learned brother in HIS named Taha, and that Brother Taha was a Salafi. Once I heard he was Salafi, I knew enough to be worried—for al-Husein, for our friendship, and for myself.

The Arabic word Salaf, from which the term *Salafi* comes, means predecessors or early generations. Those who subscribe to this school of thought seek to return to the pure Islam practiced by Prophet Muhammad and the first generation of Muslims. *Salafi*, in short, is the term that Wahhabis use to refer to themselves (although there are some Salafis who can't be classified as Wahhabis). Osama bin Laden is a Salafi.

From the outset, al-Husein was impressed by the depth of Taha's knowledge, and recognized that there was a compelling case for Salafism. Our conversations became peppered with al-Husein's comments about what "a Salafi would say." He didn't refer to himself as a Salafi, but wanted us to be aware of, and consider, the Salafi position. An angel and a devil were perched on al-Husein's shoulders arguing. Whether the Salafi was the angel or the devil depends on your perspective.

It was clear that the days when my conversations with al-Husein were far-ranging intellectual odysseys were gone. Just as al-Husein remained silent when I told him about the head office's reaction to our high school presentation, I soon found our conversations punctuated by silences. These silences would follow any criticism I offered of extremism in Islam. Perhaps al-Husein disagreed with me—but I suspected that it was something more than that. I suspected that he agreed with my criticisms deep down, but that he was trying hard to suppress these feelings. That he was ashamed of them.

Al-Husein would also more frequently take jabs at liberal Muslims with whom he disagreed. These jabs began innocuously enough after his night with the Tablighis. "On campus they always have these events," he told me. "Events like What is Islam? I don't even go to them anymore. I already know the answer. What good could they do me?"

He didn't say that because these events were basic, containing introductory information. No, it was because these were Sufi-type events that approached the faith by exploring the manner in which various people practice Islam. Al-Husein was no longer interested in how other people practiced Islam. He had found true Islam—why did he need another perspective?

As al-Husein became seduced by the Salafi worldview, we had our own Salafi visitors in Ashland. Three men came over from Saudi Arabia to produce a documentary about Islam: Abdul-Qaadir Abdul-Khaaliq, an African-American convert to Islam who now lived in Saudi Arabia and worked for Al Haramain; Ahmed Ezzat, an Egyptian sheikh who now lived in Saudi Arabia; and a Saudi man named Abdullah An-Najashi, who barely spoke English and whose main purpose seemed to be comic relief.

I later learned that there was a second reason for their visit, beside the documentary. Sheikh Hassan had recently complained to Al Haramain's head office in Riyadh that it didn't make sense to have the U.S. headquarters in an out-of-the-way place like Ashland, where there wasn't a huge pool of potential converts to draw on, and where there was a limit to the impact that publicity and *dawah* work would have. The Riyadh office wanted to have our visitors assess the wisdom of keeping the head U.S. office in Ashland.

Pete was raving about Abdul-Qaadir long before he set foot in southern Oregon. "This guy is great," Pete said. "He can come here and teach classes every night at the Musalla, teach weekend classes, and help show us what real Islam is."

So I was intrigued to meet Abdul-Qaadir, and came away impressed when we were introduced.

Abdul-Qaadir was a light-skinned black man with a broad chin and a full beard. His facial hair wasn't very thick; there were a few patches on his cheeks where I could see his skin through the hair. He usually wore a kufi and *thobe*. His clothing gave off the appearance of cleanliness and purity. I noticed that he rarely smiled, and had a peculiar way of speaking: he projected constantly, as though he were always speaking to an audience, carefully enunciating every syllable. But the main thing that struck me about Abdul-Qaadir was that he was a man of obvious intellectual gifts.

One morning Abdul-Qaadir came into the office and sat next to me. I would soon look forward to my private morning chats with Abdul-Qaadir, as each gave me a new insight into the faith. They would remind me of the walks I used to take with al-Husein around the quad, except that my talks with Abdul-Qaadir tended to leave a bitter aftertaste.

This particular morning Abdul-Qaadir described the story of his conversion to Islam. Years ago, after being raised a Christian, Abdul-Qaadir was studying music in Berkeley, California. (He would later stop playing music, believing it violated Islamic law.) Abdul-Qaadir said that he was at dinner with friends one night—at a Church's Chicken—and learned that the musicians he was eating with were Muslim. He was unfamiliar with Islam, and in fact had never before heard anybody question the Trinity. When his dinner companions not only said that they didn't believe in the Trinity, but were also able to provide good, logical arguments against it, Abdul-Qaadir was blown away. Soon after, he took his *shahadah*.

Al-Husein and I spoke that night. It was becoming increasingly difficult to relate to him. But I wasn't sure *why* it was difficult: I wasn't sure if it was because his views were becoming radical, or if it was that I lacked faith. What I knew—and what I found appealing about al-Husein's transformation—was that he now possessed the kind of absolute confidence in his convictions that I had so long sought.

Abdul-Qaadir's arrival gave me something I could discuss with al-Husein. I described Abdul-Qaadir in glowing terms, then said, "Please pray that Allah helps Abdul-Qaadir do the same thing for my faith that Brother Taha did for yours."

Many of my talks with Abdul-Qaadir were "words of wisdom" experiences. Sometimes he'd come in to tell me about a theological issue that he was thinking about. Sometimes he would talk about more general matters. One day he explained his personal growth as a Muslim.

Abdul-Qaadir had been involved in various Islamic groups, and had been close to a number of different Islamic thinkers. Some of the figures he told me about were more liberal in bent; one of them, much like al-Husein and I, used to speak constantly about "social justice." I hadn't heard of the figure before that, and can't recall his name now. But I remember Abdul-Qaadir telling me how he turned his back on that outlook. He said he thought about writing a book exposing his former mentor's heterodoxy, but decided not to: "That would be like shooting a fly with a bazooka."

Abdul-Qaadir's Islamic development culminated in him discovering Salafism. I was taken by his description of that discovery. He didn't frame it in the manner that I usually heard—that Salafism is self-evidently right, and that other Muslims who don't see that are deviants or fools. Rather, it was something he grew into slowly, step by logical step, after a few misadventures within the faith. "I'm happy to call myself a Salafi," Abdul-Qaadir said. "It's the most persuasive method of understanding Islam that I've found. Maybe there's something better out there, but I haven't found it."

A few days later Abdul-Qaadir and I spoke about my love of books. He asked me about the Islamic authors I liked, and I told him that one of the main ones I'd been reading was Abu Ameenah Bilal Philips (a Jamaican convert to Islam and a genuine radical). "It's good that you like to read so much," Abdul-Qaadir said. "People who read tend to be fooled less easily."

I nodded. While most of my coworkers would be hard-pressed to read a single book from cover to cover, Abdul-Qaadir was well read and multilingual.

I had first thought of the Salafis as men like Dennis Geren, who didn't have complex ideas and were quick to accept the answers that their sheikhs gave. Abdul-Qaadir and al-Husein didn't fit that mold. Abdul-Qaadir came across as reasonable and thoughtful, a man of conviction. When I was around him, I felt that I was the one leading an unexamined life. Abdul-Qaadir knew with absolute certainty where he stood, and his life was seemingly free of inconsistencies. He was married and had kids. He and his family had removed themselves from the un-Islamic environment of the United States to live in Saudi Arabia, a country where he didn't have to deal with the mixing of the sexes; he didn't have to grapple with such issues as the duty of *hijra*.

Abdul-Qaadir had me pick up a newspaper for him every morning on the way to work so he could clip out articles that had some relevance to Islam. He believed, though, that photographs were *haram*; after all, the Prophet told his wife Aishah that the angels won't enter a house with pictures in it. So when an article that Abdul-Qaadir clipped from the paper had a photo in it, he'd turn it over so the picture couldn't be seen.

This ability to negate all that was inconsistent with his worldview was so different from the life I was living, a life of uncertainty and compromises. It was clear that Abdul-Qaadir's purpose as a Muslim was to submit to Allah's will. He came to Salafism because he believed that the most logical way of discerning Allah's will was a literal reading of Allah's word, the Qur'an, and a return to the Prophet's example. Abdul-Qaadir embraced the truth unapologetically. How could I not be drawn to this clarity?

Previously, al-Husein had been the only one I could talk with about my struggles within Islam. Al-Husein understood the religion, understood how radicals thought, understood their arguments. He and I used to discuss the delicate balance between being true to your faith and making sure that you didn't descend into unthinking extremism. Now I had no one.

As much as I loved them, my parents' view of God did not appeal to me. To me, their mishmash of religious beliefs was more indicative of a transcendent search for beauty than a desire to submit to God's will. Nor did I think I could discuss this with Amy, since she wasn't Muslim.

Deprived of an outlet for discussing these issues, I decided to keep my spiritual struggles to myself as I veered down the road to radicalism.

You shouldn't marry that *kafir* woman."

Pete took me aside after work one day to discuss my impending marriage to Amy, and this was his advice. The consummate salesman, Pete had a pitch prepared. "There are women from the Muslim world, like Thai women, and all they wanna do when you come home from work is serve you. 'Oh, did you have a hard day at work? Here, lemme give you a massage. Lemme make you dinner and take care of you.' Those women really know how to be obedient, how to take care of their husband, not like American women."

He then turned his attention from the proffered Islamic alternative to my fiancée. "Western women are different, bro. Let's say you're able to lead her to Islam. Maybe it'll take five years, maybe seven years. . . ."

"Sooner than that, *inshallah* [God willing]!" I had given a lot of thought to Amy and Islam. I desperately wanted her to share my faith.

"Okay," Pete said. "Sooner than that, *inshallah*. But look, bro, what if she does become Muslim? Western women are raised differently than women in the Muslim world. They have their feminisms here, they're taught from the very beginning that they're supposed to be 'independent.' Even if she comes around to Islam, even if she accepts the rights that a husband should have over his wife, she's still not gonna serve you or obey you like a Muslim woman would. And do you really think, even if she becomes Muslim, that she's gonna let you take on another wife?"

I didn't want to carry the conversation any further. But it was not a topic that Pete would let go of easily.

Soon after Abdul-Qaadir arrived in Ashland, I decided to stop listening to music. This was no small sacrifice.

I had loved music ever since I was a kid, and had an enormous CD collection. Sometimes I'd find myself thinking in music. I would associate particularly strong emotions with certain songs, would associate different parts of town with other songs. I had a favorite nook near the top of Lithia Park where, when I wanted to be alone, I could sit on a large rock by the babbling creek. It reminded me of Fleetwood Mac's haunting "Seven Wonders." There was I-5 connecting the north and south ends of town, a route I'd often take to meet up with my best friend in high school, Jacob Bornstein. That section of freeway made me think of the Doors' "L.A. Woman." There were countless other spots that I associated with countless other songs.

Ever since Dawood first lectured me about the impropriety of music, I struggled with whether I should remove it from my life. It seemed unfathomable that I could simply quit something that had meant so much to me, that was so closely tied to my emotional highs and lows.

I felt, though, that I needed to make a decision. I drove my Tercel past the golf course, out toward the lake. Driving often helped me clear my head and think. As I drove, I listened to a mixed tape that I had made in college. The music seemed to fit the road. There was a dark, winding stretch where the endless guitar riffs of Golden Earring's "Twilight Zone" punctuated each turn. As I took the final, sloping drive up toward Emigrant Lake, the near out-of-control mix of a guitar and flute in Jethro Tull's "Sealion" marked the ascent. And I sat in my car, on the dirt road near the edge of the lake, letting the music wash over me. So many songs, each bringing back some long-forgotten memory or emotion.

But this would have to end, I decided. There were my coworkers, but there was also my relationship with Allah. (I used to call the Creator either God or Allah interchangeably in my thoughts; by now, I only used the name Allah.) Was music *haram?* I found some of the evidence in Muhammad bin Jamil Zino's book unpersuasive the first time I read it. But I couldn't deny the power of some of the other *ahadith.* If I really believed in Allah, I had to be intellectually honest. Even if some music were *halal* (lawful), the music I was listening to was not. Stringed instruments were well known to be *haram,* and I couldn't think of a song on my mixed tape that didn't have a guitar in it. And the themes of my music? Allah, I knew, wouldn't approve of them. There were songs about sex, songs about drugs—most of the music I listened to was religiously objectionable in some way.

I drove back toward the house, knowing that this would be the last time I enjoyed the music that I used to love so much. As I got close to home, I decided to take another lap around the block. A chance to listen to one more song.

As Jimi Hendrix's "Eazy Rider" reached its crescendo, I finally pulled into the driveway. I ejected the cassette from the car's tape player. I then held the tape in my hand and sat looking at it. Already I was regretting the loss of music. I wanted to pop the tape back in and keep listening. The ghost echoes of music reverberated through my head.

I brought the tape into my room, thinking about the temptation of music. I needed finality.

So I took the tape in both hands and squeezed until it snapped in two. In that instant, the broken tape seemed like a symbol. I was turning my back on a life of not being serious about my faith.

Then I grabbed a Kleenex from the side of my bed and wrapped the broken tape inside it. I didn't want my parents to see it. I thought about how they had introduced me to music. I remembered that they had given me a tape of the Beatles' *Abbey Road* when I was just six years old,

old enough for the album to hold my interest but too young to recognize its true brilliance.

I wasn't hiding the tape because my parents would be upset that I'd given up on music. It was larger than that. My parents had no problem with my conversion to Islam because our ideas about religion were fundamentally the same thereafter. No longer. I was careening down a new road, and didn't know where it would lead me—but I knew that my ideas about religion were no longer like my parents'. And I knew that these differences would hurt them deeply.

Since Amy and I were now engaged, it made sense that she would spend the summer with me in Oregon. We hadn't been together since her Christmas break, and I couldn't wait to see her. But I also felt hesitant.

I had undergone so many changes since I had last seen her, changes that she couldn't anticipate and probably couldn't comprehend. And now I didn't know how we fit into each other's lives. Would my views on our relationship change?

I knew that my coworkers wouldn't approve of the fact that Amy had come to stay with me for the summer. And I didn't want them to know that she was here. I wanted to keep my life at work separate from my life with the woman I loved.

If only hypocrisy were that easy.

Abdul-Qaadir, at least, had a different take on my marriage to Amy than Pete did.

Since he knew that I would be marrying a Christian woman, he broached the subject early in his time at the Musalla. He said that it was permissible for a Muslim man to take a Christian wife, but he did have some warnings.

Abdul-Qaadir first warned that the purpose of marriage was to produce Muslim children. It didn't matter if my wife was Christian; there was only one faith that my kids could be raised in.

He warned also that my first obligation would not be to my wife, but to my brothers and sisters in Islam. "There is good in this world, and there is evil," Abdul-Qaadir said. "And as long as your wife isn't a Muslim, as far as we're concerned, she is one hundred percent evil."

That remark stuck with me when I went home that evening and saw Amy: she is one hundred percent evil. I tried not to act differently toward her; I tried to put Abdul-Qaadir's remark out of my mind. But it wasn't something I could shrug off easily. Nor was it something, I realized, that I could dismiss out of hand as wrong.

One night, Pete asked me to come by his house. I hadn't been paid in a couple of months. Pete had explained that he didn't want to write me checks too frequently because it'd surely tip off the IRS that I was working for him. But now he wanted me to come by to discuss payment.

I parked by his house and walked around to the back, to the old prayer room. The sheets that hung from the ceiling were still up; Pete did not want his visitors to catch a glimpse of his wives. Pete went behind the sheets at one point and returned with a couple of plates of rice and a bottle of tahini. We sat on the floor together eating. I wasn't going to speak first; the situation concerning my payments had been awkward from the very outset, when the first check I received had ostensibly been for selling Pete a computer.

Pete took a sip of spiced tea, then asked, "How much did we agree that I was going to pay you a month? Two thousand dollars?"

"Yeah."

He looked at me sternly. "I don't remember agreeing to that number."

I was taken aback. When Pete convinced me to apply for a job, he had shown me the advertisement in *Al-Jumuah* magazine that listed the salary as $2,000 a month. When he told me I was hired, he never specifically said that my monthly salary would be $2,000—but wasn't that a reasonable assumption? Still, I didn't want to come off as defensive. I just nodded and said, "We agreed to two thousand."

Pete exhaled and looked at the floor. "Bro," he said, his voice less lively than usual, "I don't have the money to pay you. I can give you seven thousand dollars for the past few months' work and for the rest of your time here, but that's it."

My mind suddenly flashed to the concept called *fi sabil Allah*, things that you do purely for the pleasure of Allah. Intentions are important to the reward you receive for good deeds, and anything *fi sabil Allah* is done with the best of intentions. What better reward is there than working to advance Islam while foregoing some of the payment that you've been promised?

"I'll do it for seven thousand dollars, Pete," I said. "I'm happy to do it *fi sabil Allah*."

Pete nodded. We sat around chatting a bit longer before I walked to the car to head home. I didn't mind taking less than Pete had initially advertised the position for. What did bother me, as I drove home, was that Pete had first tried to claim that he never agreed to the advertised salary.

A few days later on the phone with al-Husein, I found myself saying something the significance of which neither of us fully comprehended at the time. "What they don't understand when they see how we practice Islam," I said, "is that we don't do these things because it's what we *want*. We don't suddenly wake up and decide that we hate music or silk. We do what we do because it's what Allah wills."

The Salafis were now a "we."

eight

MAN BITES DOG

Some people think you should kill them."

This was Abdul-Qaadir's response when Pete's eleven-year-old son Yusuf—whose mother had left Islam for Christianity—asked if it was possible for someone who had been Christian, then become Muslim and then returned to Christianity, to again become Muslim.

Yusuf's mom had been a source of anguish for Yusuf and his brother Yunus. Both of them looked up to Pete with the full devotion of sons who are starved for their father's attention. I never met her—she and Pete had long been divorced by the time I got to know him—but I once saw a photo of her and Pete when they were young. She was an attractive blond woman, and Pete looked different back then. Now, despite his mischievous streak, he was quite tense. He actually seemed relaxed back then. Back then he didn't have a beard, but had big, hippie-type hair. I imagined that he had been like the person I was before I began to work for Al Haramain—liberal, devoted to pluralism, probably unduly optimistic.

Pete once told me that when he met the mother of Yunus and Yusuf, his main concern was bringing her to the faith. Before anything else, he preached to her about Islam, and eventually persuaded her to convert.

Only then did they marry. (The clear implication was that I shouldn't marry Amy unless I could persuade her to become Muslim.) Eventually, though, she divorced Pete and left Islam. I never heard the story behind this decision, but I now imagine that her experience was similar to mine. I imagine that Pete first told her about a simple, beautiful, and progressive Islam. He may even have believed it when he told her about it. But as Pete became a more serious Muslim, I imagine the rules and restrictions became greater. She may have been uncomfortable with the status of women in her new faith. Pete may have asked her to wear the *hijab*. Whatever the reasons, she returned to Christianity. I remember thinking at the time that she had left Islam because she wasn't really ready to submit to Allah's will. I remember thinking that she had made an enormous mistake.

Pete had remarried since then. When I worked for him, he was married to two women at once. Pete went to great lengths to make sure that neither I nor any other man in the community met his wives face-to-face. Whenever I entered his home, I would go in through the back door and would spend the entire visit in the old prayer room with curtains blocking the view of the rest of the house. The secrecy had nothing to do with the fact that Pete was married to two women, and everything to do with Pete's conservative views on relations between the sexes.

Both of Pete's sons identified themselves as Muslim. The older son, Yunus, was more rebellious, and more troubled, than Yusuf. He had an inquisitive and scientific mind. He'd constantly ask about and latch on to the fine points of Islamic law, even though he didn't seem too devout. But he certainly enjoyed correcting others when their Islamic conduct didn't comport with the rules. Yusuf, in contrast, was a sweet kid. He was obedient to Pete, well behaved. I remember watching him play with Dawood's sons, who clearly looked up to him. At the time, I marveled at how mature Yusuf was for his age.

Yusuf did seem genuinely devoted to Islam, and he was obviously

upset that their mom had left the faith. He wanted her to be Muslim like
the rest of us. It was at a night lecture given by Abdul-Qaadir that Yusuf
asked his question about those who have left Islam and received what
must have been a very upsetting answer from Abdul-Qaadir.

I hadn't gone to that lecture, but the next morning, when Abdul-
Qaadir sat down in the office for our morning Islamic chat, he began by
saying, "Last night's lecture caused a bit of controversy."

"Oh, really?" I asked.

Abdul-Qaadir told me about Yusuf's question, when he'd asked
whether it was possible for someone who had been Christian, then
become Muslim, and then returned to Christianity to again become
Muslim.

In response, Abdul-Qaadir had said flatly, "Some people think you
should kill them."

Abdul-Qaadir said that some people were offended by his remarks.
"It's a sensitive issue for Yusuf and Yunus," he said, "since their mother is
an apostate." He was putting this mildly. Imagine telling an eleven-year-
old kid that God wants his mom put to death, and you'll understand the
level of sensitivity at play.

But that wasn't what I thought of when Abdul-Qaadir told me about
the previous night's class. I wasn't thinking about feelings or sensitivi-
ties. I wanted to know if those people really *should* be killed.

And Abdul-Qaadir had a ready explanation. "The reason a lot of
people are uncomfortable with this is because they don't understand the
notion of apostasy in Islam. They have these Western ideas about religion as something you try on to see if it feels comfortable, something
that you can take off just as easily as you put it on. They hear that you
can be killed for leaving Islam, and their reaction is 'Huh?' What they're
not considering is that religion and politics aren't *separable* in Islam the
way they are in the West. When you take the *shahadah*, you aren't just
pledging your allegiance to Allah; you're aligning yourself with the

Muslim state. Leaving Islam isn't just converting from one faith to another. It's more properly understood as *treason*."

Something had changed in me. It used to be that when I listened to Islamic edicts, the first thing I'd ask was: *Is this moral? Is this rule just?* I had stopped doing that. The question of morality now seemed beside the point. After all, where was I getting my standard for morality if it wasn't from Allah? Now, when I heard a new *fatwa* or an unfamiliar point of Islamic law, my initial reaction was purely logical. I no longer asked if it was moral. Rather, I asked whether this was a proper interpretation of the Qur'an and the Sunna. After Abdul-Qaadir explained that apostasy should be thought of as treason, I just nodded and said, "That makes sense."

I was beginning to more fully understand what made me refer to myself as a Salafi in my phone conversation with al-Husein. I didn't want to straddle two worlds with my commitment to Allah battling my passion for "social justice." I didn't want to be racked by doubts and uncertainty. I didn't want to be regarded as a heretic by my brothers and sisters in faith.

No. I wanted to live a life of conviction—like Abdul-Qaadir, like al-Husein. I wanted a clear guide for telling right from wrong. Was there a better guide than Allah's own word—the Qur'an—and the example of his last prophet?

Still, while Abdul-Qaadir's description of apostasy made sense, I wanted to know for myself: was he right about the evidence?

I read up on the matter, turning first to Muhammad bin Jamil Zino's *Islamic Guidelines for Individual and Social Reform*. I had gone from feeling trepidation whenever I saw the book, as though it were a despised enemy, to considering it an authoritative source of answers.

Flipping through Zino's book, I found that it spoke directly to the topic of apostasy. There was a *hadith*, collected by al-Bukhari, in which the Prophet said, "Whoever apostatizes from Islam should be killed." This seemed to leave little room for doubt. At the time, I felt proud that I didn't just react emotionally to Abdul-Qaadir's comment about the killing of apostates, but that I had instead recognized the logic behind the view, did the research, and found that his statement was theologically supported.

Little did I know that in just over a year, these rulings would apply to me.

The beautiful thing about our faith," Pete had told me when I first met him, "is that it's a complete way of life. The Prophet, peace be upon him, teached about everything, down to how you eat your food and how you wipe after you go to the bathroom. Islam leaves no room for question!"

I was finding this to be the case. Sometimes the rules were difficult to remember, but I followed them dutifully.

One day in the office, I was ordering a book over the Internet. When I pulled out my credit card to enter its numbers in the order form, Dennis Geren looked over and said, "Haram!"

"What?"

"Haram. That credit card is haram. Islam prohibits the paying of interest, and you have to pay interest with credit card debt."

I shrugged. "I always pay my bills on time. I never pay interest on this credit card."

"A number of Islamic scholars have considered that argument, and they concluded that even signing an agreement saying that you'll pay interest in the case of a late payment is haram."

Naturally, I stopped carrying and using my credit card after that.

Just as I had feared, that summer was not a good time to have Amy in Oregon.

I had come to accept rules and restrictions that I once thought

ridiculous. I remember how bizarre I found it when Sheikh Adly refused
to be in the same room with Suzi Aufderheide, and only considered it
acceptable when she agreed to have the door open with her young son
just outside. But now I was beginning to reconsider my views on relations between the sexes. And sadly, my relationship with Amy was the
epicenter of how these changes played out in my life.

I never saw women in the Musalla. If women were in the building,
they would be downstairs. At one point, the downstairs area was under-
going extensive renovation and was basically uninhabitable, so they
moved the women upstairs to the living room adjacent to the prayer
room. To make it Islamically acceptable, curtains were draped over the
entrances to the living room so the men wouldn't lay eyes on the women
(similar to the curtains in the back of Pete Seda's home). But Sheikh
Hassan was visiting from California that week, and protested. He said it
was wrong to have the women upstairs, because one of the men might
glimpse them through the curtain when he was in the foyer. Although
the women grumbled a bit, they were shepherded downstairs, where
they could neither hear the sermon nor pray in comfort.

By the time Amy arrived in Oregon, I wondered if it was proper to
make physical contact with her, wondered whether it was okay to even
be in the same room with her. As I worked through these questions, I
became more distant. I didn't think she could understand.

One day after work, Abdul-Qaadir gave a lecture about the importance of marriage. I felt that the sermon spoke directly to what I was
going through—the sinfulness of modern dating, the superiority of
Islamic courtship, the obligation to marry once you've decided that a
woman is right for you.

Pete took me aside after the lecture. Although I didn't want word to
get out that Amy was staying with me, he knew. "Bro, why don't you
have that woman come up to the Musalla?" he asked. Pete never referred
to her by name. "We can do a *nikah* ceremony right here. Then you won't

have to worry about being around a woman you're not married to, and all the sins that come with that."

The *nikah* is the Islamic marriage ceremony. It instantly struck me that Pete was right. Amy and I could have two different wedding ceremonies, a Muslim ceremony and a Christian ceremony. We could do the *nikah* now. It would cost her nothing, and would ensure that I was right with Allah.

I snuck off to another room and called Amy. When she answered the phone, I told her that I loved her and wanted to marry her. Those statements were vague, and were things she already knew. In her sweet, shy Carolinian accent, Amy said that she felt the same way.

"Well, why don't we get married?" I asked. "Why don't we get married now? You can come up here, we can have an Islamic marriage ceremony, and then everything between us will be okay in God's eyes." As I moved deeper into Islamic fundamentalism, I became worse at explaining myself. My demand that we have our Islamic wedding ceremony immediately was completely unexpected, and I never really justified it.

There was a long pause. Unlike when I asked Amy to marry me back in January, this was an awkward pause. Finally, Amy said that she'd think about it, but didn't really feel comfortable. I told her to give it serious thought, that it was very important to me.

This wouldn't be our last discussion about an Islamic wedding ceremony.

A few days later, I walked into the main prayer room to make *salat*. Abdul-Qaadir and Dennis Geren were there. Abdul-Qaadir peered down at my ankles, then said, "Roll your pants legs up two inches."

"Why?" I looked over at Dennis's ankles and he proudly showed me that his pants were already rolled up a couple of inches.

"I'll tell you later," Abdul-Qaadir said.

I was puzzled, but complied. Abdul-Qaadir, Dennis, and I prayed. It was the height of summer in Ashland, the time of year when I loved to thank Allah for all the beauty he instilled in his creation. The prayer room's windows offered a peek at the green grass outside, the lazy traffic on I-5, the mountains beyond that. But this year I was far less interested in the world's beauty. The only beauty I cared about was the beauty of the hereafter. To get there, I didn't need to appreciate the aesthetics of a warm summer day; I needed to follow Allah's rules.

When we finished our prayers, Abdul-Qaadir said, "There is a *hadith* where the Prophet, *alayhi salaatu was salaam*, told one of his followers, 'Have your lower garment halfway down your shin; if you cannot do it, have it up to the ankles. Beware of trailing the lower garment, for it is conceit.' This was a serious issue for them. As Prophet Muhammad, *alayhi salaatu was salaam*, said in a *sahih hadith*,* 'The dress that is under the ankle is in the Hellfire.'"

Dennis nodded with satisfaction. He was improving as a pupil.

And so was I. After that conversation, I dutifully checked before each prayer to make sure that my pants legs came up above the ankles.

Unique among the Muslims I was close with in Ashland, Abdi and Mary didn't mind Amy's presence in my life—nor did they mind her presence in town.

One day, Amy and I went out for a meal with Abdi and Mary at an Indian restaurant in nearby Medford. I was somewhat reserved during the meal, interested in watching Abdi and Mary's interactions with Amy. They treated her like family, like a dear friend whose presence couldn't make them happier. It was just like things should be when you

---

*The *hadith* were evaluated based on the confidence that one can have in their authenticity. A *sahih hadith* is considered sound.

go out with friends: easy conversation, a bit of humor, no feeling of being watched and judged. I actually found the ease of our meal together odd.

Before we finished eating, I asked them about things I should make sure I did with Amy while she was in town. Mary suggested that we head to Southern California, and I take her to Disneyland. Amy had never been there, and it sounded like a nice idea.

Haram, ya sheikh!"

Pete shouted that at me in the middle of a phone call we were having with Sheikh Adly. Dennis and both of Pete's sons were also in the office. He was chastising me in front of them for doing something that was impermissible Islamically. What I had done was begin to play a game of Freecell (a Solitaire-type computer card game).

Pete had wanted me to sit at the computer while he spoke with Sheikh Adly, in case he needed notes taken. They had been talking for a while, and no notes were needed. While waiting for Pete to finish up, I opened up the Freecell application and started a game. That's when Pete yelled, "Haram, ya sheikh!" Haram—it is prohibited.

Yunus, Yusuf, and Dennis stopped what they were doing. Their attention turned to me and Pete. We had Sheikh Adly on speaker-phone, and Pete said, "Sheikh Adly, one of the brothers here is thinking about playing a card game on his computer, and he wants to know if it's halal to play this game."

"No, it is haram," Sheikh Adly said. "It is haram to play cards and gamble for money."

Pete didn't want to leave any doubt, though. "Ya sheikh," he said, "our brother here wants to know if it's haram if he isn't gambling for money, if he just wants to play his game on the computer but there's no money at stake."

Behind me, I heard Yunus say, "It's idle time." Ever the brash young man, he wanted to jump in with an answer. I almost laughed when he said that. In Islam there was a prohibition on idle time, on wasting your time when you could be studying the Qur'an and *ahadith* or doing other things that are pleasing to Allah. But I almost laughed because Yunus would fritter away his own time: watching TV, playing military games on his computer, sitting in the office and making meaningless conversation. But despite all of his own wasted time, he would cheerfully denounce a few moments of Freecell while waiting on Pete.

"It's *haram*," Sheikh Adly said to Pete. "There are human faces on the cards and that is against the teachings of Prophet Muhammad, *alayhi salaatu was salaam*. And playing the cards is idle time, which is also against Islam." I saw Yunus smirk out of the corner of my eye.

I closed the game of Freecell. Yunus and Yusuf left the office. My interaction with Pete had been a spectacle for them, a somewhat charged confrontation that was resolved when I closed the game.

Though I wasn't happy with the way the interaction went, it would be a long time before I'd again take up Freecell. After all, the game was a temporary diversion: its value paled in comparison to the need to be right with Allah.

I took Amy to Disneyland in mid-July.

Just like the rest of that summer together, the trip was not without its drama. I was still pressing her on the *nikah* ceremony, having trouble understanding why she wouldn't accede to it. It seemed to me that it wouldn't cost her anything, and would make me feel better about our relationship. I didn't understand at the time what is now obvious: Amy didn't want to submit to a religious ceremony that she didn't understand, didn't think was necessary, and meant nothing to her.

The stress that Amy's refusal caused me was palpable. "I think that we're sinning in our time together," I said during the long drive to Anaheim. "All I want is for us to have this ceremony and then this won't be a concern anymore. At all." Amy didn't reply, but she had made her view clear when I first broached the subject of a *nikah*: she didn't share my religious beliefs, and didn't think we were in a constant state of sin. Trying to give her some incentive, I added, "This would probably make Pete happy. He might even give me time off for a honeymoon."

Amy wasn't persuaded. We weren't having premarital sex; she didn't understand why I viewed our relationship as sinful. "What do you think would be okay?" Amy shot back. "Sitting on the porch together holding hands?"

I didn't answer. She meant the remark sarcastically, but I wasn't sure that even that would be acceptable. After all, if we were holding hands, our skin would be touching.

I was amazed by Amy's ability to put aside the awkwardness of the moment and enjoy our time together in Anaheim.

From the moment we entered the theme park and began our stroll down Main Street, U.S.A., I loved every moment that I spent with Amy. We strolled through New Orleans Square together, watched a street band perform, and ventured into Disney's Haunted Mansion. We took a jaunt through the pioneer days at Frontierland, circled the small lake in the middle of the theme park in the three-story *Mark Twain* Riverboat, munching the whole time on fried cinnamon-sugar churros.

More than the whimsy of our time together in Disneyland, the break from Al Haramain made a difference. It was as though I was back in college with Amy, with nobody watching over me to make sure my behavior comported with proper Islamic conduct. Visiting Disneyland is like taking a trip into the imagination, and part of the imagination for me during that weekend was being whisked back to a world where my own moral reasoning mattered, where I didn't have to be constantly on my guard, where I didn't have to worry about whether people should really be killed for leaving Islam.

My return to Ashland signaled a return to my daily checklist beamed down from heaven. Eating: right hand only. Pants: below the knees but above the ankles. Touching: not okay for dogs or women. Sneezing? If you sneeze, say, *"Alhamdulillah."* If someone else sneezes and says *alhamdulillah*, you reply: *"Yarhamukallah."* (Arabic for "May Allah bless you.") Music: forbidden. Paying interest: forbidden. The beard: required.

The rules were voluminous, but I was beginning to master them. Abdul-Qaadir helped me work on my *tajweed* (pronunciation during recitation of the Qur'an), and it too was improving. Earlier, I noticed that the serious Muslims in Ashland seemed to derive a great deal of personal worth from how well they followed these strictures, and would evaluate others based on their ability (or willingness) to do the same. At first I thought that was wrong. I once told al-Husein, "Other people's faith is between them and Allah. It's not my business to judge their Islam." But I increasingly viewed these rules as a way to judge where my own faith stood—and to judge the strength of others' faith as well.

When it came to following the rules, Abdul-Qaadir was head and shoulders above the rest of us. At one point, an unfamiliar car turned up the long driveway toward the Musalla. It belonged to Dawood's parents. Dawood was still in Saudi Arabia, and they had come by to pick up some mail and other miscellaneous items for him.

Dawood's parents were at least in their sixties. As they entered the Musalla, I carefully watched how the other Muslims greeted them. Dawood's mom was an older lady, so was it okay to shake her hand? Pete greeted them first, with his charm in high gear. He shook her hand. Dennis Geren also shook her hand, declining to mention that he thought this was the first step toward marriage. I came next, and shook her hand as well. I stood next to Pete, and we watched while Abdul-Qaadir greeted Dawood's parents. He shook the hand of Dawood's father, and when Dawood's mother held out her hand, he didn't shake it. Instead, he fluidly placed in her hand the mail for Dawood that we had collected over the past couple of months.

"He's smooth," Pete whispered to me, admiringly. "Did you see that? *So* smooth."

Late in the summer, the PBS show *Frontline* broadcast an episode about the twin bombings of U.S. embassies in Kenya and Tanzania that al-Qaeda carried out the year before, in August 1998. The show twice mentioned that the terrorists had received support from an Islamic charity with offices in Africa; both times, Al Haramain's logo flashed on the screen.

I learned of this while reviewing the daily crush of e-mail one morning. One of the messages was from Pete, and there was a video clip attached to it showing the *Frontline* segment.

Pete was livid. He called the office less than two minutes after I looked at the video clip. "Bro, did you see that clip from *Frontline?*" His speech was loud, rapid, and interspersed with Farsi curse words. "They have *no proof* that Al Haramain was involved in those acts of terror, no proof at all!" Pete had about a dozen different plans, all of which he wanted to put into effect right away. He wanted us to write a letter to *Frontline* demanding a retraction; he wanted to file a lawsuit against PBS; he wanted to immediately hire a PR consultant to repair what he viewed as Al Haramain's now-tarnished image.

Pete came to the office later that day and we placed a call to Soliman al-But'he, an Al Haramain director who was born in Egypt but now worked in the head office in Riyadh. Pete frantically explained the *Frontline* clip to Soliman, then asked, "These guys are completely wrong, aren't they? There's no way our offices in Africa were involved in these bombings, right?"

Soliman wouldn't give a straight answer. "Brother, there are many volunteers who come in and out of our offices in Africa, who might work there for a few weeks and then move on. We can't really know who's gone through there."

"You don't *know* if people in our Africa offices supported the embassy bombings?" Pete sounded incredulous.

"No, brother, we don't know," Soliman said.

When the phone call ended, Pete was despondent. "We're finished," he said. "After this show, people are gonna think of the embassy bombings whenever they hear Al Haramain's name. We're through."

"Pete," I said, "they only flashed our logo twice, for about five seconds each time. If Al Haramain really wasn't involved, this isn't going to permanently change people's view of us."

Pete wanted to press ahead, immediately, with a response. Like so many of Pete's ideas, it started with a bang but ended with a whimper. I drafted a letter to *Frontline* on his behalf that he decided not to send because it sounded "too angry"; Pete and some directors from the Riyadh office met with attorneys at a Washington, D.C., law firm and paid them a $50,000 retainer for a defamation suit against PBS that, as far as I know, went nowhere; and we met with a PR consultant a couple of weeks later but never implemented her ideas.

I didn't give much thought at the time to Al Haramain's logo appearing in connection with the embassy bombings. It certainly didn't make me question my affiliation with Al Haramain. My view was that Western governments and the Western media misunderstood and feared Islam, and this seemed to be another case of their misunderstanding.

I probably should have been more suspicious. I had seen Al Haramain's ideology firsthand and knew about its international reach. Al Haramain was originally formed as a private charity in Riyadh in 1992.

By the time I came to work for the group, it had offices in more than fifty countries and an annual budget of $40 to $50 million. Years later, after Islamic extremism finally came crashing into the public consciousness, I would learn about some of the activities that Al Haramain's branch offices were involved in.

Further evidence would come to light, for example, about Al Haramain's role in the embassy bombings. The U.S. Treasury ultimately designated Al Haramain's offices in Kenya and Tanzania as sponsors of terrorism for their role in the plot. The Treasury designation listed multiple connections between Al Haramain and the embassy bombings, including the Al Haramain offices' involvement in planning the attacks, funding by a wealthy Al Haramain official, and a former Tanzanian Al Haramain director's role in making preparations for the advance party that planned the bombings. The Al Haramain branch in the Comoros Islands was also designated because it "was used as a staging area and exfiltration route for the perpetrators of the 1998 bombings."

Nor was this Al Haramain's only connection to terrorism. The *New York Times* reported in 2003 that Al Haramain's Indonesian office had been a conduit for funds to Jemaah Islamiyah, the terrorist group responsible for the October 2002 bombings in Bali, Indonesia, that killed 202 people, primarily foreign tourists. In designating the office a sponsor of terrorism, the Treasury Department also noted that it provided financial support to al-Qaeda, and that money donated to the Indonesian office may have been diverted to weapons procurement.

A number of other Al Haramain branches were similarly designated by Treasury after 9/11. The Afghanistan office was designated for supporting the bin Laden–financed Makhtab al-Khidemat terrorist group prior to 9/11, and for its involvement in a group training to attack foreigners in Afghanistan after the Taliban were toppled. The Albania office was designated because of its ties to al-Qaeda and the Egyptian

Islamic Jihad, which led the Treasury Department to conclude that the office "has been used as cover for terrorist activity in Albania and in Europe." The Bangladesh office was designated after one of its officials sent an operative to conduct surveillance on U.S. consulates in India for a potential terrorist attack. The branch in Ethiopia was designated because of its support for al-Ittihad al-Islamiya, a terrorist group that has carried out attacks on Ethiopian defense forces. And the Pakistan office was designated for supporting the Taliban and the terrorist groups Lashkar e-Taibah and Makhtab al-Khidemat. The Pakistan office also had several employees suspected of being al-Qaeda members, including one who was thought to have financed al-Qaeda operations and another who reportedly planned to carry out terrorist attacks in the United States.

With offices in more than fifty countries and a very conservative approach to Islam, Al Haramain has also been at the center of controversy concerning the radicalization of Muslim populations throughout the world. This was an issue in Bosnia, where Saudi charities were disappointed in the kind of Islam that Bosnian Muslims practiced and made it their mission to usher them toward Salafism. It was also an issue in the Netherlands, where Dutch intelligence found "financial, organisational and personnel interconnection" between Al Haramain and the radical El Tawheed mosque in Amsterdam. El Tawheed is the mosque where Muhammad Bouyeri reportedly prayed. (Bouyeri brutally killed Dutch filmmaker Theo van Gogh after van Gogh directed a film called *Submission*, which dramatized the mistreatment of women born into Muslim families. He shot van Gogh six times, slit his throat with a kitchen knife, then used the knife to impale a five-page note to his chest.)

I didn't know any of this about Al Haramain's international activities at the time. Much of it I couldn't have known, since the bulk of this information would come to light after the 9/11 attacks. But in the late summer of 1999, I wasn't concerned about Al Haramain's alleged connections to the East Africa embassy bombings. Perhaps I should have been.

Although there were plenty of rules that I still didn't follow to my satis-faction, I had at least begun to internalize them. I now felt ready to tackle the most difficult laws.

It was time to read the essay on jihad in the back of the Qur'an that Dawood had mentioned when I began work at Al Haramain. I sat at my kitchen table late at night and turned to it. Entitled "The Call to *Jihad* (Holy Fighting in Allah's Cause) in the Qur'an," it was written by for-mer Saudi chief justice Abdullah bin Muhammad bin Humaid.

In the essay, Chief Justice bin Humaid outlined the three historical phases of jihad in Islamic jurisprudence: "[A]t first 'the fighting' was for-bidden, then it was permitted, and after that it was made obligatory— (1) against them who start 'the fighting' against you (Muslims) . . . (2) and against all those who worship others along with Allah."

There was support for his view that these were the three stages of jihad. Initially, despite the severe persecution that the Prophet faced from the Quraysh tribe in Mecca, he didn't permit his followers to fight against the Quraysh. Rather than fighting, Muhammad and his followers fled from Mecca to Medina in the *hijra*.

After the flight to Medina, the Muslims gained in political and military strength. It was then that Muhammad received new Qur'anic revelations allowing the Muslims to engage in combat in certain cir-cumstances. The Qur'an says in Sura 22, Verses 39 and 40: "Permission to fight is given to those who are fighting them because they have been wronged, and surely Allah is able to give them victory. Those who have been expelled from their homes unjustly only because they said: Our Lord is Allah."

And after that, in subsequently revealed verses, jihad became obliga-tory upon the Muslims. The second Sura of the Qur'an, Verse 190, no longer uses permissive language but rather the language of obligation:

"And fight in the way of Allah those who fight you." And Sura 9, Verse 29, contains an even broader instruction:

> Fight against those who (1) believe not in Allah, (2) nor in the Last Day, (3) nor forbid that which has been forbidden by Allah and His Messenger . . . (4) and those who acknowledge not the religion of truth among the people of the Scripture, until they pay the *Jizyah* with willing submission, and feel themselves subdued.

It was significant that Chief Justice bin Humaid analyzed the order in which these verses were revealed. Although the Qur'an isn't organized in the order of revelation, this order is important because of the concept of abrogation. Muslim commentators have traditionally held that when two Qur'anic verses are in conflict, the latter verse nullifies, or abrogates, the verse that came before it.

So Chief Justice bin Humaid argued that the order to refrain from the fighting was abrogated by subsequent revelations making it permissible, and that these latter verses were in turn abrogated by verses making jihad obligatory. There was indeed a marked difference in the language as the revelations progressed. The permissive language used to describe the fighting in Sura 22 was replaced by descriptions that used the imperative tense. Thus, Chief Justice bin Humaid argued that believers don't simply have the *option* to fight against unbelievers. Rather, Muslims have the affirmative duty to engage in jihad against unbelievers when the unbelievers fight against them (*ayah* 2:106), and when unbelievers refuse to believe in Allah and the Last Day, accept Islamic *sharia*, and pay the *jizya* (*ayah* 9:29). Chief Justice bin Humaid implored, "Jihad is a great deed indeed and there is no deed whose reward or blessing is as that of it, and for this reason, it is the best thing that one can volunteer for."

I thought that I wasn't ready to read this essay before. And indeed, I wasn't ready when Dawood first mentioned it. At that time, I was trying to focus on points of agreement with my coworkers, believing that over time I could lead them toward a more moderate view of Islam. But the opposite had occurred. Over time, I became persuaded by the case for a more conservative Islam.

And now, reading Chief Justice bin Humaid's essay on jihad, I found myself persuaded by his argument.

A few minutes later I set up my prayer rug, facing toward Mecca. I made *salat* for the fifth time that day, the nighttime prayers. All Sunni Muslims make *salat* in the same way—speaking the same words and going through the same pattern of standing, bowing, kneeling, and prostrating. But after the standard form of *salat*, Muslims will often pray silently to Allah about their specific needs or desires. This is called *du'a* (Arabic for supplications). And after *salat*, for the very first time, I prayed for victory for the mujahideen.

This is what I had so long resisted, what I had so long believed I was fighting against. But over time my ideas about the faith were transformed, and I now believed this was the *right* thing to pray for. If it felt uncomfortable for now, that was a problem with my faith. And I had nothing but time to make my faith blossom.

The four of us sat on the couch, cowering. A very filthy animal was threatening to rub up against us—and potentially, to dirty us. The animal was a beautiful tan and dark black dog named Abby, a cross between a greyhound and a heeler (a herding dog that herds other animals by nipping at their heels).

We were working on the Islamic documentary that Abdul-Qaadir and his companions had come to the United States to make. After surveying the various production companies in the area, we selected one in nearby Medford called Landmind Productions, whose stock footage of explosions and flames would later be used by the NFL as a *Monday Night*

Football graphic and in the movie *Charlie's Angels*. One of the reasons we selected Landmind was that a man ran it. Most of the other local companies had women in top management positions, which was awkward for us.

It was a hot, bright day when we drove out to Landmind. It was located in what had once been a pear-packing plant in an old industrial part of Medford. The building was gray near the front entrance, with a large black horizontal stripe running down it. It had the kind of large block windows that I've always associated with Elks clubs and Masonic temples.

After a short wait we were escorted into the building to meet John Foote, the president and founder of Landmind. I noticed that we passed a basketball hoop on the way in, as well as some very comfortable-looking couches along the wall.

I liked John. He was wiry, standing about five feet ten with brown hair; his clothing reminded me of a skateboarder. We might have been friends in another context. John was twenty-nine years old, running his own business, and had a bubbling enthusiasm for what he did. Within the first hour of meeting him, he took us on a complete tour of the two warehouses that comprised Landmind's work space.

John was particularly proud of a jail cell set that he had created for the music video "Criminal" by local punk band Virus Nine. There was a life-size plastic model of a man in an orange jumpsuit and a black skull-cap sitting on a wire bed in the cell, looking despondent, a grimy toilet standing against the opposite wall. Landmind did the special effects for his electrocution. There was another set that I also appreciated, a horror scene of a graveyard featuring a zombie in an army jacket, a mummy rising from a coffin, a wooden grave saying "RIP" in white, and a television on the ground that played a looping horror film.

I loved John's passion for his work, and found him easy to get along with. But when I looked at him, I saw far more than that. I homed in on how his personal appearance and habits fell short of Islamic norms. He wore an earring—*haram*, as Sheikh Adly would surely point out, because men are not to wear women's clothing or accessories. He had a tattoo, also *haram*. Some of the guys in his crew were even worse; there was a kid named Mike with short black hair and an almost shaved head who smoked like a chimney and wore shorts that didn't cover his knees, leaving part of his thighs exposed. But of all the ways that the appearance and habits of John and his crew fell short of Islamic norms, surely his dog was the biggest offense.

I had first learned about the problem of dogs in Islam when al-Husein and I visited Turkey together, and he told me about a *hadith* where the Prophet said that angels will refuse to enter a house with a dog in it. I had made an effort to study the *ahadith* in greater depth since then. And I learned that dogs were held in even lower regard than I initially believed. In one *hadith*, Muhammad said, "Were dogs not a species of creature I should command that they all be killed." The Prophet also said that dog owners would lose the reward of their good deeds. And he specifically prohibited commerce in dogs—regarding the price of a dog as illegal, along with the earnings of a prostitute and the charge of a soothsayer.

Our encounter with Abby the dog came while we were waiting for John in one of Landmind's meeting rooms. Pete, Abdul-Qaadir, and Ahmed Ezzat were also in the room, and we all sat on a large light blue couch. When Abby entered, she paced around in front of us, inquisitive, as though expecting that these new visitors would pet her.

But we didn't react like your average visitors. Instead, everyone on the couch leaned back as far as they could, trying to prevent the dog from coming into contact with them. I saw that not only was Ahmed's body recoiling, but he also craned his head back as far as it would go, as though that could somehow protect him. Ahmed said something in Arabic that I didn't understand.

When John entered, he instantly read our body language. "Out of curiosity," he said, "does Islam have some kind of problem with dogs?"

"We shouldn't be around them," Ahmed blurted out. He exhaled the words as though offended by John's audacity in leaving us alone in the room with a dog.

John nodded and smiled. He was taken aback, but did his best to smooth everything over. "Don't worry," he said, "I'll make sure that she doesn't come back in and bug you." He tenderly led Abby out of the room. She wagged her tail and took one wistful glance back at us, disappointed that she never got the attention that she had come to expect.

When John was out of earshot, Abdul-Qaadir asked me in a whisper, "Do you know enough Arabic to understand what Ahmed said?"

At the time, I did not.

"I said that if that dog touched me, I was going to kill it," Ahmed said. Everybody laughed.

Later, as we left the studios, the close encounter with the canine was still fresh in everybody's mind, particularly Ahmed's. As we drove back toward Ashland, he told a story about when he was a boy growing up in Egypt. There had been some dogs in the neighborhood. His mother had warned him about the dogs, since they were at best impure. So when one of the neighborhood dogs finally bit him, he was ready. Ahmed bit the dog right back.

Ahmed's story provoked delighted howls of laughter. At the time, we thought of his biting a dog as a minor act of heroism.

nine

THE JEWS' PLAN
TO RUIN EVERYTHING

When I saw that my dad had picked up a book about Islam from the public library to learn more about my religion, my first response was to carefully screen the book for deviance. If there was any question about whether I had truly begun to accept the ways of the Salafis, my instincts in this exchange with my father should have put those doubts to rest.

I had noticed this Salafi tendency to "correct" others on theological matters early on, before I even began to work at Al Haramain. I wasn't the only one to notice this. The Naqshbandis' U.S. Web site, Sunnah.org, had an amusing cartoon called "Forbidding the Good." I first ran across it in March of 1999, when I was pondering how the Islam practiced at Al Haramain differed from the religion I thought I was embracing when I took my *shahadah*.

In the cartoon, a young man decides to convert to Islam after reading a book explaining the faith. The next panel comes a few weeks later in a mosque, when the young man—now wearing a green tunic and sporting a full beard—kisses the Qur'an after reading a chapter. The man sitting next to him, a Wahhabi/Salafi, reprimands him: "Why are you kissing the Qur'an? This is *bida*—innovation."

The Wahhabi/Salafi then sees the new convert with prayer beads, and again corrects him: "This is *bida*, too!" The Wahhabi/Salafi says to himself, "It is my duty as a Muslim following the right creed, *aqida*, to help this misguided new Muslim." Eventually he hounds the new Muslim so much that the young man runs out of the mosque, screaming, "Let me get out of here!" (There was, however, a happy ending: after running out of the mosque, the young man encounters Naqshbandi Muslims, who are able to reignite his passion for Islam.)

I found the cartoon funny when I first read it, so reflective of the Wahhabi tendency to correct others in matters of faith. And now, that was my first impulse when I saw my dad reading a book about Islam. And I *did* find something to correct him on.

The book, I saw, was written by Mirza Ghulam Ahmad, the founder of the Ahmadiyya religious movement. This was a movement about which I had done much studying. I initially encountered it when working on my honors thesis. At first I came away impressed by the Ahmadis, given their early *dawah* efforts to bring Americans to Islam. At the time, I viewed them as a mainstream Muslim group, given that they didn't have the Nation of Islam's theological deviations. But since I started working for Al Haramain, my impression became far less positive.

The biggest problem I had with Mirza Ghulam Ahmad was his use of the terms *nabi* (prophet) and *rasul* (messenger) in referring to himself, which seemed to contradict the finality of Muhammad's prophethood. There were also several other Ahmadi beliefs that contradicted more theologically sound accounts. I was now regularly praying for the mujahideen's victory. Mirza Ghulam Ahmad, in contrast, had argued that jihad could only be used to protect against extreme religious persecution, and that it couldn't be used as a reason for invading neighboring territories. This, to me, contradicted the Qur'anic account.

So I told my dad, "Be careful with that book. There are a lot of people out there who put out information that doesn't represent the most carefully considered Islamic view, and Mirza Ghulam Ahmad is one of them. He even claimed to be a prophet, which is completely contrary to Islamic teaching since Muhammad said there would be no other prophets after him."

Just like when I told my dad about Mike's argument for Jesus' divinity, this statement upset him. "I just wanted to learn more about Islam," he shot back. "I'm not going to go out and start worshipping Ghulam Ahmad!"

"They don't *worship* him," I said. "His followers merely think he was a prophet. But that in itself is unacceptable Islamically."

The words coming from my mouth were cold and humorless. I remembered how, early in my encounters with Wahhabis, I noticed that they were eager to correct me on any Islamic shortcomings. Now, evidently, I was doing the same to my own family.

It was nearing the end of July, and it remained light outside well into the evening. I left work around five o'clock and parked my Tercel near the Daniel Meyer Pool. Stone walkways crisscrossed the perfectly cut grass of the fields outside the pool. These fields sprawled for hundreds of feet, up until they met the railroad tracks that cut across the town.

I sat down on the grass to read a book. It was the perfect scene for some summer reading. But instead of light fiction, I was curled up with a book by Abu Ameenah Bilal Philips, *Tafseer Soorah al-Hujuraat*. I felt a vague unease, aware that I was having trouble appreciating the beauty of this warm summer evening. I discarded this feeling, telling myself that this life was temporary, and I was surrounded by people so wrapped up in this world that they had lost sight of the larger picture. An image flashed through my head of Dennis Geren scoffing at them dismissively and muttering, "The *kufar*."

Tafsir is Arabic for explanation and interpretation of the Qur'an. (Bilal Philips transliterates the word differently; his system of transliteration is predominantly used by the Salafis.) I was interested to read Bilal Philips's account of the history of *tafsir* and the various schools of *tafsir* that developed over time. He outlined a clear system for interpreting the Qur'an, with a hierarchy of interpretive methods. Most desirable, naturally, was *tafsir* by the Qur'an itself: sometimes the Qur'an will ask and subsequently answer questions, and in other places it makes general statements that are later explained with greater specificity. Failing that, there was *tafsir* of the Qur'an by the Prophet, where he personally clarified verses in the holy book. If Muhammad's companions were confused about a verse and couldn't find an explanation in the Qur'an or one that was provided by Muhammad, "they would use their own reasoning based on their knowledge of the contexts of the verses and the intricacies of the Arabic language in which the Qur'aan was revealed." Likewise, if we—the Muslims of the twentieth century—were unable to find the answer in the Qur'an or Sunnah, we would next turn to the sayings of Muhammad's companions for enlightenment. And the last method of *tafsir* in this hierarchy was *tafsir* by opinion. These opinions would have to be based on the first three steps, and would only be considered valid if they didn't contradict the previous steps.

Clearly, there was a science of *tafsir*. And, typical of the books that I got through Al Haramain, Bilal Philips outlined not only the proper methods of *tafsir* but also the dangers of deviant *tafsirs*. These included *tafsirs* that placed too much emphasis on the spiritual over the material, those that attempted to interpret revelation according to human logic, and those whose errors were based on an obsession with the Prophet's descendants.

I paused for a second and put the book down. It was a beautiful day. The sun was setting, couples were strolling past, and a gentle breeze ruffled the grass. But the beauty of the evening wasn't doing anything for me. I no longer appreciated nature the way I once did.

I thought about the book. I had at one point recoiled from passages such as the one I was now reading, which condemned different ways of interpreting Islam. I once thought that there were *many* Islams, a diversity of practice within the faith. I once thought that I could learn from other people's practice even if it differed from mine. But now Bilal Philips's writing resonated rather than repelled. He was offering a more objective guide for telling right from wrong, for distinguishing between sound and shaky methods of Qur'anic interpretation.

I thought back to the conversations that al-Husein and I had with my parents when he visited Ashland. Those days were long gone, separated by time and by the changes that al-Husein and I had gone through. I remembered how al-Husein and I had agreed with my parents on so many spiritual matters. If al-Husein were here today, we would no longer have those long conversations with my parents. Now, I felt, I had finally developed the correct understanding of religion.

Even after converting to Islam I had at first believed that I should forge a relationship with Allah that felt comfortable. I thought back to my conversation with Joy Vermillion in Venice, when she asked if I would ever consider leaving Islam. Back then, I had told her that I wouldn't: "I can find everything I need in this faith. I can have a mystical relationship with God. And if I'm looking for greater literalism, I can find that, too. There are plenty of directions that I can grow within Islam."

I had no desire to leave Islam, but my response to Joy had been wrong. I had approached the question from the perspective of what felt comfortable to me. Absent from my answer was a consideration of what was *true*. I had spoken with Joy about my spiritual needs, but they are irrelevant if Allah exists. If Allah exists, *none* of our spiritual needs can be fulfilled if our relationship with Him is based on falsehood. If Allah exists, we don't forge a relationship with Him. Instead, He dictates a relationship with us. Salafism led me to comprehend this in a way that I never did before. The scientific methodology espoused by Bilal Philips and others like him was an effort to ensure that our understanding and actions accord with Allah's will.

Salafis carefully interpret the Qur'an and Sunna because they believe that the best way of interpreting Allah's will is going back to the earliest understanding of Islam. The earliest generation of Muslims is a pious example because if Muhammad were truly a prophet, those who were closest to him and experienced life under his rule would best understand the principles on which an ideal society should be built.

I now understood why I had long resisted this logic: it was leading me to conclusions that I once considered unacceptable. I was reevaluating my ideas about jihad, about the role of women, about religious minorities and individual freedoms. I was reevaluating my ideas about the Taliban.

But I felt a pang of loss that I could no longer sit down at the dinner table with my parents and talk about all the areas where we agreed spiritually. I felt a pang of loss at the freedom of intellect I had once cherished. I used to enjoy trying to reason through any complex and controversial issue, from abortion to health care policy to Middle East politics. Now I had embraced a creed that answered even the smallest of questions, such as what hand to wipe with after using the bathroom.

But why the pang of loss if this was *right*? Shouldn't I instead feel a joy of discovery?

I realized that I had stopped reading the book about twenty minutes ago, and had been lost in thought.

I was unhappy, but the conclusions I had reached, the method of interpretation I was using—they were *right*. Happiness, I was sure, would come later.

Charlie Jones was fired as July drew to a close.

His depressive tendencies were obvious from the first time I met him, and they only grew over time. They were reflected in his speech, his bearing, and his work. Sometimes Charlie wouldn't show up at the Musalla for weeks at a time. At least a couple of times his wife called to see if we knew where Charlie was; his whereabouts were a mystery to her as well.

Most of the office backlog that I had been forced to deal with had been Charlie's responsibility. He was, for example, supposed to write the reports for the head office in Riyadh that had been months late. But most egregious was his failure to pay our bills on time. We were so late in bill payments that at one point our long-distance provider bounced us from the standard plan and started billing us at random. One month our charges came to over four hundred dollars, an outrageous total.

Charlie had been diagnosed with a chemical cause to his depression, but refused to take medication. "Maybe this sounds silly to you guys," he said, "but rather than taking this medicine that the doctors claim is supposed to make me better, I just pray to Allah. If Allah wants to cure me, He will."

Pete arranged a meeting at the Musalla that was one part intervention, one part termination. It was getting close to evening and five of us—Charlie, Pete, Dennis Geren, Abdul-Qaadir, and me—sat on the prayer room's thick blue carpet. The session was far more compassionate than I expected. Pete made clear to Charlie that we all loved him, saw him as our brother, and wanted what was best for him.

"But, bro," Pete said, "this job isn't good for you. It isn't making you better. You're a guy who loves the outdoors. You love riding horses, being around trees, working with your hands. You're not gonna be happy cooped up in an office all day long, staring out the windows and wishing that you could be outside instead."

Charlie quickly became defensive. "Look, I know that sometimes I haven't shown up for work as I should, but I can honestly say that I've never charged a penny for work I didn't do," he said. "Things have been rough for me, but I've been praying to Allah, and I know Allah can cure me if He wills it." Charlie nodded at the four of us, his eyes wide.

Pete was whispering in my ear. "Say something," he said. "Say something." Pete and Dennis knew Charlie far better than I did, and Abdul-Qaadir was a superior religious scholar to me. I saw my role as moral support more than anything else—but complied with Pete's order.

"Charlie," I said, "I know that you say you haven't charged anybody for work you didn't do, and we appreciate that. But it isn't that simple. Sometimes your failure to show up has other costs, like with the phone bill. We were being charged three hundred and four hundred dollars a month for a few months because we had been so late in payments that they bounced us from their standard plan."

I instantly wished that I hadn't followed Pete's order to speak. Our purpose was not to show Charlie that he'd been an inadequate employee. He already knew that. Our main purpose, rather, was to show him compassion, to let him know that we wanted to be with him as he moved forward from this difficult point.

Fortunately, my remark didn't turn the meeting sour. As the intervention/firing ended, Charlie said, "Thank you, guys. You're great brothers. I really feel loved, I really feel like you guys would do anything to help me get better. I appreciate it."

"We love you, bro," Pete said. "More than anything else, what we care about is that you get well again." The rest of us nodded.

Although I saw Charlie at *juma* prayers a few times after this, it would be the last conversation of substance that I ever had with him.

Not only was Allah watching me; so were my coworkers.

This time, Dennis Geren watched my sandwich with an eagle eye. "Is that *bacon* on your sandwich?" he asked incredulously.

I knew that it looked bad, and stammered a bit. "It's, um, actually turkey bacon," I said. "A Muslim friend at Wake Forest tipped me off to it."

Dennis looked skeptical.

"It's all turkey, no pork," I continued.

"Okay," Dennis said. "If it was real bacon, I was going to tell Amu Pirouz and you'd be in big trouble." Amu Pirouz was one of Pete's many nicknames: *Amu* was Arabic for "uncle," and Pete's actual name in Farsi was Pirouz. Dennis would refer to Pete as Amu Pirouz to Dawood's sons, Zaki and Zayd. Usually, Amu Pirouz would enter the equation when Zaki and Zayd were misbehaving. Dennis would threaten: "If you do that again I'll tell Amu Pirouz, and he'll send you downstairs *for the rest of your life!*" The threats were apparently so traumatizing that the younger son, Zaki, once burst into tears when Pete entered the office.

Dennis said the remark as a joke—that he'd tell Pete and I'd be in big trouble. But really, what *would* he have done if I'd brought a sandwich with bacon to the Musallah? Wouldn't he have told Pete?

I felt *watched*. But I now wondered if that should make me feel uncomfortable. Did my discomfort reflect a lack of *gratitude?* Weren't they doing me a favor by trying to watch over my religious life?

I had told myself this so often that it was becoming a mantra: the problem must be with me.

As Amy was on the verge of leaving Ashland, we took a walk through Lithia Park together. I had always loved coming to the park, strolling through the trails beside the gurgling creek. It felt peaceful, set apart from the rest of the world.

Over the course of the summer, I hadn't shared much with her about my changing beliefs. There had been signs, of course. My (thwarted) insistence that we have our *nikah* ceremony now had been one sign. There were others. I would no longer condemn Islamic radicalism to Amy. Occasionally when I came home from work I'd parrot a remark or analogy that Abdul-Qaadir had made in his lecture (such as parroting his criticism of feminism), thinking it important that Amy get more of an authentic Islamic perspective. I had a harsher edge around Amy and my parents than ever before, and would tell them far less of what was going on in my life. I remembered how, at one point during the summer, my dad remarked sadly that he and I didn't really talk anymore. He was right; surely Amy saw the difference too.

But when we walked through the park together, I was astounded by the kind of unconditional love she displayed toward me, an unconditional love that I knew I could not possibly deserve. As we chatted about our time together that summer, Amy mentioned that my dad had told her that he expected some of my coreligionists wouldn't be happy that I was marrying a non-Muslim.

"I told him that I didn't think that would be a problem," Amy said. "If they're not happy with you marrying me, I expect that to be a problem for *them*, not for me."

I nodded my head, saying nothing. I realized that even here, she perhaps had too much faith in me.

It is the Jews' plan to ruin everything."

We were gathered in the prayer room, sitting on the floor, and this was Ahmed Ezzat's remark.

People often ask me if other Muslims accepted me as one of them despite my Jewish background. The answer is that they did. Sometimes al-Husein would make jokes about my Jewish heritage, but they were always friendly, the kind of ethnic or religious jokes you can make about your friends if you're truly comfortable with them. I was never the *target* of anti-Semitism during my time as a Muslim. Whether I *witnessed* anti-Semitism during this time is a different question. It would, I submit, have been impossible not to. From anti-Semitic conspiracy theories being peddled in a Turkish bazaar (the merchant blamed Israel for the Ottoman Empire's dissolution; anyone with a passing familiarity with history will understand that this is quite impossible) to themes pervading the literature that Al Haramain distributed to offhand comments about "the *yahoods*," anti-Semitism was undeniably present. But never more present than in Ahmed's remarks that evening.

We were gathered in the prayer room because Abdul-Qaadir was teaching a class that night. I enjoyed seeing Abdul-Qaadir teach: he really *had* helped to transform my practice of Islam. He spoke with the same kind of confidence and world-is-watching-me presence when addressing a group that he used when it was just the two of us in the office. I was impressed by his knowledge of Islam, his knowledge of Arabic, and his thorough methodological approach to the faith.

Because of my Jewish background, other Muslims would often ask me questions about Judaism. We frequently had visitors stay in the Musalla for a few days at a time. One of our visitors this time around was, like Pete, Iranian. I no longer recall his name, but I remember the question he asked me during one of the breaks: "Daveed, what is the Talmud?"

As I was about to answer, Ahmed Ezzat, the Egyptian who worked for Al Haramain in Saudi Arabia, jumped in. "It is the Jews' plan to ruin everything," he said. I felt a moment of shock. I had begun to see the world through the same theological lens as these guys, but that didn't mean that I bought into crude conspiracy-mongering about the Jews.

And the Talmud, which is a record of rabbinic discussion of Jewish law, ethics, and customs, was far from a plot to ruin everything.

Ahmed continued, "It shows how the Jews plan to have the gentiles do their will. They planned to create a financial system based on interest, which we now have, and they planned to destroy morals. Why is it that Henry Kissinger was the president of the international soccer federation while he was the president of the United States? How did he have time to do both? It is because part of the Jews' plan is to get people throughout the world to play soccer so that they'll wear shorts that show off the skin of their thighs."

Dennis Geren was lying on his back on the floor. His back often bothered him, causing him to lie down in an effort to relieve his aches and sprains. "Henry Kissinger was the secretary of state, not the president," Dennis said. Then he got to his feet and left the room. I wondered what he was thinking. Although Dennis was often possessed by anger, he was no anti-Semite—and I was sure that he thought Ahmed's paranoid delusions were just as ridiculous as I did.

Pete's reaction was different. "Wow, bro, this is amazing," he enthused. "You come to us with this incredible information. You need to get on the microphone so you can tell the sisters about this." Pete handed the microphone to Ahmed.

Ahmed seemed embarrassed by the attention, but spoke into the microphone anyway. "There is nothing else to say," Ahmed said. "I have talked about the promoting of interest, soccer, the shorts, and the showing of the thighs. That is all, I've covered it."

I wasn't sure what to say. Ahmed's statement was false and dangerous. He hadn't described the Talmud or anything close to it. Instead, Ahmed was thinking of the Protocols of the Elders of Zion, a fraudulent document produced by Czarist Russia purporting to evidence a vast Jewish conspiracy. It is a document that the scholar Norman Cohn aptly described as part of Hitler's "warrant for genocide" against the Jewish people.

But I knew how things would go if I argued. Since Ahmed's Islamic knowledge surpassed my own, he thought he was also more qualified to speak on all other matters, including Judaism. And the others in the room probably agreed. As I had noticed almost two years before, when I first encountered Sheikh Hassan, argument and debate didn't take place here the way I was accustomed to from college. Purely logical arguments could be brushed away as Islamically improper, and the only time you didn't have to worry about slipping up in a way that could diminish your standing in the community is when you took the most hard-line position.

What would happen, I wondered, if I took issue with Ahmed's explanation? Perhaps he would argue with me, using pathos in place of logos.

But this wasn't an area where I was on unfamiliar ground, grasping for the theologically correct position through the haze of Qur'an and Sunna. I *knew* that what Ahmed said was false, and I knew the impact that this kind of conspiracy-mongering had on Jews in the past.

And yet I remained silent. Somehow I knew that if I argued with Ahmed, I would persuade no one.

It was one of the rare moments in which Yunus did not annoy me. He was talking about his father, Pete.

The degree to which Yunus and Yusuf looked up to Pete was apparent. They were both starved for his attention. In the limited time that he spent with his two sons, Pete obviously came across as a hero and a role model. Today, Yunus was telling me how beloved Pete was in the community.

Yunus's story was a small example, yet also a window into how Pete was seen. In January 1997, there were heavy rains in southern Oregon. Ashland Creek leaped its banks and washed out much of Ashland's downtown area. The flooded town was without indoor running water for days. Yunus told me how Pete drove a truck to the nearby town of Talent and returned with drinking water. He glowed when he described how happy this made people.

I thought about how it seemed that everyone knew Pete around Ashland, from all quarters. The hippies, the business owners, and the rabbis would ask me how he was doing and insist that I say hello. Thinking of the teachings within Al Haramain, Pete's offhand remarks about the *kufar*, his willingness to believe in the truth of alleged Jewish conspiracies, I thought about how none of them knew the real Pete Seda.

Then I further thought about Pete's almost unwavering sincerity, even when faced with the seeming contradiction between the idea that Islam was a religion of peace and the hateful views that his organization propounded. Even Pete, I realized, may not know the real Pete Seda.

It was a beautiful August day in Lithia Park's Japanese Garden. Stone paths snaked through the garden, there were scattered benches, flowers of many colors were in bloom. And as usual, I didn't appreciate the beauty.

The film crew from Landmind Productions was there, shooting footage of the local Muslims as we talked about how we came to Islam and what our faith meant to us. I watched them shoot a scene where Yunus Sedaghaty talked about the impact of Islam in his life. It didn't come across as sincere. I wandered toward our food spread. (When Pete gave the film crew money to buy refreshments, he gave three provisos: "Don't spend this money on alcohol, pork, or pornography.")

A man named Muhanid Khuja was sitting by the food, some sandwiches that the crew had picked up from the local Subway. Muhanid was from Guam. He had shown up in Ashland a few weeks back, seemingly at random, saying he was on a mosque tour through the United States. Some of the mosques he had encountered apparently horrified him with their deviant practices. But he took a liking to us and Pete took a liking to him. Soon, Muhanid became Pete's new right-hand man. Pete was in the process of buying a new house, and Muhanid was trying to guide him through the thorny process of making the purchase without paying interest.

Muhanid had a large beard and a large gut. I chatted with him for a few minutes, and the topic turned to my impending departure for law school. Muhanid was skeptical. "As a lawyer you have to take a pledge to defend the Constitution. There are some things in the Constitution I like, but a lot of things in the Constitution are completely against Islamic principles." Muhanid then talked about how he had once served in the U.S. Armed Forces. At the time, when he was a less serious Muslim, he didn't give much thought to whether it was wrong to do so. Now, in retrospect, he realized that it was wrong—the oaths he had made, the allegiances he had given contradicted his oath and allegiance to Allah.

"What in the Constitution is against Islam?" I asked.

"Well, for example, abortion."

I shook my head. "No. The word *abortion* is never mentioned in the Constitution, and nothing in the Constitution says that you have to be for abortion rights. There are a lot of Christian lawyers who practice in the U.S. but bring lawsuit after lawsuit trying to overturn *Roe v. Wade*."

"Well," Muhanid said, "if you were a Muslim living under the Roman Empire, what would be the right thing to do? Would you practice in Roman courts, or would you steer clear of them entirely?"

During a break in the filming, I caught a piece of Pete's conversation with John Foote. Pete was describing Yunus's interest in learning how to make videos, and wanted to see if Yunus could go by Landmind from time to time for training on video production.

"I do landscaping," Pete said. "I'm a landscaper. If Yunus came by from time to time and you showed him how to do film production, I could do landscaping work for you in exchange." He smiled conspiratorially. "And then we won't have to worry about taxes or anything like that, 'cause no money is changing hands." (When I interviewed John Foote for this book, I learned that the training that Pete envisioned never took place.)

I smiled and gave a half-laugh. I was no expert in tax law, but I knew that an exchange of services like that should be taxable. At the time I thought it was just another example of good old colorful Pete.

Later, it was time to shoot a scene with Yunus. For the shot, the film crew had us sitting on a couple of rocks, with a stream flowing gently past. They wanted to film our dialogue—a young Muslim man (me) sharing his wisdom with a Muslim teenager.

As the cameras rolled, Yunus asked me the same question I had heard on my first day of work. That day now seemed like a lifetime ago, and in some ways it was. "How are Muslims able to find the right person to marry," he asked, "if they aren't able to date?"

This was no mere theoretical question for him. It was a question that—with Pete as his father and Islam as his religion—he would have to grapple with. I remembered how at one point he and Dennis Geren were poring through correspondence from people requesting Islamic literature. Every time they came across a letter from a woman, they'd ask aloud whether she was single. My response at the time was gentle mockery: "Grow up, you two!" And Yunus had earnestly replied, "We *are* grown up. There are very few things more grown up than this." And you know? He was right. He wasn't thinking about a fling or a one-night stand. Yunus was just trying to do the best he could with the rules that were supposed to guide him.

I hesitated when Yunus asked his question. The hesitation was probably so small as to be unnoticeable, but my thoughts immediately turned to my relationship with Amy. I thought of how we had met, remembered our first kiss on a van ride back from Carrollton, Georgia, recalled the first time that Amy had told me that she loved me. There was a year of courtship before I asked her to marry me, a full year before I knew with certainty that Amy was the woman with whom I wanted to spend the rest of my life.

That's what I thought about in my moment of hesitation. But I almost immediately turned to Yunus and parroted the explanation that Pete had given on my first day on the job. "We believe that our method of courtship is *better* than the Western courtship process. There is a right way and a wrong way to tell whether someone is right for you, and the Islamic courtship process is devoted to quickly figuring out whether a potential mate is someone with whom you can spend the rest of your life. Often Western relationships are very superficial. You might not start to discuss deeper issues that are central to how you view the world for months or years. In the Islamic courtship process, you don't date. You want to know if someone is marriage material. And so you don't work toward a discussion of those deeper issues. Instead, that's where you *begin*."

Yunus nodded. He actually seemed satisfied. Of course, none of that is what I did with Amy. But I *believed* the words that I spoke. I loved Amy deeply, but actually regretted that we had met and dated in the traditional Western way. We weren't even married under Islamic law yet. Every time she and I were alone in a room together, every time we touched, every time we kissed—all of this was sinful.

I loved Amy deeply, but I was racked by doubt.

As the scene wrapped up, Yunus came up to me and said, "Good job with your comments on marriage." I nodded, somewhat surprised. It was the first time Yunus had said anything positive to me.

It was now dusk, and the production crew was packing up their cameras. I walked to my car. There was a lot to think about. Normally, this would be one of those drives where I'd pop in a tape and let the music wash over me while I drove, lost in my thoughts. But today there was no tape to play.

It was an event that most Americans didn't even notice. Islamic militants from Chechnya invaded the neighboring Republic of Dagestan on August 7, 1999. Somewhere between a thousand and four thousand fighters entered Dagestan and declared the land they occupied to be an Islamic state. Three days later, Russia responded by sending in fifteen thousand ground troops and initiating hundreds of bombing runs, killing thousands.

To most people, it seemed like one more skirmish occurring half a world away. I realized immediately, when I first ran across news of the invasion, that it would prove significant to me. It went to the heart of so much of what I had been thinking about and praying for over the past several months. Chief Justice Abdullah bin Muhammad bin Humaid had argued at great length that jihad was not just an acceptable means of establishing an Islamic state, but that undertaking jihad was an affirmative duty. And now the jihad had come.

I spoke briefly with Mahmoud Shelton, the Naqshbandi Sufi who had graduated from Stanford, about the situation in Chechnya. He stood in the office, and was flipping through a newspaper. When he came across a story about the invasion of Dagestan he skimmed it and seized on a line that described the invaders as Wahhabis. "But I didn't think the Wahhabis were heavily involved in the war of liberation from 1994 to 1996," he said.

I shrugged. "The details aren't clear yet. It doesn't seem to be the same group as in the first war, and this definitely wasn't defensive."

"So, what, is this just some group of random yahoos who are invading Dagestan in the name of creating an Islamic state?"

I didn't reply. I knew that of all the people here, Mahmoud would be the most antagonistic toward Wahhabi fighters. Though I had more than a little sympathy for where he was coming from, my mind kept returning to Sura 9:29, the order to fight those who do not "forbid that which has been forbidden by Allah and His Messenger." Wasn't that just what these mujahideen were doing?

Soon I would learn that this is exactly how many of my coreligionists viewed the invasion.

I was never a fan of good-byes. Even when al-Husein graduated from Wake Forest a semester before me, our farewell was poignant yet short. My last day of work at Al Haramain was unceremonious.

I packed up the limited personal items that I had in the office, gave Dennis Geren a firm handshake, and called Pete on his cell phone. I told him that my work there was complete. "I'll keep you in my prayers, bro," Pete said. "And when you're in law school, just make sure you remember . . ."

As so often happened, Pete's cell phone lost reception. It was almost fitting. This way, I could at least imagine that he had some piercing insight to share with me. In reality, he probably would have just interrupted himself before he could have finished the thought.

I recognized that I left Al Haramain a completely different person than I was the day I traipsed through the front door, ready to take part in the presentation to Ms. Thorngate's high school class. My views of God, the world, and myself had been drastically transformed. I had no idea whether I preferred the new me or the old one, nor did I know whether I was sad or happy to be finished at Al Haramain and on to law school.

ten

NEW YORK, NEW YORK

Aastaghfirullah!" It was an Arabic phrase literally asking Allah for forgiveness that al-Husein and I sometimes used in our conversations.

This time, al-Husein used the phrase while we were standing in line to buy various casebooks for my first semester of classes at the New York University School of Law. The guy ahead of us in line reminded me of your typical Wake Forest frat boy, both in his appearance and his chosen topics of conversation. He was speaking into his cell phone, loud enough that al-Husein and I could hear every word. He gave an all too predictable description of what he had done last night: "Man, we got *so* drunk!"

We both chuckled. Wake Forest was far behind us. We had changed far more in the sixteen months since al-Husein's graduation than either of us could have imagined, but suddenly we were back on common ground: making fun of arrogant frat boys for their toxic lifestyle. It was one of those rare moments where it seems like old times really can be recaptured.

Al-Husein had come to New York to help me move into my new room in D'Agostino Hall, NYU's high-rise student residence at the corner of MacDougal Street and West Third in the heart of Greenwich

Village. I was still trying to sort out how we now fit into each other's lives, but I was glad to have him around.

Al-Husein flipped through the various orientation materials, helping me pick out the organizations that I should be a part of. At the top of both of our lists, naturally, was the Middle Eastern Law Students Association (MELSA), the one student group with an Islamic orientation.

It was great to see al-Husein, but different. It was as though we were getting to know each other anew. At one point we had been comrades in the struggle to create a more progressive Islam. Since then, we had both become more serious about the faith. But how did our newly formed worldviews mesh? Neither of us knew the answer.

We spent some time exploring the city together. New York City has a heavy Islamic presence, and al-Husein was eager to encounter other Muslims on the street. "You can tell another Muslim by the way he dresses," al-Husein said. "You look for the beard, for the loose-fitting clothes." I nodded.

And we spotted other Muslims almost right away when we left D'Agostino Hall and stepped onto bustling West Third Street. D'Agostino was right across from Vanderbilt Hall, a large red brick building where the bulk of the law school's classes are held. Another block down, just past Vanderbilt, was Washington Square Park.

We walked east on West Third, toward Broadway. This was to be another of the many long walks that al-Husein and I took together, where we'd both reflect on life's meanings, and our place in this world and the next. Only I had far less of an idea about what to expect from the conversation than I did in the old days, when we had circled Wake Forest's quad together.

We didn't get more than half a block before glimpsing a couple of other Muslims across the street. One of them was black and the other was South Asian. And it wasn't beards or loose-fitting clothes that gave them away: they both wore kufis.

We waved at them and crossed the street. We all exchanged Islamic greetings. It turned out that both men taught at the university level. "We're scientists," the black convert said. "We're involved in *changing paradigms*. We take our faith, and we bring that to our scientific work." Although al-Husein was in divinity school at the time, he was still thinking about going to medical school as his father had done. This enthused our two conversational partners, as they thought that he too could be involved in the important task of changing paradigms, in the medical field. They were less interested in the fact that I was beginning law school—probably because there was no need to change paradigms there. We all knew that *sharia* was the perfect law: what more innovation did the field of law need?

While al-Husein spoke with the black convert, I spoke with the South Asian man. He gave me his phone number. "We should stay in touch," he said. "There are so many situations right now that affect us as Muslims. There is this situation in Chechnya. That's something we need to watch."

I nodded. Just as I had thought when the mujahideen first invaded Dagestan, this conflict was proving to be far bigger, far more important than most Americans realized.

This is a much different place than college was," I said. "You probably have better insight into this than I do. Who are our natural allies?"

I was asking one of the female members of MELSA, who was in her third year of law school. We were talking on the phone. I clutched my large green plastic receiver while peering out the dorm window at West Third Street. I felt that I had to ask this question because I found NYU confusing, unfamiliar. Most Wake Forest students were apolitical—but if anything, the average Wake student was right of center. So the various minority student groups formed a sometimes ill-fitting alliance. But the average NYU student was hardly right of center. In class, whenever I thought of raising my hand to make a left-of-center point that would have been vaguely revolutionary at Wake Forest, at least two or three students would beat me to it. I wasn't sure there was such a need to work with other campus minority groups. And with my deepening commitment to Islam, I wasn't sure that these ill-fitting alliances would be productive anymore.

But I wasn't expecting the answer I got. "I wouldn't trust any of these groups," she said. "There are so many *yahoods* here that we can't really trust anybody."

I was taken aback. *Yahood* was Arabic for "Jew." I said, "You know that my parents are *yahoods*, right?"

"Of course," she replied. "I could tell by your name. Why do you ask?"

I wasn't sure what to say. Why did I ask? Wasn't the reason obvious? If both of my parents were Jewish, then perhaps I wouldn't find the assertion that we couldn't trust anybody at NYU because there were so many Jews all that appealing. But instead I said, "No reason. Just making sure you knew."

This was not the Daveed Gartenstein-Ross of Wake Forest campus activist days. I normally wouldn't remain silent in the face of bigotry of any kind—particularly when it was directed at people like me. But since my time at Al Haramain, things had changed.

My one solace during my first semester at NYU was prayer. When I undertook my five daily prayers, that was the one time that I knew I was doing something unambiguously good.

After that rather upsetting phone call, I went through my afternoon prayers. Making *du'a* at the end, I supplicated Allah to cure the *Ummah* of this disease of anti-Semitism.

Those prayers were bizarrely interspersed with supplications for Allah to grant victory to the mujahideen.

The first time I went to a Yankees game, what struck me most was the music they played after the game ended. As the final out rolled in and people began to rise from their seats, I recognized the opening bars of Frank Sinatra's "New York, New York" piping through the loudspeakers. Although it was one of the many songs to which I'd never devoted much attention, this time I really listened to the lyrics—and found that I disagreed with them:

> If I can make it there,
> I'll make it anywhere.

If you can make it here, you'll make it *anywhere?* Hardly. I thought of Ol' Blue Eyes—an alcoholic, a womanizer, and a musician—trying to make it in Mecca. Frank Sinatra *did* make it in New York, but I doubted that he could make it in the world that I had been inhabiting.

In fact, I knew that I too could make it in New York—but didn't know whether I could make it as a true follower of Allah. This is what I thought about as I shuffled out of the Yankees game with the rest of the crowd.

I still spoke with Pete from time to time. In one of our first discussions after I got to New York, he told me that he wanted to do something to protest the brutality with which the Russians were carrying out their military campaign against the Chechens.

"Bro, now they're gonna use chemical weapons against the mujahideen," Pete said. "I saw pictures on TV of some of these Russian soldiers with gas masks on. They claim that they're wearing gas masks because the mujahideen are gonna use chemical weapons against them, but that's a lie and I can prove it." Pete paused for dramatic effect, then said, "Would *you* use chemical weapons in your own backyard?"

I thought about that. "You have a point," I said.

"These *kufar* think they can just go in and brutalize the Muslims. But they're gonna learn that it isn't that easy."

I didn't know at the time that Pete may already have had in mind plans to ensure that the Russians wouldn't have it that easy.

My classes, at least, were going well. My favorite professor was Larry Kramer, who taught civil procedure. Kramer was in his early forties, a graduate of the University of Chicago's law school and a former clerk to Supreme Court Justice William J. Brennan. He would later go on to become the dean of Stanford's law school.

The thing I appreciated most about the class was Kramer's Socratic method. He was able to pierce to the heart of a student's argument and eviscerate it in a way that none of our other professors could. Because of that, the class's opinions on Kramer were sharply divided. He was simultaneously loved, hated, and feared—at times all by the same person. Testament to Kramer's skill as a teacher is the fact that I found his class engrossing, even though it focused on the technical details of civil litigation.

Part of the reason I enjoyed the class was that it didn't force me to compromise my Islamic principles. My criminal law course often focused on theories of punishment. I knew that it would never be acceptable to say in class, "The right punishment for a thief is to have his hand cut off, because that's what the Qur'an demands." In contrast, what could be inappropriate Islamically about a system of civil procedure? *Sharia*-compliant courts would also need to have procedures for dealing with civil litigation.

As part of his Socratic method, Kramer would often put his students into roles, as lawyers or judges. One day, Kramer put me and one of my friends, a leftist from California named David Alonzo-Maizlish, into the role of attorneys who were supposed to debate the legal issues from one of the cases we had read.

My background in college debate did me well. From debate I had garnered a certain approach to analyzing arguments and organizing my thoughts. The margin notes in my casebook broke down all of the court's analysis comprehensively, detailed the arguments that had been presented to the court in a manner I could quickly assess. And thinking on my feet came naturally.

After my brief debate with David Alonzo-Maizlish was done, my friend Sadik Huseny—himself a lapsed Muslim of Albanian descent— whispered to me, "That's the best I've seen anybody do in this class." Sadik, who was a remarkably articulate individual, had described the "flush effect" that occurred when you were called on in Kramer's class: suddenly everything you had thought of, everything you had prepared for, was flushed right out of you.

When I saw Professor Kramer in the hallway later, he nodded and said, "Good job today in class." I appreciated his manner of giving the compliment. He didn't even slow down to say it. Instead, he nodded and congratulated me while walking past, never breaking his stride. But I also knew that Kramer wouldn't give a compliment lightly.

But in the end, I wished that I felt like my good performance in class *mattered*.

I found my studies to be an excellent diversion. I knew that most students thought it was tedious to come back to their rooms and pore carefully through the massive red-and-black casebooks with highlighters and pens in hand. To me, class preparation—like my five daily prayers— was a moment to get away. When I was preparing for class, I felt that I was inhabiting a more whimsical universe than usual. The universe of the law was one where I could approach analytical problems using pure logic, where I could venture my own moral opinions. Not, I thought, like the real world. There was a pronounced difference between how I felt when I picked up my Aspen Law casebook to read about tort law and how I felt when thumbing through the Noble Qur'an and trying to reason through the obligation of jihad, or *hijrah*.

Anytime al-Husein announced that he had a question for me, I would brace for what was coming. Today it seemed that he was probing my practice of Islam. "I know that at one time you and I both believed in the need for an Islamic reformation," he said. "I want to know if this is something that you still believe in."

I looked at the street outside while holding the receiver. There was one guy in the dirty clothes of a homeless man aggressively shaking his coffee mug at passersby, looking for change. "I never really believed in an Islamic reformation," I said. That was true, at least partially. I would never have used that phrase to describe what I had believed. I had tried to reconcile my passion for social justice with a sincere belief in Allah and an effort to stay true to His religion. I used to think the two could be reconciled. But I was rapidly concluding that I had simply been wrong about that.

I continued, "An Islamic reformation was far more at the forefront in your thinking than in mine. I always wanted to be as true as possible to the Qur'an and the example of the Prophet, *alayhi salaatu was salaam*. What has changed is my idea of what it means to be true to the Qur'an and Prophet Muhammad, *alayhi salaatu was salaam*."

It seemed that Al-Husein was satisfied with the response, and our conversation continued. I wondered how he would have responded if I

had told him that I *was* still committed to the idea of an Islamic reformation. It seemed like, as during my time at Al Haramain, he was probing for deviant beliefs.

The end of finals was not as sweet for me as for most first-years. The
other students saw the end of finals as a last hurdle cleared, allowing
them—at least for the next three weeks—to go back to enjoying life. I
continued to see law school and exams in the opposite way. They were
no obstacle, but rather a somewhat pleasant escape.

After our last finals were done, there was a champagne toast to celebrate. John Sexton, NYU's legendary law school dean (and now the university's president) came out to lead the toast. I of course did not drink,
but afterward went with other students to a bar to celebrate.

Looking at the other students, it was obvious that I was living in a
different universe. They were jubilant to be done. There was drinking,
some dancing, loud music often drowning out tepid attempts at conversation. They seemed happy. Though I wasn't drinking, I wondered if
even *this* was wrong: being around alcohol and loud music, in a place
where the sexes mixed freely.

The other students were blissfully unaware of the various rules that I
struggled with constantly. They never had to worry about whether a full
beard was required, whether it was okay to shake hands with a woman,
whether you could wear shorts in the summer. They didn't have to worry
about whether music was unlawful, about rolling up their trousers before
they prayed. And they never had the burden of wondering whether the
Taliban and the holy warriors of Chechnya were *right*.

I thought back to when al-Husein visited me when I was moving
into my dorm room, and our trip to NYU's professional bookstore. I
thought of al-Husein's remark—*"Astaghfirullah!"*—when we heard the

frat boy–looking guy talking about his drinking exploits. Things had seemed so clear to me at the time. That confused kid was lost in his own sins and error, unlike me.

But now, as I watched my classmates, I had to wonder: if I had the truth and they were in error, why did I envy their ignorance? Why did I wish that I too could suck down a beer and ignore events that were unfolding half a world away?

The pervert Jews whine about their so-called Holocaust. But how much worse is this, when it is being done in the open with all the world watching?"

These were not Abdul-Qaadir's words, but he was the cause of this e-mail arriving in my in-box. Indeed, one thing that made it difficult to ignore events occurring half a world away was the constant stream of e-mail that discussed these events.

Abdul-Qaadir, the black convert to Islam who had helped mentor me down the road to Salafism, had set up an e-mail list just as I was beginning law school. On it, he would send out information on the Chechen mujahideen. I never doubted what his perspective would be on events in Chechnya, and he did not disappoint with his raw enthusiasm for the holy warriors. Sometimes he would send out his own reports on the fighting. Other times, he would send out e-mail that came from other sources, like the fiercely pro-Chechen Qoqaz information group, which included e-mail written by people throughout the world who sympathized with the Chechens' cause. (Qoqaz was the Arabic word for the Caucasus region, where Chechnya is located.)

The message about the "pervert Jews" and their "so-called Holocaust" was part of a compilation of messages that had been sent to Qoqaz expressing various Muslims' support for the Chechen mujahideen. These messages were compiled in a single e-mail. I presumed that the e-mail had been sent from the Qoqaz group to Abdul-Qaadir, and from Abdul-Qaadir it had been passed along to me. Some of the messages sent to the Chechens were about as innocuous as messages sent to a group of Islamic radicals trying to establish a *sharia* state by force could be—but the innocuous ones were the minority. The message that struck me, the message about the pervert Jews whining about their so-called Holocaust, went on about how the so-called Holocaust was at least carried out in secret by the Germans, while here the Russians were slaughtering the Chechens with all the world watching. So how much worse is this than the Holocaust? With my old activist impulse, I thought about replying with a message saying that you don't have to attack the Jews to support the Chechens or the Muslims—perhaps even pointing out that I was from a Jewish background but had come to embrace Islam. But what good would that have done?

Abdul-Qaadir eventually established his own Internet news group about the events in Chechnya. It was called Ansaarul-Mujahideen, "News from the Chechen Mujahideen point of view." It may be somewhat difficult to believe in the post-9/11 world, but Abdul-Qaadir ran this news group right out of Yahoo.com. This was the world before the September 11 attacks, where the jihadists weren't under much scrutiny, and little seemed out of place about running this news group on one of the Internet's most popular destinations. (After 9/11, Abdul-Qaadir sent out an indignant e-mail stating that "some views, such as those I have passed forth in this egroup now for two years, may now be viewed not just as passing on of information but advocacy of terror!" He added, "I do know that as a person, a MUSLIM American, who has a hard time shutting up or being told he has no right to have an opinion, I find it repugnant that the only things that can be said or expressed are those things which are deemed suitable by those who do not share our faith. I believe this breeds extremism and hatred, exaggeration and misunderstanding.")

In this pre-9/11 world, Abdul-Qaadir's news group even featured reports sent to him directly from the field of combat. One of them stands out to this day. I remember coming back to my dorm room after class, opening my e-mail, and seeing a message from Abdul-Qaadir announcing that he had "bittersweet news": One of the Chechen mujahideen, with whom Abdul-Qaadir had carried on a long-running correspondence, had been killed. The holy warrior had longed for martyrdom. He was a long-time international jihadist, fighting on battlefields that ranged from Afghanistan to Southeast Asia to the Caucasus. Wherever he went, this young man sought to die in Allah's cause. Abdul-Qaadir had received a report of the death from some of his comrades-in-arms. They reported that when the young man died, he had been standing up and praying for death—and then had been hit by an incoming Russian rocket.

Abdul-Qaadir finished the e-mail by imploring the readers to think of how much more the dead mujahid had done for the *Ummah* than any of us, the readers.

But was that really what the religion was about? Fighting in various battlefields scattered throughout the world, trying to topple secular governments, and praying for death? Even though the mujahideen were in my prayers, my doubts were growing.

A Web site that al-Husein showed me in December made me feel that I was the only one with doubts. I was in Orlando, where al-Husein grew up, because he was about to get married. It was a few days before the *nikah* ceremony, and al-Husein was only partially focused on his own wedding. He was preoccupied with guilt, Islamic rules—and the Chechen mujahideen. Al-Husein was showing me his favorite Internet picture of those holy warriors.

It was a photo of the Chechen mujahideen lined up for a battlefield prayer. Al-Husein explained that he had this photo up on the wall of his room back in Boston.

A number of al-Husein's cousins had come to Orlando for the wedding. They were young, beautiful, and vivacious Indian-American women. One of them looked at the computer screen and asked what to her must have been the obvious question: "Are you joking?"

Al-Husein flatly informed her that he was not joking. He wasn't harsh, but his response suggested that she shouldn't have had to ask such a question. I thought that al-Husein's response must have made her feel the same way I felt when al-Husein had no answer to my story about Al Haramain's head office getting upset over male and female high school students being in the same room together. It was not what she expected, and it suggested this was not the same al-Husein she had known and loved.

She may have realized then that she was losing him, but didn't realize how much. Al-Husein still joked around with his cousins and seemed to have a genuinely good time around them (although it was surely a good time punctuated by guilt), but he did something that the old al-Husein would not: after he'd been with his cousins and before he went to pray, he would make *wudu*, the pre-prayer ablutions. He would do that because his cousins were female, and coming into contact with members of the opposite sex breaks one's ritual cleanliness.

I remembered a conversation I had with Abdul-Qaadir. He told me that one of the most difficult things he had to do after becoming a serious Muslim was break off his friendship with his female cousins. "Growing up in D.C.," he told me, "I'd do everything with my cousins. I thought of them as being just like my *sisters*. But when I became serious about Islam, I realized that I couldn't be around them anymore. Even if I was close to them growing up, they *aren't* my sisters. The fact is, they're *legal* for me to marry, so the normal restrictions for male-female relations apply." First-cousin marriages are common in the Arab world and expressly permitted in the Qur'an.

On one night leading up to the *nikah*, al-Husein told me that he was going to stay out late with his cousins. "I want to spend some time with them," he said. "I want to get my time in with them now, because it can't be like this once I'm married." I figured that what he said was not what he meant. Being *married* wouldn't change the way he could spend time with his cousins. It was becoming a more conservative Muslim that changed everything.

In fact, al-Husein's transformation into a more conservative Muslim had caused him to get married so quickly in the first place. Shortly before the miracle that transformed him, al-Husein had begun to date an attractive woman named Liana Sebastian from an Indian-British background. Liana had been raised Christian, then converted to Sunni Islam after a brief involvement with the Ismaili community. But Sunni Islam was still new to her, and there was so much that she didn't know.

One thing she couldn't have anticipated was an e-mail that she got from al-Husein early in the fall, shortly after I began classes at NYU. He sent the message to both me and Liana. The e-mail was a forward of a message that al-Husein received through the Harvard Islamic Society. The message began by discussing how university students needed to avoid the trap of shaking hands with members of the opposite sex. Even though doing so has become customary in Western colleges and universities, it is still sinful. The message then went on to outline relevant *ahadith* about relations between the sexes, and made the case for complete separation. No kissing, no holding hands. Even being alone in a room together before marriage was verboten.

Al-Husein didn't send this e-mail as a mere point of interest. He wasn't simply considering its argument; he was *convinced*. I spoke with al-Husein on the phone shortly after he sent the e-mail, and he told me how guilty he felt about becoming emotionally attached to a woman who was not his wife. In the ultra-orthodox version of Islam that al-Husein had come to embrace, this was considered *haram*, impermissible.

There was a certain tone in his voice. My experience with al-Husein was that he was intellectually inquisitive, that almost any argument was on the table for him. But the urgency with which he said this suggested that there was no reasoning with him on this one. He had made up his mind, and to argue with him would be insensitive.

But there was a way out: the *nikah* ceremony. When I spoke with him, al-Husein viewed the *nikah* similarly to how I saw it when I tried to get Amy to agree to it. After the *nikah*, al-Husein and Liana would be husband and wife, and all would be legal. (Of course, al-Husein wanted to have the *nikah* and spend his life with Liana for many more reasons than mere feelings of guilt. But this is what I homed in on at the time because I was grappling with similar feelings.)

Al-Husein went down to Orlando in November to talk things over with Liana, their families, and a local imam who agreed to consult them on the matter. I didn't learn the details of this meeting at the time, but the end result was that Liana decided she loved al-Husein, wanted to spend her life with him, and thought that sanctifying their relationship through the *nikah* was the right step to take next. They proceeded to have the *nikah* on December 25, which not only marked Christmas Day but also fell in the middle of Ramadan that year.

I was in Orlando as al-Husein's best man. I would also be a witness to the signing of the marriage contract, and—with the limited skills I had picked up after a semester of law school—even drafted a large section of the *nikah* contract for them.

Al-Husein's obsession with following the rules could not have been more pronounced when I was in Orlando with him. He had told me to bring my suit and tie when I went down. But the first time I put the suit on, al-Husein looked contemptuously at my tie. He grabbed it, putting two fingers underneath and running his thumb down it. "Is this *silk?*" he asked.

It was. "I don't know," I stammered. My response was unimpressive: would Allah forgive you for wearing silk simply because you had forgotten to check?

Al-Husein's parents were also seeing him in a new light. As Ismailis, they were used to Sunnis regarding them as outside the fold of Islam—and they now realized that their own son saw them that way. They tried to be supportive, but didn't know what to make of these changes.

Early one morning I overheard a telephone conversation between al-Husein and his parents. There had been a lot of argument because al-Husein wanted to make sure that everything was, as he put it, "done by the Book." The *nikah* ceremony had to comply entirely with Islamic law—but since his parents were Ismailis, the question frequently arose of *whose* Islamic law would be followed. In this conversation, he told them that under his interpretation of Islamic law, they weren't Muslims; they were *kufar*. I winced when I heard this, but didn't say anything. Instead, I was just trying to be a good friend. I was trying to guide al-Husein as best I could, trying to be a calming influence on a potentially explosive situation.

Eventually it was time for the *nikah* ceremony. As al-Husein was getting dressed in his wedding robes, his dad handed him a black kufi with gold threads on the outside. Al-Husein looked at the kufi suspiciously. "Is it *real* gold?"

Under Islamic law, men are not to wear gold.

"Husein," I said, the first time in all the many moments leading up to the *nikah* that my voice had a note of reprimand, "get over it."

He quickly did and wore the kufi to the ceremony. The ceremony itself was a brief and formal affair that took place in the main prayer area of an Orlando mosque. Al-Husein had mused earlier that for many of his relatives, it would be the first time they had ever set foot in a real mosque. And indeed, I was amused at the time by how clueless some of his relatives were about proper Islamic conduct. There was the uncle who wanted to drink alcohol at the wedding; there was the aunt who thought that al-Husein was a fundamentalist because he was fasting for Ramadan; there were the relatives who wanted to take him to a strip club the night before the ceremony.

I had mixed feelings about the *nikah* as I headed to the Orlando airport when it was finished. I would be traveling to North Carolina to spend the rest of Christmas break with Amy and her family. I thought of how both al-Husein and I had taken a turn for a much more orthodox practice of Islam. Although we were heading in the same direction, our theological transformation was driving a wedge between us. We were not the same people who had first become friends three years ago.

On the other hand, I sensed that Liana was a truly special person, a good influence on al-Husein. I thought of how the religious changes I had gone through made Amy uncomfortable, but never changed the core of her love for me. Liana displayed the same kind of patience, support, and love for al-Husein. I was happy for al-Husein to have a woman like that in his life.

As I boarded the plane, I thought about how much I had changed. At one point, I would have found everything that al-Husein had insisted on over the past several months and at his *nikah* ceremony to be bizarre—al-Husein's refusing to be alone in the same room as Liana, his interrogation about whether my tie was made of silk, his concern about whether the threads in the kufi he would wear for the ceremony were made of real gold. But over the past few months, I had come to view these as weighty moral issues.

Al-Husein and Liana were now married under Islamic law. He no longer had to feel conflicted about the time he spent with her. He no longer had to worry about contravening any Islamic laws.

Boarding that plane to spend the rest of Christmas break with Amy, I realized that I envied al-Husein. He was marrying a Muslim woman. Even if she didn't agree with his extremely narrow approach to Islamic law, she was willing to have the *nikah* sooner rather than later. Amy didn't share my faith and didn't sympathize with my concerns. And I knew that, while I wanted the days of vacation that I spent with her to be a time of bliss, there would always be guilt lurking just below the surface.

The bottom line is that I realized that the religious proscriptions that I was falling short of *could* be followed. I was *capable* of following them. Having a beard rather than a goatee wouldn't be difficult. While it might be awkward at first to refuse to shake hands with women, eventually people would understand that this was something I didn't do and would stop asking. And I could have kept all my money in a checking account rather than a savings account to make sure I didn't receive interest. (My student loans were another matter; the lenders were unlikely to look kindly upon me refusing to pay the interest that I owed them.)

So what was going on? I was just beginning to admit to myself what my hesitations were. But I vaguely understood that I had trouble separating the small things I did from the big picture. And I was beginning to have grave doubts about that big picture. I had begun to question whether women should really be relegated to the socially inferior position that a Salafist society would place them in. I had begun to question whether ideals like freedom of speech and freedom of religion were really so wrong. I had begun to question whether it was indeed right that my religion should be spread by force. I had even begun to question whether the Chechen mujahideen were really right. They weren't fight-

ing a war of liberation; instead, they had initiated the conflict by invading
Dagestan in an effort to establish an Islamic state governed by Taliban-
like rules.

I thought back to my days as a campus activist. I thought about the
psychological theory, self-perception theory, that al-Husein and I had
both latched on to. The theory holds that people develop their attitudes
by observing their own behavior, then reasoning backward from the
behavior to determine what their attitudes must be. As campus activists,
we embraced the idea that if you could get someone to act in a certain
way, their beliefs would eventually fall into line, and we'd try to get
people involved so they might come to define themselves as activists.

But I realized that my development into a serious Salafi had been
influenced by the same principles. There were the small steps I took.
There was my refusal to shake hands with the female schoolteacher who
wanted to bring her class to the Musalla. There was my decision to stop
listening to music, to grow a full beard, to roll up my pants legs before
prayer, to stop wearing shorts or anything that left my thighs exposed. I
now saw even these as small but definite steps toward radicalism.

No, it wasn't that the various strictures were too difficult to follow. I
could have happily followed all the rules that were thrust upon me if I
knew they were right. But I had developed so many doubts about the big
picture.

Islamic radicals want to reestablish the caliphate. Many Muslims feel
that a calamity struck the *Ummah* in 1924 when Mustafa Kemal Atatürk
broke up the Ottoman Empire and replaced it with modern Turkey.
Before that, the Ottoman Empire had served as the caliphate; that is,
the Muslim world had been under unified leadership. Many radicals believe that modern nation-states are illegitimate, and that only a caliphate
is worthy of authority over the Islamic world. The radicals would have
this new caliphate ruled by a Taliban-like regime, not by the liberal, progressive "true Islam" that al-Husein and I had once propounded. And

the caliphate would become a reality through jihad. Were *these* the mujahideen for whom I was praying?

As my plane lifted off, I prayed to Allah to cure me of the disease of my doubts.

Early in 2000, I called Pete and told him that I was going to pay taxes on the money that I was paid while working at Al Haramain.

Ultimately, my parents persuaded me to do this. I had been so surprised when Pete insisted on writing that the first check had been for a computer that I told them about it. They strongly advised that since I was going to law school, I should steer as far from trouble with the law as I could. And I was paid less than $10,000 for my entire time at Al Haramain. I could make more than that in a month as a lawyer. It simply wasn't worth getting into trouble over such a trivial amount.

Pete sounded surprised when I told him I was going to pay taxes, but didn't try to talk me out of it. "There was also a computer that you sold to us back in January," Pete said. "Are you going to pay taxes on that too?"

"Yes, Pete, I am. There was never a computer. That check was for work that I did for you."

"I just wanted to check to make sure, bro."

In January 2000, Pete called me to tell me that he had prepared a letter to the Russian ambassador outlining his plan to drive a peace convoy into Chechnya. "Take a look at the letter," Pete said. "You might need to change some of the language."

I remembered Pete's "peace convoy" idea during the Kosovo war—a convoy that would enter Yugoslavia, distribute humanitarian supplies, and send a signal that the war had to end. The peace convoy represented the best and worst of Pete's thinking. He was able to think big and think creatively, coming up with Rube Goldberg–like solutions to the world's problems, with himself as the star of the show. But like Rube Goldberg's fantastic machines, there was always a hitch or two in Pete's ideas that would prevent them from becoming reality.

Pete had a similar peace convoy plan for Chechnya. He wanted to take a large convoy filled with food and medicine into Grozny, the capital of the Chechen Republic. There, the convoy would evacuate the wounded and show the world that the Russian invasion of Chechnya had to end. The peace convoy was never a realistic response to the Kosovo war, but at least you could understand why the Serbs might be interested. Sending a signal that the NATO bombing had to end would, after all, *help* them.

There was no such incentive for the Russians, since Pete wanted them to invite him into Chechnya to signal to the rest of the world that the Russians had to end a war that *they still wanted to carry out*.

But Pete e-mailed the letter to me. When I opened it, I was greeted by the salutation: "Dear Ambassador Bonehead." The letter went on to say that if the Russians would allow the peace convoy to enter Chechnya, "I will personally kiss your filthy ass." The letter was somewhat amusing, but also provided a telling look at Pete's attitude.

There was no question where Al Haramain as a group stood on the war in Chechnya. In January 2000, the charity's main Web site, run out of Riyadh, featured prayers for the Chechen mujahideen:

O Allah! Aid our Mujaahideen brothers in Chechnya. O Allah! Unify their rows, and gather them on the word of truth. O Allah! Aim their firing and strengthen their determination, and make their feet firm, and descend upon them tranquility, and satisfy their hearts and guide them to that which is all good.

Pete's sympathy for the mujahideen was also clear from my phone calls with him.

By February, it was obvious that Pete's full attention was devoted to Chechnya. I received a short e-mail from him on February 8:

> Salam
>
> I am outraged this Russians bluntly giving the finger to human-itarian Orgs even killing some smashing cameras and more recently begun a systematic genocide since the western world has told Rus-Putin finish them while we make some noise so as we are against this genocide
>
> ISNA of Canada send us money for Chechnia [sic].
>
> Call me collect ASAP

When I called Pete after getting that message, he was vague about his plans. He wanted to do something about the situation in Chechnya, and he might need my help.

"I'm happy to help, Pete," I said. "Let me know what you need me to do."

It would be a little while before I heard from him again.

What I didn't expect was for Pete to take his anger toward the Russians to the next level, to actually help the mujahideen. But it seems that this is exactly what happened. And but for my growing doubts, I too might have gotten entangled in this plot.

Pete called me in the middle of March 2000. I hadn't spoken with him in a few weeks, but when I answered the phone, he acted like we were still back in Ashland, like I were still working for him. "Bro," he said, "Soliman is flying into town tomorrow. I want you to go out to the airport, bring him flowers, tell him how glad you are to see him, and make him feel at home in New York." He was referring to Soliman al-But'he, another Al Haramain director who worked in the Riyadh office. Although I had never met him, I had spoken with Soliman on the phone several times while I was working in the Ashland office, and had exchanged e-mail with him on countless occasions.

"What?" Amy was visiting me over her spring break. She sat on the bed while I stood by the window of my dorm room, holding the green receiver. No doubt she heard the surprise in my voice.

"Bro, Soliman doesn't come into the U.S. too often, and it'd be real nice if we could show him the kind of hospitality that people really appreciate in the Arab world."

"Pete, I have a full schedule, and it's about a thirty-dollar cab ride to the airport. It'd cost me sixty dollars or more to see him."

"I know it's an inconvenience, but look, bro, I'm trying to get you a law school scholarship from Al Haramain. I told them how good you are and said that we *need* this guy. You're one of those young Muslims who could be a future leader in the *Ummah,* and I wanna make sure that you don't have to worry about money all the time while you're in school, and you don't have to go through the problems with *riba* [interest] that come with taking out loans. So I wanna get you to meet Soliman, so you can treat him like a good host while he's in New York and he can see that you're legit. Whaddaya say to that, bro?"

"I don't know, Pete. You say Soliman is coming into New York tomorrow, right?"

"Yeah."

"So look, let me think about this. I'll get back to you."

"Okay, bro," Pete said. "It'd be best if you can meet up with him. That would mean a lot to him."

I hung up the phone and gave the matter some thought. It seemed like an imposition at first, but Pete claimed he was trying to get something for me. I talked it over with Amy. But, as had become routine, I didn't give her enough of a window into my world. There was so much that I wouldn't, and probably couldn't, explain. There was the fact that my religious inexperience and uncertainty had locked me into an unfortunate pattern with Pete and the others. It was a command-and-respond pattern, where someone would tell me what to do and I would do it. Since religion influences every aspect of one's life in Islam, this had boiled over into an uncertainty even on secular matters.

And so, even when Pete called to ask me to spend a few hours and about sixty dollars on a lark, my reflexive reaction was to agree. After all, I was beginning to believe that I did not know best. Instead, the people with Islamic knowledge superior to mine knew best.

But then I thought about the reaction I could expect from Soliman. And when I thought about Soliman, my thoughts turned to my facial hair. I grew a full beard when I was at Al Haramain, but shaved it off in favor of a goatee months ago. What would Soliman think? Would I spend sixty dollars to get to the airport only to find Soliman chastising me for my physical appearance?

On top of that, something just didn't sound right about Pete's request. What it was, I couldn't put my finger on. But intuitively, there seemed to be something strange about Pete's desire to have me go to the airport and meet Soliman.

I called Pete later that day and told him apologetically that I couldn't go. "I have a lot of work to do and can't really afford to spend sixty dollars to take a cab out to the airport and back," I said.

Pete sounded annoyed, but said it was fine. Clearly, though, if he really had been pushing to get me a law school scholarship from Al Haramain, my refusal made him give up on the idea.

My decision not to meet Soliman was more significant than I could have realized. Part of the significance lay in the fact that I had stood up to Pete. This small act of rebellion would grow into something more, although at the time I couldn't imagine by how much.

And part of the significance lay in what Pete and Soliman may have had planned for me. Since I didn't go to the airport, there is no way of knowing precisely. But I would later learn that at the time Soliman was passing through New York, he was in the process of smuggling about $130,000 out of the country—money that federal investigators believe was used to fund the Chechen mujahideen. It is only my growing doubts that prevented me from heading to the airport and discovering what they had in mind—and ultimately, these doubts may have saved me from involvement in a plot to fund terrorists.

eleven

RESURRECTION

It was a Sunday morning, and it felt right.

I woke up around nine o'clock, showered, shaved, and put my suit on. I had a quick breakfast, then walked out the front doors of D'Agostino Hall. It was a hot day. As was the case every Sunday morning, the corner of West Third and MacDougal was littered with trash: paper plates, beer bottles, old newspapers, nightclub flyers. I walked past the panhandlers, the early-morning risers, and those who never quite found their way to bed last night.

I walked to the Washington Square Church, a United Methodist church up the street from Washington Square Park. It was the first time I had been to church in four years. Last time was with Mike Hollister in Bellingham. Back then, the experience did nothing for me. This time, I didn't know what to expect.

The church had a woman pastor, a marked contrast from the various Islamic ceremonies I had been to over the past several years. Although I had little knowledge of Christian doctrine, I realized that most Christians would probably see her sermon as objectionable. It focused on Marion Zimmer Bradley's book *The Mists of Avalon*, a retelling of the King Arthur legend. The pastor explained that *The Mists of Avalon* has a different holy trinity than the Father, Son, and Holy Spirit of Christianity—and that the trinity presented in Marion Zimmer Bradley's book was more woman-affirming.

After the sermon, they invited everyone present, Christian and not, to take communion. The preacher mentioned that their communion used grape juice rather than wine. On hearing this, I decided to participate. I wouldn't have done it if they used wine, which was *haram* to drink.

Walking home afterward, I tried to gauge my emotional reaction. Despite the questionable religious content, I felt invigorated. Thinking of the reaction that men like W. D. Muhammad and the Naqshbandis received in Islamic extremist circles, it amazed me that in the world of Christianity you could give a sermon like the one I had just heard without instantly being branded a heretic and apostate.

As I walked back into my dorm room, I wondered if I would go to church again. As I faced my prayer rug in the direction of Mecca for my afternoon prayers, I acknowledged the obvious. If everything were all right with my faith, I wouldn't have set foot in a church in the first place.

I would finish work early in those days. I worked as a summer associate for a small law firm called Cooper, Brown & Behrle, located on the corner of 57th Street and Madison Avenue, near Central Park. There were only four lawyers at the firm, and only one was under fifty. The good part? I was usually out the door by five o'clock.

Once outside, I often found myself strolling through Central Park. Ever since I was young, I would always go to a park when there was something I needed to think about.

But lately, I wasn't sure what it was I needed to think about. I recognized that I wasn't the same person who I had been a few years ago. I thought of how I felt when I had graduated from college—full of passion for creating social change, confident in my political and moral convictions, enthused about building a deeper understanding of my faith. All that remained now was a vague, hazy memory of feelings that had probably been illusory at the time. That, and the feeling that I missed the person I had been.

Sometimes, when I got home from work, I would read fatwas online. I used to actively avoid Islamic rulings that I feared I wasn't prepared for. But lately it seemed there was no point in fleeing from the inevitable.

One day I was reading through a Web site called Islam Q & A, which had an impressive array of fatwas on various subjects. The Web site's readers would write in with topical questions, and a team of Islamic legal scholars would answer them. One question caught my eye: "Is it permissible to allow a Christian wife to practise her religion in the home?" I immediately thought of Amy, whom I would marry the following summer when she graduated from Wake Forest.

The questioner stated that he knew that Allah permits us to marry Christians and Jews. But, he wondered, "Can she practice her religious rites in the same house and have pictures of the crucifiction* of Jesus (A)** and celebrate Thanksgiving, Christmas and etc. Can her kids join her? If no, would not it hurt her feelings? Please, answer me on this issue."

I felt numb as I read the sheikh's response:

Praise be to Allaah.

It is not permissible for a Muslim to allow his wife from among the People of the Book to celebrate her festivals in his home, for the man

---

*"Crucifiction" is obviously a typographical error, but a somewhat telling one. For example, the Muslim polemicist Ahmed Deedat wrote a pamphlet entitled *Crucifixion or Cruci-fiction* that argues (in accord with standard Islamic teachings) that Jesus was never crucified.

**"(A)" is short for *alayhi salaatu was salaam,* or "upon him be prayers and peace."

is in charge of that woman and she does not have the right to openly celebrate her festivals in his home, because of the resulting effects of corruption, forbidden things and display of the symbols of kufr [disbelief] in his home. He should keep his children from taking part in those innovated festivals, because the children belong to the father and he should keep them away from these forbidden celebrations. At the same time he should direct them towards what will benefit them, even if that affects his relationship with his wife. The aims of sharee'ah and protecting one's religion—which is one of the most important aims of sharee'ah—take priority over everything else.

Imaam Ahmad ibn Hanbal was asked about a man who had a Christian wife—could he let her go out to join in the Christian festivals or to go to the church? He said, no.

In *al-Mughni* (1/21), Ibn Qudaamah says: "(Treatment of women): If his wife is a dhimmiyyah [a Jew or Christian living under Islamic rule], he can prevent her from going to the church, because that is not an act of obedience to Allaah."

If these scholars said that the husband should stop a Christian wife from going to church, then what do you think is the case with regard to her celebrating these innovated festivals in the house of her Muslim husband? Especially when we know the harm that results from these festivals, which is far worse than her merely going to the church. And Allaah knows best.

I thought about how much Christmas meant to Amy. I thought back to 1998, when I spent Thanksgiving with Amy's family in her hometown of Elizabeth City, North Carolina. When Thanksgiving ended, they began to prepare for Christmas. Their enthusiasm was infectious. I watched as Amy and her sisters decorated the tree, putting up ornaments and sprinkling it with tinsel. They put old Christmas records on the phonograph that they had listened to from the time they were kids.

Growing up, I had never celebrated Christmas. Seeing Amy and her sisters preparing for the holiday, my instinctive response was to seriously engage the idea of Christmas from a Muslim perspective. I paid close attention to the lyrics of one of the songs about Santa Claus:

He sees you when you're sleeping
He knows when you're awake
He knows if you've been bad or good
So be good for goodness sake

My first impression was that Santa Claus sounded an awful lot like God: keeping track of your good deeds and bad, constantly aware of whether you're sleeping or not. But almost immediately, I realized that I was taking myself too seriously. They didn't believe in Santa Claus. They didn't think he was actually watching them when they were sleeping and awake and keeping a balance sheet about their deeds. Santa was one of the myths of Christmas, one that everyone recognized as a myth. Eventually, Amy persuaded me to put on a Santa hat.

I thought of the photograph that one of Amy's sisters later took of Amy and me, sitting on the couch in her parents' living room with these hats on. We looked so happy together. I had managed to put aside my instinctive and overblown objections to Christmas, and was—like the rest of Amy's family—enjoying the spirit of the season.

But my thoughts quickly turned from my memories of Christmas to the fatwa I had just read. Was I really to prohibit Amy from celebrating Christmas in our home? This was the kind of idea I once would have laughed at. But now I resisted that impulse. Instead of laughing, I repeated one of my mantras: *It isn't about what you want. It is what Allah wants.*

So there was no neat conclusion when I finished reading the fatwa, no elegant way to summarize its meaning. I just felt numb.

A few days later, I again found myself wandering through Central Park. High-rises towered over the glistening waters of the lake at the south end of the park. I walked down a stone path, past the large rock formations. There were ice cream vendors, Frisbee tossers, furiously pedaling bicyclists.

Something felt different this time, though. Before, I felt lost when walking through the park—feeling that I needed to think about something, but unable to pinpoint what it was. It was as though my time as an Islamic fundamentalist had dulled me, stripping me of the ability to think for myself.

But this time I started to work my way through a few basic, glaringly obvious principles.

When you became Muslim, you thought that the moderate interpretation was clearly right. You thought that extremists were either ignorant or manipulating the faith for their own gain. Your time at Al Haramain has made you question this. As your cherished vision of Islam collapses, you're left feeling depressed, helpless, confused.

I stopped and bought an ice cream sandwich. These thoughts were self-apparent. I already *knew* them. What I hadn't done before was systematically analyze my state: why was I unhappy?

At Al Haramain, you began to do things that you never would have before. You once ridiculed a legalistic approach to Islam, but you've now adopted it as your own. You once unreservedly condemned the "extremists"; now you say prayers for the mujahideen. *But you still have doubts, and you're not happy with where you are.*

I finished the ice cream sandwich and tossed the wrapper in a trash can. It was starting to grow dark, so I turned to leave the park and head back to the subway. There wasn't much more to think about anyway: the conclusion was obvious.

Allah has given you a summer job where you're off work around five o'clock every day. You need to take advantage of all the time you have. Your problem is that you don't know where you stand. Sheikhs and learned members of the community have been trying to spoon-feed you answers since the minute you arrived at Al Haramain. You need to find your own answers. Reread the Qur'an, study the ahadith, study the works of scholars whom you trust and respect. Discover where you stand.

I continued to read through the Islam Q & A Web site, and continued to come across interesting fatwas.

One questioner wanted to know if it was okay for a husband to marry a second wife without the consent of his first wife. The answer was that he didn't need the first wife's permission, since "no evidence appears either in the Qur'an nor *sunnah* requiring the permission of the first wife if her husband wishes to marry another wife, and therefore he is not required to ask her permission."

I also found a question about the punishment for apostasy in Islam. Although I already knew the answer, it may have come as a surprise to the questioner. His question took a deeply skeptical tone: "I am currently in a philosophy of religion class and my teacher is an atheist. He claims that under an Islamic state if a born Muslim converts to another religion he is killed. Please tell me if this is true."

The answer:

Praise be to Allaah.

The punishment for apostasy (*riddah*) is well-known in Islaamic Sharee'ah. The one who leaves Islaam will be asked to repent by the

Sharee'ah judge in an Islaamic country; if he does not repent and come back to the true religion, he will be killed as a kaafir and apostate, because of the command of the Prophet (peace and blessings of Allah be upon him): "Whoever changes his religion, kill him."

It is well-known in Sharee'ah that the punishments (*hudood*) are not carried out on minors, because they have not yet reached the age of responsibility; but in the case of those who have reached the age of responsibility, the punishment (*hadd*) applies, without a doubt.

The person who knows the truth and believes in it, then turns his back on it, does not deserve to live. The punishment for apostasy is prescribed for the protection of the religion and as a deterrent to anyone who is thinking of leaving Islaam. There is no doubt that such a serious crime must be met with an equally weighty punishment. If the *kufar* do not give people the freedom to cross a red light, how can we give freedom to people to leave Islaam and disbelieve in Allah when they want to?

That last line actually made me laugh. "If the *kufar* do not give people the freedom to cross a red light, how can we give freedom to people to leave Islaam?"

Islam Q & A wasn't an amalgamation of fringe rulings. Rather, these were the kind of fatwas that I had grown accustomed to during my time at Al Haramain. And I had learned that the theological basis for these rulings was far more sound than you might glean from throwaway lines comparing apostasy laws to traffic lights.

Fatwas like the two I had just read, with conclusions that my moral impulses rebelled against, once made me deeply uncomfortable. But increasingly, the effect these rulings had on me had changed. It used to be that I'd go numb and withdraw when I read them. Now, I felt emboldened. When I read that there was no need to get your first wife's permission before taking on a second wife, when I read about the killing of apostates, I felt that this knowledge helped me build my case. I didn't know what this case was for, or what it was against—but the feeling was there.

I thought about Prophet Muhammad frequently. Al-Husein had recently told me that whenever he heard of someone's approach to Islam, he would ask himself one question: "Would it embarrass the Prophet?" That is, would Muhammad see this interpretation as such a distortion that he would disavow it?

I wondered what Muhammad would think of me and my practice of Islam. And whenever I thought of Muhammad, the feeling of inevitability crept back. Where my views diverged from those of the Salafis, wouldn't my ideas embarrass the Prophet?

More and more, I found myself in church on Sundays. I would go alone each time, and would generally try a new church each week. I found something satisfying in church that I did not find in my daily life. I couldn't put my finger on what it was.

The churchgoing experience was no longer punctuated by guilt. I no longer wondered whether it was wrong to enter a church in the first place, whether I should avoid a worship service so heavily based on music, whether I was sinning by taking communion. I often thought about the summer of 1996, when I had visited Mike Hollister in Bellingham and he had asked me to become a Christian. At the time, the idea that I would convert to Mike's religion seemed far-fetched. Now I wondered how my life might be different had I done so. Would I be happier?

I was thinking about that decision on the way back from church one day as I wandered through Washington Square Park. I paused for a couple of minutes to join the crowd watching the break-dancers in the park's enormous fountain but mainly I just walked, lost in thought. *But you made your choice*, I told myself. *You chose Islam, not Christianity.*

That was the brick wall I always hit when thinking about Mike and Christianity. I had made my decision, and I knew the rules. Islam was not an easy-in, easy-out religion.

Suddenly, another glaringly obvious point came to me, one that I was surprised hadn't occurred before. It was as though I was just now awakening from a long intellectual slumber in which I had missed both the subtle and also the obvious. I realized that my goal was to please God, not to cower before Islam's apostasy strictures. And I realized that I wasn't sure that I *had* found the truth in Islam.

The biggest reason I converted to Islam in the first place was that it felt comfortable. I paused when I fully understood that. A man in blue jeans and a wife-beater shirt pushed past, almost running into me. Shifting my focus away from myself for a moment, I looked at the throngs of people in the park. Some of them watched the dancers and other street performers; some were here to sell drugs; others rushed through the park at a breakneck pace on a Sunday afternoon. The familiar feeling of inhabiting a different universe than other New Yorkers hit me. But this time, I didn't envy them. Instead, I was on the cusp of discovering something, and it felt exhilarating.

I took a seat on one of the benches. I noticed a big-haired African-American magician, one of my favorite showmen, performing nearby. I smiled ruefully upon seeing him. When I first encountered him a couple of months back, I was determined *not* to enjoy his act. Magic was *haram*. One of Muhammad's companions even had a punch line of sorts after beheading a magician: "Let him use his magic for his own benefit now." Just as attending church no longer made me feel guilty, I now watched his act free of moral questions.

As I watched, I turned back to my realization that I had converted to

Islam because it felt comfortable. I now believed that one's level of comfort shouldn't be a factor in *any* religious decision; the only consideration was God's will, not one's own. *But if my original decision to become Muslim was based on what felt comfortable, maybe it too was wrong.*

I couldn't believe that I hadn't understood this before. And this realization changed everything.

When I got back to my apartment that evening, the first thing I did was call Mike Hollister. It had been a while since we'd spoken. Certainly, he was surprised by what I asked when he picked up the phone.

"Is there a particular translation of the Bible that you like, Mike?"

"Um, well, there's a great New International Version student bible that Amy and I like to use."

"Could you send me a copy? I want to read the Bible."

I didn't really discuss my spiritual struggles with anyone else, not even Amy. But sometimes I'd drop a hint.

I got an e-mail from Amy in the middle of the summer with a link to an NPR story critical of the madrassas in Pakistan (the Islamic religious schools where many of the Taliban were educated). Along with the link, Amy commented, "Talk about stereotypes!"

She was suggesting that the story contained unfair stereotypes about Islam. At one point I would have agreed without even considering the matter, simply assuming that the piece was full of bias. But this time, I sent Amy a message that said that the radical teachings in Pakistan's madrassas were indeed a problem. My e-mail included a number of links to articles describing in greater depth these teachings and the radicalization that they produced.

It felt strange to send that e-mail. I was so used to defending Islam

against people's misconceptions, and accusing the Western media of distorting the faith. It was the first time I weighed in to defend an article
critical of some facet of my religion.

When I spoke with Amy on the phone later that day, I asked if my
e-mail had surprised her. She said that it did. I knew that there were
more surprises in store for her.

When I opened the cardboard box that arrived a few days after I spoke
with Mike, I found a religious "care package."

There was a beautiful leather-bound New International Version student edition of the Bible. There was a book by Josh McDowell, whose
exposition of the "liar, lunatic, or Lord" dilemma I remembered well.
There was a book defending the doctrine of predestination by the
acclaimed reformed theologian R. C. Sproul. Mike had also thrown in
C. S. Lewis's *Mere Christianity*.

The books that Mike had sent were soon joined in my dorm room by
stacks of religious volumes. If you were to walk into my room during this
time, I would seem mired in study for a very difficult exam—and that
impression wouldn't be far off the mark. Various books covered the floor,
the desk, the shelves.

I listened to audio debates between Christian and Muslim scholars,
read books of apologetics on both sides, followed debates between Muslims and Christians on the Internet, pored through the Bible and Qur'an
and filled both holy books with yellow tabs.

I still prayed five times a day, but my supplications to God after I finished
my prayers were now drastically different.

It used to be that in my supplications, I would ask for what I thought
God wanted me to ask for—like the mujahideen's victory. This notion

of what God wanted was filtered through my experiences at Al Hara-main. I was afraid to ask for anything too liberal, anything that might conflict with what the sheikhs and visiting scholars assured me was right.

I had now begun to supplicate God not for what the most conserva-tive interpretations of Islam asked for. Instead, I asked for what I knew I needed; and for the first time, my supplications began to reflect my grow-ing doubts.

I once thought I knew the truth; I now asked God to lead me to it.

In church the next Sunday, the sermon was about God's love.

For months, I was sure that I couldn't possibly be worthy of God's love. How could I be? Here I was racked with doubts, unable to trust myself to do the right thing or to follow basic rules.

The sermon had an angle that I didn't expect: that we really weren't worthy of God's love. "Nobody deserves salvation," the preacher said. "We are all tarred with sin; we are all dead in our own sinfulness. None of us is worthy of standing before God on the day of judgment."

Long pause. "But He loves us anyway. He loves us with a perfect, divine love. The only way we can be worthy of standing before God is through the sacrifice of the perfect embodiment of humankind, the sac-rifice of one without sin. That is why God gave us the ultimate sacrifice, the sacrifice of His only begotten son, the Lord Jesus Christ. It is the ulti-mate sacrifice, and the ultimate gift, a gift none of us deserves but one which we are privileged to be able to accept."

As had become my post-church tradition, I strolled through Wash-ington Square Park and thought about the sermon. This was the first time that I had considered that God might love me even though it was a love that I didn't deserve. The idea appealed to me deeply on an emo-tional level. But was it the truth?

It was a Friday night. Most of my friends were out drinking. I was in my dorm room, hunched over my desk, thinking about a death that may or may not have occurred two thousand years ago.

I found that Islam and Christianity had two very different accounts of what became of Jesus. Christianity holds that Jesus was crucified, died, was buried, and rose from the dead. Islam holds that Jesus was never crucified. In the Muslim account, his enemies were deceived into believing that Jesus had been crucified—but in reality, he wasn't.

I once thought of this as an area where the two faiths' different accounts made no practical difference. But as I learned more about Christianity, my mind changed. There may, in fact, be no two events more important to Christianity than the crucifixion and resurrection. It was Jesus' sacrifice that allowed the forgiveness of sins. And Jesus' resurrection—his ability to conquer hell and come back from the dead—shows that we too can return from death.

It was understanding the importance of these events to Christianity that made them my topic of study tonight. As I had so often done lately, I tried to tease out one principle at a time.

Before Jesus' disciples saw him rise from the dead, they were scattered, demoralized, and frightened. With his resurrection, their faith was reinvigorated. The disciples believed that they saw Jesus alive again, saw him resurrected. The disciples preached this and were persecuted for it. Some of them were put to death while swearing by the resurrection.

I wondered whether their account could be believed. I turned and opened the Qur'an that sat in another corner of my desk. Verse 4:157 addressed the crucifixion: "That they said (in boast), 'We killed Christ Jesus the son of Mary, the Messenger of Allah';—but they killed him not, nor crucified him, but so it was made to appear to them, and those who differ therein are full of doubts." Which one was right?

What principle could distinguish between the two accounts? I thought of the persecution that Jesus' disciples suffered because of their belief in the crucifixion and resurrection. *They didn't die for a set of ideals—it was for a set of facts. Do people die for a set of facts that they know to be false?*

I felt that I was onto something. Slowly, with each layer that I pulled back, I felt my ideas about God shifting.

It had been a summer of internal upheaval. But when I first told Amy about the religious changes I was experiencing, I did so casually.

She was down in North Carolina, and we were talking on the phone. I told Amy about the religious works I had been reading, like the Bible and C. S. Lewis's *Mere Christianity*. For the first time since I started work at Al Haramain, I sounded enthused about religion.

There was one key comment that actually mattered to me in this discussion. I slipped it in near the very end, as though it were the most natural thing in the world. "I guess I'll eventually have to get baptized, then," I said.

There was silence on the other end of the line through which I could feel Amy smiling. "I have to say that makes me happy," she said.

She sounded as though her happiness embarrassed her.

Late one night, with religious tomes spread out on my desk and strewn about my room, I found myself thinking of Abdul-Qaadir. I thought about the confidence with which he had told little Yusuf that his mother should be killed for leaving Islam. I absentmindedly picked up my hardcover copy of Muhammad bin Jamil Zino's *Islamic Guidelines for Individual and Social Reform*. I turned right to the *hadith* that had been bothering me: "Whoever apostatizes from Islam should be killed."

I exhaled deeply, wondering how seriously one should take these injunctions in the twenty-first century, in the United States of America.

I thought back to the night that I took my *shahadah*. I had woken up the next morning knowing that everything was different. I had woken up as a Muslim, and couldn't wait to find out what my new life had in store. What would the future hold if I became Christian?

twelve

A QUIET NORMAL LIFE

was sitting across the table from a gray-haired, bearded Urdu speaker, discussing religious matters. My lunch companion wasn't from Pakistan (where they speak Urdu); he was a white American from New Jersey.

Shortly after I converted to Christianity in late 2000, I reached out to some of the Christian groups that minister to Muslims. One day I got a phone call from a man named Dick Bailey. He had worked as a missionary in Pakistan for years. This was our first meeting, and it wouldn't be the last. I met him just as fall was turning to winter, with crisp winds and overcast skies.

We were going to have lunch together. Dick said he was fine with all kinds of food, but didn't like goat meat—a reference, no doubt, to the time he'd spent in Pakistan. We walked a few blocks to Johnny Rockets, the hamburger chain. An odd place for our first meal together.

Seated in the faux 1950s-style diner where the jukebox blasted 1980s pop tunes, I told Dick about how I was born into a Jewish family, and about my conversion to Islam and later to Christianity. It was a story that, at the time, was unfamiliar and difficult to tell. As I spoke, I felt how disjointed and elliptical I must have sounded. I told Dick about my friend al-Husein, and how I soon needed to tell al-Husein that I was no longer Muslim.

In an effort to boost my spirits, Dick told me of other people who had been Muslim and eventually came to Christ. After relaying one of the stories, Dick concluded by saying, "But he's had to pay a price for becoming Christian."

"What price?" I thought I knew the answer.

"Within Islam, the penalty for leaving the faith is death. There are a lot of Muslims who take that very seriously, even in the West."

"I'm worried about that," I confessed. "Here I am in law school, exams are coming up in about a month. I have a good job lined up for the summer, and I want to do well. I don't want to deal with someone threatening to kill me. I don't even want to have to think about something like that."

"We all pay a price for our belief in Christ," Dick said. "This isn't the same kind of persecution, but when I go back and see my old friends from high school, a lot of them think I'm weird for becoming a devout Christian. The point is that all of us sacrifice in some way."

I looked at Dick blankly. He was right: it wasn't the same, at all. People thought I was weird when I became Muslim. I could deal with people thinking I was weird. Living under the constant threat of being killed, that is a different story.

I told Dick that I didn't want to tell al-Husein that I had become Christian. I wasn't afraid of al-Husein; he wasn't a threat to me. Or so I hoped. It was just that so much was new and uncertain. It would be hard enough to tell al-Husein that I wasn't Muslim. I didn't want to tell him that I had become a Christian on top of that. Dick turned to me as we stepped out onto Eighth Avenue. "Promise me something," Dick said.

"What's that?"

"I'm not saying that you *need* to tell al-Husein that you've become a Christian. But I want you to promise me that if he asks, you won't lie to him. He might ask you, 'If you're not a Muslim, then what have you become? Are you an atheist? Have you gone back to being a *Jew*?'"

I nodded. "I won't lie to him." But I hoped that the question wouldn't arise.

I think you need someone to come out there, spend a weekend with you, pray with you, and help you reconnect with the faith."

This was al-Husein's reply when I told him that I had ceased to believe in Islam. I was hesitant, but I recognized that this is what a good friend does. If you're having a spiritual crisis, a good friend takes the time to see you and try to shepherd you through it. Nonetheless, he could tell that I was hesitant.

"Look, I'm going to come to New York this weekend anyway, to spend time with Liana's family," al-Husein said. "I don't have to stay with you. I'll just come out to see you while I'm there."

We met up on a Sunday, in the early afternoon. We walked into the West Village together. Last time we had walked through the West Village was when al-Husein had come to help me move into my dorm room. Then we had both been disdainful of the decadence, the materialism, the disbelief that was so prevalent.

We went to an Indian restaurant where I was a regular. Al-Husein handled the entire interaction impressively. As we strolled through the West Village, he didn't mention Islam. He didn't mention Allah. He asked about law school, and seemed genuinely interested in the classes I was taking, in the plans I had for the summer, in what I wanted to do when I graduated. It was this kind of proficiency with people that had so impressed me about al-Husein when we first got to know each other.

After I spent a while telling him about law school, about my plans for the summer and my plans after graduation, I asked al-Husein about his life. He filled me in on how things were going at the Harvard Islamic Society, and told me about how he had continued to grow in his faith. Then al-Husein gently asked, "How is your study of Islam going?"

He didn't demand that I explain myself or my spiritual crisis. He wasn't interrogating me. His transition felt like nothing more than an innocuous question.

I nodded and smiled, aware that the conversation was about to become more serious. "As you know from our previous conversations," I said, "I feel that the foundation for my belief in Islam has crumbled. I feel that I came to the faith for the wrong reasons. When I became a Muslim I was assured that the progressive vision for the faith was the true one, a version of Islam that upheld women's rights, human rights, religious freedom, social justice. A version of Islam that was perfectly at peace with all other religions. But as I learn more about Islam, I realize that much of what I was at first told about it wasn't accurate."

"Are you angry?" al-Husein asked. "Do you feel that people misled you?"

He wanted to know if I was angry at *him*, if I felt that *he* had misled me into believing in a version of Islam that wasn't real.

"No," I said. "I'm not angry at anybody. I think everybody who helped me along my path to Islam was genuine in what they believed. I don't think anybody lied to me or purposefully misled me. But that doesn't change the fact that I feel like my foundation for belief has been cut from under me."

Al-Husein nodded thoughtfully. "I know that you had a bad experience with the people you worked for out in Oregon. But you can't let what a few people did sour you to the whole religion."

"I'm not. This is deeper than that." I didn't tell al-Husein that, when he had decided to become more serious about Islam, his own views were often indistinguishable from those of my coworkers at Al Haramain.

Nor did I tell al-Husein that what ultimately led me away from Islam wasn't dissatisfaction with any of the social teachings: it was the fact that I was persuaded by the case for another faith.

"Let me give you some advice," al-Husein said. "This is a very important issue. There are few issues more important than what you're struggling with now. It isn't important because of your friendship with me. And I'm not just saying that it's important because I'm a Muslim. This is about your relationship with God. What happens to you in the next life could hinge on what you decide now."

I nodded. Everything that he said was correct.

"Here's my advice," al-Husein said. "You need to ask yourself two questions. First, you need to ask yourself whether you *believe* in God."

I smiled. "That answer is easy."

"Then if you decide that you believe in God, the next question you have to answer is why Islam is the right religion."

I don't think the surprise showed on my face. Al-Husein was perfectly right up until this second question. He was correct that the first thing anybody needs to ask is whether he believes in God. But the second question couldn't be more wrong. I had once been so focused on Islam that I was unable to even conceive of following another faith, so I understood where al-Husein was coming from. But the second question to ask is not why Islam is right. If you think God exists, the next step is to *compare* various faiths.

I didn't say this, though. My concern was not to score any debating points. My concern was al-Husein himself. I grew up without siblings, but while I was in college I had come to regard al-Husein as my brother. That may have changed after I left Islam, but I still cared for him. At the very least, he was still my half-brother.

"Your ultimate duty is to God," al-Husein said. "The question isn't what I want; the question isn't one of *my* pleasure. The question is what is pleasing to God."

"I agree with that," I said. "I remember at Al Haramain we used to call it *fi sabil Allah*, that which is for the pleasure of Allah."

Al-Husein nodded. "That is a vital concept. Your intentions matter. As you struggle with your spiritual questions, you need to make sure that you're seeking God's desires and not following your own."

After the meal, al-Husein asked if there was a place around here where he could make *salat*. I told him that he could pray in Vanderbilt Hall, the building where the bulk of the law school's classes were held. The dining area where snacks were served during the day was empty at night; I had made *salat* there during my first week at NYU. I suggested that al-Husein go there to pray.

I walked al-Husein to the bathroom, where he would purify himself before prayer with *wudu*, the Islamic ablutions. "Why don't you come and pray with me?" al-Husein asked.

The offer was made with genuine warmth, and it was the right thing to ask. But I had the right counter. "It wouldn't be *fi sabil Allah*," I said. We had already discussed the importance of intentions. If I were to pray with al-Husein, my intentions wouldn't have been pure. I wouldn't have been trying to please God. The prayers would have been for al-Husein's pleasure.

We parted with a long hug. I told al-Husein that I would be there for him if he needed anything. If I could do anything for him as a friend, as a lawyer, whatever. Al-Husein had treated me in the way that a brother would. I realized that I should have told him about my new beliefs. But I couldn't bring myself to do so, not yet. And he wasn't the only one who I couldn't yet bring myself to tell.

It wasn't until Amy's last semester of college that she finally settled on law school. She had given some serious thought to going into education, but decided against it after a semester as a student teacher in a Winston-Salem high school convinced her that she had not the gift.

She thought about getting a policy degree and thought about Peace Corps, something that wouldn't fit too well with married life. Even if law school was a last-minute choice for Amy (as it is for many people), she unsurprisingly aced her LSATs and got into most of the top schools to which she applied. When she finally decided to join me at NYU in the fall of 2001, I was overjoyed.

I was at lunch with Sadik Huseny, the lapsed-Muslim classmate who took civil procedure with me during our first year. The first-year experience is intense in law school. You take all your academic courses with the same group of about a hundred other students. It makes for *very* large classes, but you nonetheless end up getting to know the other hundred students quite well. Sadik and I had formed a study group together in our first year, and he became a close friend. But we had seen far less of each other in our second year of law school. He seemed a little uncomfortable around me, like there was something he wanted to discuss.

I let him direct the conversation. There was some small talk about classes and our plans for the summer, but Sadik finally got to what must have been the purpose of the lunch. "So you're Christian now?" he asked.

I nodded. "Yes, I am."

"Why is that?" he asked. "I first get to know you and you're a devout Muslim, you're praying five times a day, then suddenly you're Christian. If you were dissatisfied with Islam, why didn't you just stop believing in anything? Why did you latch on to Christianity so quickly?"

"Because I believe in God," I said. I wasn't sure Sadik would understand this; I knew that many people would not. "I believe in God, and

Islam was part of my search to understand who God really is. I didn't just leave Islam and become Christian because I was unhappy with Islam, Sadik. I left Islam and became Christian because I became convinced that my earlier ideas about God were wrong. I became convinced that I could find the truth in another faith."

Sadik shrugged. "I hear what you're saying, but I'm not sure it makes sense."

"Some people believe in God, and others don't," I said. "If you can see this through my eyes, you'd understand that the truly surprising move would have been if I simply ceased to believe."

Sadik nodded, but I'm not sure he would ever come to understand this second conversion.

I had come to believe in the resurrection, but I wasn't yet fully resurrected.

I still felt uncomfortable telling the story of my religious conversions—not only for personal safety reasons, but also because my story was so unusual that I doubted many other people could understand it. People were more likely, I thought, to see me as crazy, or as someone who couldn't make up his mind and was bouncing erratically from religion to religion.

Nor was I finished with the rules that had been drilled into me at Al Haramain. They would crop up at strange times. When Amy and I were shopping for our wedding bands, for example, I remembered the *hadith* where Muhammad had said that it was forbidden for men to wear gold. While Amy got a yellow gold wedding band, I selected one that was white gold—one that didn't *look* like it was made of gold. The only thing that I had in mind when selecting this wedding band was that *hadith*, even though I was no longer Muslim.

So Al Haramain's legacy lived on even after I had left Islam.

Pete was next, after al-Husein. The last time I'd had substantial interaction with Pete was the previous spring, when he wanted me to meet Soliman al-But'he at the airport and I had refused.

Pete had called me just a few days earlier. He would greet me with the traditional Islamic greeting when he called: "*Assalaamu 'alaykum.*" Desiring to live without deception, I wouldn't offer the Islamic reply. Instead, I'd say something like, "Hi, Pete, how are you?"

Pete immediately noticed my failure to respond to his Islamic greeting in kind. But during his first phone call, before Amy came to New York, Pete told me what he wanted without remarking on the fact that I didn't reply to his Islamic greeting.

"Look, bro," Pete said. "I know that the Jewish state has elected this Ariel Sharon as its leader. This makes me sick to my stomach. This guy shouldn't lead a nation-state. He's a war criminal and should be thrown in prison for what he did to the Palestinians at the Sabra and Shatila refugee camps. What I want you to do is to talk to some of your crazy professors there at NYU to see if they have an idea for how we can take this guy to court."

I told Pete I would look into it. I knew that I had to tell him that I had left Islam. I figured that the next time we spoke should be the time. As luck would have it, Amy was in town for the second significant conversation that I'd have with Pete in the course of a year. I told her that a phone call with Pete was coming, that I needed to tell him I had left Islam. She could see that I was nervous. "You shouldn't worry about this," Amy assured me. "The worst he can do is yell at you and tell you that you're going to hell."

There was so much more he could do, though. But I hadn't told Amy about the traditional punishment for leaving Islam. I didn't really speak with anyone about it. I didn't want to worry her, nor did I want people to know that I could, at some point, face death threats for my new faith. I viewed it as a sign of weakness. All I wanted was a normal life.

I locked myself in my room for almost an hour and got on the phone with Pete. He could see on the caller ID that I was on the line, and he answered in typical fashion, "*Assalaamu 'alaykum,* my dear brother Daveed! How are you?"

"I'm doing well, Pete. Thanks."

I again hadn't responded to his Islamic greeting. So now he had to ask. "Bro, are you even practicing Islam at all?"

"I'm really having my doubts, Pete. Grave doubts. I don't think I'd call myself Muslim at this point."

Pete, like al-Husein, responded with a soft touch. I should have known that he would. His first wife had left Islam and returned to Christianity: he'd been forced to deal with this kind of thing before.

Pete made me promise that I'd continue to seek out God. "Bro, you might live for a hundred more years. But what you gotta understand is that this life, long as it is, is nothing compared to the next one. We're living for the next life, bro, and we're living to please God."

"I agree with all of that, Pete."

Pete went into a long-winded story about how he had recently bought a new house, and he took out a loan to do so, a loan that would charge him interest. Paying interest, as I knew, was *haram.* But here he had a beautiful house, and he began to wonder what the harm was. Wasn't it easier to just take out a loan? Then Pete found that there was a termite infestation that he hadn't caught on first inspection. He would have to get new floors put in. That, to Pete, was God's way of showing him the consequence of taking out an interest-bearing loan.

The application to what he was telling me was obvious. I might be living a life that I think is good, but if I'm defying God, I will eventually pay for it.

Pete ended by saying, "Bro, I want you to know that it's okay with me if you experiment. If you end up belonging to some crazy religion or something else, I won't be mad at you. What matters to me is that you continue to seek the truth."

I was impressed with the way Pete handled that call. For the next couple of years, whenever I returned to Ashland, I'd always think about meeting up with Pete for coffee, to see him in person again. I didn't ever manage to see him, though, and within a few years it would be impossible to do so.

Amy and I were married on Sunday, June 3, 2001.

The festivities were a weekend-long affair, kicking off with desserts at her parents' house in Elizabeth City, North Carolina, on Friday. For the first time in years, I was surrounded entirely by friends and by those who wished the best for my future with Amy. I hadn't seen my parents since wrapping up work at Al Haramain; the expense and travel time between New York and Ashland were prohibitive.

I had four groomsmen, including Mike Hollister—people who had known me before, during, and after my time as a Muslim. Al-Husein and Liana did not come to the wedding. Although they were invited, it was a tepid invitation; I didn't know if I wanted al-Husein there. Nor did I know whether I would have made him a groomsman if he was able to come. The changes that we had both been through had created a distance between us.

Other friends and family members had made the trip to North Carolina from Florida, New York, Washington, D.C., Virginia, and beyond. My parents would later describe the weekend as "heaven on earth." They weren't too far off the mark.

Some friends of Amy's family, who had a beautiful riverside home, offered up their property for a Saturday bash. I went out in a kayak with Jacob Bornstein, my best friend from high school and one of my groomsmen.

As with most of my other friends, he was aware of my movement toward and eventually away from Islam, and he was interested in hearing about what the journey had meant to me. I was unable to cleanly summarize it. There were so many things that I had been through and believed while at Al Haramain that I didn't want to acknowledge, let alone discuss. And there were issues I was still struggling with, like what the punishment for apostasy in Islam meant for my life.

The wedding location had been set while I was still a Muslim, and, at the time, I didn't want to have it in a church. We were married at the Albemarle Plantation, a country club in Hertford, North Carolina, bordered by the Albermarle Sound and Yeopim River. The skies were clear, and everything seemed to glow: the grass, the guests, and the waters behind us.

The minister asked Amy and me to look into each other's eyes as we said our vows. As I looked at Amy, I realized how much she had sacrificed for me. She had seen me descend into fundamentalist Islam and emerge on the other side as a Christian. She had politely resisted my demands to have a *nikah* ceremony before the wedding. I thought of how unpleasant I had been—to Amy, to my parents, to my friends—during my time in radical Islam. It was testament to the strength of Amy's love for me, the strength of my parents' love, the strength of my friendships, that they had been able to endure.

As I looked into Amy's eyes, I knew that I couldn't possibly deserve her love. The best I could do was accept it, and try to love her with the same kind of understanding, forgiveness, and passion.

On the morning of September 11, 2001, I was working on my computer in my sixth floor apartment in Mercer Hall, a law school dorm just a block off Broadway in the West Village.

When I first heard the screams that morning, I thought there might have been a celebrity sighting. That's what it sounded like from outside the window—like a rock band had shown up, and their fans couldn't contain themselves. It was only when I looked out the window that I realized something was terribly wrong. I saw NYU students outside, in the brick walkway leading toward Mercer, some of them in the street. They didn't look happy or excited. They looked scared, anguished. I noticed that the crowd was staring south down the street, toward the World Trade Center.

I turned on CNN and found that the south tower had already collapsed. The north tower was still standing, with an ominous column of smoke rising from it.

Amy was upstairs in the computer lab. I rushed up to get her. Another student was there also, but I ignored him. "Have you looked at the news?" I blurted out.

"No." We'd been up late the night before, and she was still trying to wake up.

"There's been a terrorist attack on the World Trade Center. One of the towers has collapsed. The other's on fire."

"What?"

"Let's go outside."

We rushed out to the street where the students had gathered. There was a red SUV parked nearby with the tailgate open. The speakers were pointed toward the rear of the car, and they were blaring the news. In the confusion, there were a lot of false reports: bombs outside the Supreme Court, a dozen hijacked airplanes.

I looked around at the other NYU students, some of them close friends. They looked scared and confused. I saw one guy, blond with pale skin, leaning on a cast-iron fence, his head buried in his arm, bawling. They didn't see this coming, and they had no idea why it had happened.

I felt that I had a better idea. This, after all, was essentially what I had been praying for during all the time that the mujahideen had been in my *du'a*.

I thought of the end of my first semester of law school, when I had gone out with the other students in my section. I envied my classmates then for the fact that they didn't have to think about the issues that radical Islam had thrust upon me. But now, on September 11, as the north tower smoldered and eventually crumbled, I realized that my old world had been vividly brought to them.

I called Pete shortly after 9/11. It was one of the typical calls that many Americans made to their Muslim friends after the attacks. I wanted to make sure he was okay, and that people on the streets weren't openly calling for his blood. (As though such vigilante justice could ever find a home in Ashland.)

He sounded shaken up when we talked. "I haven't been able to do anything for days," he said. "I can barely eat. You know me, terrorism makes me real upset."

I had never known that about him, but he did sound upset now. I had no reason to doubt his sincerity.

The 9/11 attacks provided the ammunition for another of Pete's Rube Goldberg schemes. Although Pete would undertake it a few days after I spoke with him by phone, I wouldn't learn about this one for a couple of years.

Pete sent a letter to the White House, the State Department, and prominent members of Congress arguing that "[t]his unusual time calls for unusual answers and unusual actions to cope with these heinous crimes." He wrote that the key question was who carried out the 9/11 attacks—and to that extent, Osama bin Laden's knowledge of the inner workings of terror was invaluable, and it would be a tragic loss to kill him without getting information from him.

So Pete argued in his letter that bin Laden should be interviewed by a four-person team. One of the people on the team should be an American-born FBI agent who is a Sunni Muslim of Afghan descent. Two of the team members should be American-born Christian FBI agents who know the Bible well enough to quote from it. And the final member of the team would be "a U.S. citizen, not an FBI agent, a Muslim male who understands the Afghani, Pakistani, and Saudi cultures and traditions, the intricacies of Muslim sects and laws, and knows the language." That fourth person, who would serve as the team's leader, would be . . . Pete Seda himself.

The team would go into Afghanistan to interview bin Laden. "If bin Laden did not do it," Pete wrote, "then he should be willing to have these discussions. Under Islamic law, he has to help his Muslim brothers and sisters by helping expose the enemies of Islam. And whoever did this is an enemy of Islam. If it is brought up to him that Muslims are suffering globally because of this . . . he will have to respond."

Another grandiose plan. Pete never changed. As usual, nothing ever came of it.

I shuddered when I heard that the law school would hold a town hall forum for students that Friday to discuss the attacks. I already knew what NYU's outspoken leftists would say. But I couldn't keep myself away from the forum.

It seemed that everybody felt the need to express their feelings about 9/11. Middle Eastern and South Asian students understandably wanted to know if they would be harassed or profiled, and how their lives would change. NYU's hard left feared an upsurge in patriotic sentiment and nationalism, and needed to express their concerns about people taking a simplistic black-and-white approach to the attacks rather than "thinking critically" ("critical thinking" was code for realizing that the United States bore the ultimate responsibility for the 9/11 attacks).

I had worked for a Wahhabi charity that stood in solidarity with the enemy ideologically. I myself had become radicalized. Yet while I knew that NYU aspired to be a "safe place" for dialogue, this aspiration was one-sided. It was a "safe place" for those who thought the United States had brought 9/11 upon itself, and not for those who disagreed.

I knew this prior to NYU's town hall meeting, but went anyway. Some NYU professors spoke, saying nothing interesting or insightful, before the floor was opened to students. The student speeches were exactly what I had anticipated. Somebody talked about how this was because of U.S. support for Israel over the Palestinians. One woman gave a long-winded and incoherent speech. Flights were just now getting off the ground again, and she began by saying, "It's important to take a critical view of why this happened. I want you to take a look around and see what's going on in this country today. There are people of Middle Eastern descent who are, right now, being profiled in airports across the country." The awkwardly named World Conference Against Racism, Racial Discrimination, Xenophobia, and Related Intolerance, held in Durban, South Africa, had reached its conclusion just before the 9/11 attacks. After Arab states hijacked the conference by turning it into another occasion to attack Israel, the United States walked out. The speaker referred to this also, trying to show how all these factors fit together, amounting to U.S. culpability in 9/11.

Eventually I stood up. When the moderator handed me the microphone, I said, "Let me just say that I love this country. And one of the things that I love most about this country is its freedom of expression." It was an attention-grabbing opening—one that would also be appropriate

for any of the America-bashing speeches of the day. It would be typical
for the other students to talk about how they love the country's freedom
of expression before making use of that freedom of expression to excori-
ate America.

"Today I've heard other students exercise their freedom of expression
by talking about how the U.S. brought the attacks upon itself. I understand that there are a lot of things that NYU students don't like about
the U.S. or its foreign policy, but I want to remind people of the bigger
picture. I've noticed a tendency to assume that the terrorists, in attacking us, are attacking all the things that the average NYU student hates.
But the attacks are also aimed at those aspects of the U.S. that most
people here love. The attacks aren't just over our foreign policy. They're
also about the fact that we don't execute homosexuals; that we don't
make women wear burkas and treat them as second-class citizens; the
fact that we have the freedom to question or reject religion, and to practice it as we see fit. You can skewer the U.S. all you want. But I fear that
in doing so, a lot of the students here misunderstand the larger context."

After the town hall meeting ended, a few people came up to me and
thanked me for my speech. I was somewhat surprised when I passed by
Stephen Schulhofer, a very left-of-center professor with whom I had
taken a criminal procedure class the semester before. He nodded and
said, "I appreciated what you said."

The response to that speech was atypically positive. I received a
much different reaction a few days later in my federal courts class.

My federal courts professor, Barry Friedman, wasn't sure how he
should respond to 9/11. We had a class e-mail distribution list where he
sent out a message shortly after the attacks talking about how anxious
he was to get back to class. This was understandable. In the face of a
tragedy like 9/11, it's natural to want to get back to one's routine. But
the 9/11 attacks fundamentally changed our lives, presenting us with a

set of problems and moral dilemmas that none of us had anticipated. It was natural to want to get back to our normal routines and schedules, but I thought we would have been better served by time to regroup and assess how our lives had been altered, against our will.

While Professor Friedman wanted to return to our routine, he also wanted to be sensitive to students by asking if anybody had anything that they wanted to say to the class. I listened to a few student speeches. They were coded, speaking of the need to view the attacks through a "critical lens," referring cryptically to U.S. misdeeds abroad.

I had been following the discussions about 9/11 on various NYU leftist e-mail lists, such as that of the National Lawyers Guild. A great deal of weight was given to the "quick reaction" that MIT professor Noam Chomsky penned the day after the attacks. He began by conceding that the 9/11 attacks were "major atrocities," albeit atrocities that "do not reach the level of many others, for example, Clinton's bombing of the Sudan with no credible pretext, destroying half its pharmaceutical supplies and probably killing tens of thousands of people." Chomsky then opined that the proper response to 9/11 was to try to enter the minds of the perpetrators:

> As to how to react, we have a choice. We can express justified horror; we can seek to understand what may have led to the crimes, which means making an effort to enter the minds of the likely perpetrators. If we choose the latter course, we can do no better, I think, than to listen to the words of Robert Fisk, whose direct knowledge and insight into affairs of the region is unmatched after many years of distinguished reporting. Describing "The wickedness and awesome cruelty of a crushed and humiliated people," he writes that "this is not the war of democracy versus terror that the world will be asked to believe in the coming days. It is also about American missiles smashing into Palestinian homes and U.S. helicopters fir-

ing missiles into a Lebanese ambulance in 1996 and American shells crashing into a village called Qana and about a Lebanese militia—paid and uniformed by America's Israeli ally—hacking and raping and murdering their way through refugee camps." And much more.

I was interested, at the time, in the irony of statements like Chomsky's. On the one hand, he urged Americans to "enter the minds of the likely perpetrators." This is sound advice: it's advisable in any conflict to know what your enemy stands for. But on the other hand, Chomsky made no real effort to enter the minds of the perpetrators. Instead, he simply projected his own grievances against the United States onto them.

I was hesitant, but decided to address the class. Knowing what was being said in various NYU circles and knowing full well that the student comments had amounted to calls for Western self-flagellation and admissions of guilt, I wanted to offer a different perspective. I walked up in front of the class and turned toward the other students so I could see them when I spoke. I heard someone laugh. Getting out of my seat and walking in front of the class probably seemed presumptuous (none of the other speakers had done so), but wasn't meant to be.

Trying to explain why I had chosen to address the class, I began by saying that I had once been Muslim. It wasn't a good way to begin. I provided no context, no background. I didn't mention Al Haramain, nor did I mention that I had once believed in the global jihad. All my classmates and professor saw was this Jewish-looking kid getting up, claiming to have been Muslim once, and lecturing to them about the current world crisis.

I said basically the same thing that I had said at NYU's town hall meeting. I said that I was disturbed by some of the anti-American views I saw expressed around campus, on e-mail discussion lists, and otherwise. I said that there was much that is good about the United States, and part of taking a critical view of the current conflict is to understand what the enemy stands for, not just to project our own problems with the United States onto them. While my speech to the class was similar to the remarks that I made at the town hall forum, it was more disjointed at a time when the audience was more hostile.

When I finished speaking, some of the other students glared at me. I knew that I had upset some of them. A few days later, I ran into a woman of South Asian descent on the street outside Vanderbilt Hall. We had been acquaintances since my first year of law school, when we were in the same class section. When I greeted her, she told me she didn't want to talk to me. "I was upset by some of the things you said in class about un-Americanism," she said.

She meant anti-Americanism, but I wasn't surprised that she remembered my remarks as more McCarthyite than they had been. Her refusal to speak to me burned more than she realized, and burned more than it should have. It burned because I had once been so intimately involved in left-of-center politics. Some of the tendencies I now saw from NYU students had been my own tendencies when I was a campus activist. Since the far-left bases so many of its positions on principle rather than practical outcome, it generally views most issues as black-and-white moral choices, and perceives those on the other side as possessed by some moral defect. Here, those who favored a military response to the 9/11 attacks were seen as flag-waving jingoists—the kind of people who would appeal to concepts like "patriotism" while undertaking a bloodthirsty push for war and revenge. I was placed in this category for the rest of my time at NYU.

Another part of what burned was realizing that the school's aspiration of providing a "safe place" for dialogue about the attacks was false. This "safe place" amounted to embracing a stock narrative of 9/11: on the one hand, you have the vast majority of Americans calling for blood and revenge. On the other, you have some thoughtful liberals who want to look deeper at the root causes of the attacks, and who may be reviled for doing so. NYU's goal was to make students feel comfortable expressing the liberal position. My background did not fit this stock preconception: the conversion to Islam, the radicalization and the long slow climb out, the potential problem of apostasy. I knew that NYU was not, for me, a safe place to talk about this.

I never came to terms with my time at the Al Haramain Islamic Foundation while at NYU. As I moved further into the legal profession, I preferred simply to pretend that it had never happened. But in my first job out of law school, I found it impossible to do so.

In August 2002, I began working as a law clerk for Harry T. Edwards, a judge on the D.C. Circuit Court of Appeals, a federal appellate court in Washington, D.C. My second day there, the secretary handed me a form, and told me that we'd have to apply for a security clearance. She mentioned that some terrorism cases might come through the D.C. Circuit, so all the clerks had to apply for clearance.

I nodded and took the form. All I could think about when she handed it to me was Al Haramain. Just a few weeks earlier I found out that Al Haramain was named as a defendant in a civil lawsuit filed by the families of 9/11 victims. The plaintiffs claimed that Al Haramain was connected to the 9/11 attacks and should be held civilly liable. When I heard that news, it worried me, but I assured myself that the plaintiffs were casting an overly wide net. I wanted to believe that the fact I had worked for Al Haramain wouldn't have much of an impact on my life.

The security clearance form made me revisit those hopes. What would they do with the fact that I had been at Al Haramain? Would I be deemed a threat? Would they deny my security clearance?

I thought about not filling out the form, explaining that I didn't want to go through the hassle of applying for a clearance and didn't want to be involved in the D.C. Circuit's terrorism cases. But I handed it in, nonetheless, wondering what would happen.

A few days later, one of the court's administrative personnel told me that my clearance form had been red-flagged. I tried to appear surprised. "Any idea why?"

"Do you have anything to do with the Middle East on your application? Like Israel, for example?"

"Yeah, there's something related to the Middle East on there." I didn't elaborate.

"Well, that may have been it. They're really focused on the Middle East and tend to be concerned when someone has connections there."

What I didn't know at the time was that a federal investigation of the U.S. branch of Al Haramain was already underway. When I had filled out my routine background check form before beginning the clerkship, I had listed Al Haramain as an employer. The background form was then referred to the FBI team that was heading up the investigation. That team orchestrated the security clearance check. There was no need for all the clerks to apply for clearances; it was an elaborate ruse to allow them to talk to me. The FBI wanted to get my consent to investigate me, so they could determine whether my real purpose in clerking on the D.C. Circuit was to kill a judge or otherwise help the terrorists.

There was an initial, routine FBI interview related to my clearance application. A heavyset retired agent conducted the interview. He obviously hadn't read the form before coming to the courthouse for the interview. He flipped through it, seemingly asking me questions at random.

He didn't ask about Al Haramain, but at the end of the interview, he did ask if there was anything we hadn't discussed that might interfere with my ability to hold a security clearance.

I wasn't sure what to say. *I worked for a radical Islamic charity for almost a year but it isn't a problem now?*

I shrugged mildly. "No," I said. "My life is pretty aboveboard."

In January of 2003, I got a phone call from the FBI. A woman clerk said that they wanted to conduct a follow-up interview related to my security clearance application. The interview, she said, would take place at the Washington Field Office, which was just up the street from the E. Barrett Prettyman Courthouse where I was clerking. She said that the interview would focus exclusively on my time at Al Haramain, which was no surprise.

A few days later, when I was leaving the courthouse to head to the field office on Fourth Street, I ran into some of the other clerks.

"Where are you off to, Daveed?" one asked.

When I said that I had an FBI interview, he assumed it was a job interview. Nodding at my tan trench coat, he said, "Well, you look the part!"

I didn't correct him. I didn't tell him that I had actually been singled out for additional screening because of my time working for a radical Muslim charity.

When I got to the Washington Field Office, I had to wait in the lobby. I looked at the photographic displays of agents who had been killed in the line of duty. I was struck by a feeling of how honorable it must be to work for the FBI, particularly at a time like this. Then my thoughts turned to my time at Al Haramain. It had already jeopardized my security clearance. Even though I had tried to keep my past life separate from my current life as a young lawyer, after 9/11 I began to wish that I could contribute something to the war on terror. But I was resigned to the fact that my time at Al Haramain would probably be an insurmountable barrier to doing so.

Two agents interviewed me. One of them, Christopher Rogers, had obviously been with the Bureau for much longer than the other. He took the lead. I saw that Christopher was reading from a list of questions that someone else had typed for him. I would later learn that the questions had been written by Special Agent David Carroll, who worked out of Medford, Oregon. I would meet Dave Carroll in person a little over a year later.

Most people feel nervous when they have to sit in a room with FBI agents for questioning. This feeling is probably magnified when their past associations include the likes of Al Haramain. I was somewhat nervous when I was walking toward the Washington Field Office, but had formulated a simple plan: whatever they asked, I'd be completely honest. I hadn't done anything illegal, and didn't have anything to be afraid of.

I found the interview unexpectedly liberating. I had never really explained my story—my time working for Al Haramain, my conversion to Christianity, all of it—to anyone, not even my close friends. Those who had known me when I was Muslim were aware that I had worked for an Islamic charity between college and law school. They weren't aware of what went on there. Most of them didn't know that I had been radicalized. Nor was I eager to tell anybody that the charity I had worked for was now being sued for alleged ties to 9/11.

The FBI interview was the first time I sat down and tried to tell my whole story. The forum made it easy. I spoke with two people who were being paid to hear what I had to say. I hadn't known them before and in all likelihood wouldn't see them again.

The agents asked a lot of questions about Pete Seda. They wanted to know Pete's views on non-Muslims, and I outlined those views in some detail, pulling no punches. The agents often glanced at each other during the interview. My frankness surprised them, and they seemed pleased that I wasn't trying to disguise what was happening on the inside at Al Haramain.

But while I didn't want to mince words, I didn't want to exaggerate who Pete was or what he stood for. Near the end of the interview,

Christopher Rogers asked, "After 9/11, do you think Pete might have been *happy* that those attacks occurred? Did he say anything like, 'Good, the U.S. had this coming'?"

"I think Pete was horrified by the attacks," I replied. "I called him just afterward to see how he was doing, in the way that everyone was calling their Muslim friends just after 9/11 to make sure they weren't being beaten in the streets by rampaging mobs. Pete sounded upset. He said he was having trouble eating, and told me that he was horrified. He sounded genuine. I think there's a disconnect in his thinking between attitudes he might have toward non-Muslims or jihadist groups and his views on terrorism. And I think when terrorism is right in front of him, it genuinely shocks and offends him."

The interview lasted about an hour. When it ended, I told the agents that, with all I had been through, I wanted to help them if I could. I told them that they should get in touch with me if they had any other questions about Al Haramain, or about anything else where I might be of service.

A little over a year later, I would discover that things at Al Haramain were more serious than I had realized.

thirteen

INFORMANT

What did you do between college and law school?"

I was now a promising young associate at Boies, Schiller & Flexner, the law firm of superstar attorney David Boies, the man who sued Microsoft and represented Al Gore in the 2000 election litigation. I joined the firm in September 2003. I was at lunch with another of the firm's associates, Steve Miller, a gregarious man with a somewhat colorful past.

Despite how liberating it felt to tell my whole story during the FBI interview that I'd had while clerking on the D.C. Circuit, that was not the approach I had chosen since then. "I worked for a charity," I said.

"What charity did you work for?"

"It's not important."

"NORML?" Steve asked.

I thought he was asking if the charity was normal. Instead, he was asking if I had worked for NORML, the National Organization for the Reform of Marijuana Laws. It was a marijuana legalization group. "Kind of," I said.

Steve laughed, thinking I had admitted to being part of a marijuana legalization group.

The encounter was insignificant, but was typical of my cluelessness about how to deal with my time at Al Haramain. I was usually quick enough on my feet to deftly avoid discussion of this period of my life. My conversation with Steve was one of the rare instances where my evasiveness showed.

A few months later, I wouldn't be able to avoid the issue at all.

It was early February, and I had been working on a fairly important case for a couple of weeks. I had trouble believing that I'd been called onto this case only two weeks ago, and I had no idea how many hours I'd billed since then. I'd put in a lot of time, that's for sure.

I had just pulled an all-nighter putting the final touches on our brief, and had stolen maybe three hours of sleep the night before, three or four hours of sleep the night before that. I was tired, but the end was in sight.

I had been working for Bob Silver, who was regarded as the firm's unofficial number four partner; he was David Boies's protégé. Bob had a reputation at Boies Schiller, as Boies had once called him the smartest person he'd met in the field of law.

The most noticeable thing about Bob at first glance was his tan, which was too strong for a guy who spent so much time cooped up in an office. But the fake-and-bake was inevitable. The summer before I began working as an associate at Boies Schiller, I'd briefly been over to Bob's house in Connecticut. At the time, it was the most impressive private residence I'd ever set foot in, mansion-sized with perfectly trimmed grass in its expansive backyard. There was even an Olympic-sized swimming pool. It came equipped with poolside Internet access, so Bob would never have to leave his work behind.

During the visit, I met Bob's celebrity personal trainer, a perky bleach-blond who went by the name of High Voltage (and even showed Amy her credit card to prove that the world really knew her by that name). I found out later that Voltage, who was fifty-five years old when I met her, boasted a stable of clients including Katie Couric, Kelsey Grammer, and RuPaul. Voltage didn't feel that her job ended with retooling Bob's fitness routine and diet. She was also actively revamping Bob's wardrobe and image.

Sadly, Amy and I were unimpressed by the "upgraded" friends that Voltage urged upon Bob. These included a mother and daughter tandem (with the daughter a mere sixteen) who were both discussing their recent Botox injections, as well as a male neurologist who had a Botox practice on the side. At one point, Amy, a Boies Schiller paralegal named Ken Lashins, and I were sitting at a table with the neurologist when he started to tell us about a letter to the editor he had written (unpublished) which said that 9/11 was foreseeable and there should have been a missile battery on top of the World Trade Center. When we began to argue the point, the neurologist switched subjects and began to describe a different letter to the editor he had written on a less interest-ing topic. I quickly determined the man was a bore and left Ken and Amy at the table with him. Both Ken and Amy were too bashful to get up and leave the other alone with the neurologist, so ended up spending an entire hour listening to stories about the man's full repertoire of let-ters to the editor.

Back at the office, Bob openly flouted the firm's ban on indoor smok-ing, going through cigarette after cigarette while we worked on the case. He also had the most explosive temper that I had then seen. It seemed as if he was perpetually livid, every third or fourth word out of his mouth an obscenity, even when he was relatively happy. My first day on the case, Bob screamed at our cocounsel for fifteen minutes over the speak-erphone. They sat there and took it, sometimes offering a timid defense of their performance.

Now, with the sun inching over the horizon, my work for Bob was almost done. I put the finishing touches on this draft of the brief and then eyeballed it, looking for typos, blue-booking errors, bad writing. Satisfied, I e-mailed the brief to Bob and our cocounsel.

I was running on nothing but adrenaline at this point, but felt oddly peaceful. I watched cars pull into the parking lot outside, another work-day beginning. I thought about how, in just a few hours, mine would end. I could already feel myself curling up in bed back at my apartment, in a warm blanket, with the heat on, getting my first sustained sleep in a long time. It was a Thursday, and Bob had promised me Friday off.

A predictable flurry of last-minute suggestions followed my e-mail. Eventually I incorporated the last of them into the brief; my work was done. As I headed out, I stopped by Bob's office to see if he needed any-thing else. Bob sat at his desk, looking genuinely relaxed for the first time since the case began.

Bob took a drag from his cigarette, exhaled, then leaned back in his chair. "You're good," he said, reclining slightly. Then he nodded. "You're *good.*"

"Thanks, Bob."

He offered to call a car service for me, but I declined. I lived only twelve minutes from the firm in White Plains, and had enough energy to make it back to my apartment. I walked to my car and, when I got there, took a look back at Boies Schiller's offices. The firm's Armonk, New York, office was in a three-story neo-Georgian building reputedly mod-eled after David Boies's house. It was a crisp February morning, I'd fin-ished the brief, Bob Silver had been impressed by my work, and my three-day weekend was beginning. Does it get any better than this?

The victorious feeling wasn't gone when I woke up later that day. I grabbed a beer, flopped down on the green leather couch in our living room, and flipped aimlessly through the TV channels. When Amy came home she gave me a kiss, and I told her how work on the brief had gone, how pleased Bob Silver was with my work.

Amy has the most expressive face I've ever seen, one that communicates many thoughts with no spoken words. In response to the crinkle of Amy's eyebrows and her amused grin, I said, "Yeah, I know he's crazy. But he's the number four partner at Boies Schiller. I want him to like my work."

Amy was cooking dinner when the phone rang. It was my parents. They sounded worried.

"What is it?" I asked.

"It's Pete," my dad said. "Al Haramain's offices got raided."

"*What?*" Suddenly the victorious feeling vanished completely. I had hoped to keep my life at Al Haramain separate from my current life, but now Al Haramain came crashing back in.

"It's in all the papers," my dad said. "The FBI raided the offices yesterday."

"Not good." I'd only begun to think through the consequences. Would I be investigated? Was I already being investigated? Almost involuntarily, my thoughts turned to my security clearance.

My dad voiced these concerns. "Is this going to affect your ability to get a security clearance from the government?" He knew that I had applied for one when I clerked on the D.C. Circuit.

I put the best face on the situation for my parents. "Who knows? It might actually help me get a clearance, since they'll be able to see all of Al Haramain's records now."

Dad wasn't buying it. "How could it *help* you get a security clearance?"

I walked to the balcony outside and looked at the playground across the street. The night remained peaceful, in contrast to the panic that I felt. "Now that they've raided Al Haramain, they'll be able to verify what I told them in my last FBI interview. I didn't sugarcoat what was going on behind closed doors. They'll be able to see some of the hateful things that Pete said about non-Muslims."

Dad sounded surprised. "Pete said hateful things about non-Muslims?"

"Yeah, he would. What went on behind closed doors there was different than their public image."

"Do you think Pete was just tricking Rabbi David when he built their friendship?" my mom said. She was referring to David Zaslow, a local rabbi who had been friends with Pete, and who was his biggest defender after Al Haramain garnered unwanted attention for alleged ties to al-Qaeda.

"I don't know. I didn't hear him say anything about David while I was there." My answer was curt. It was cold outside, and the living room's lights seemed appealing. "Look, I'm tired. I've been working on a case nonstop for the past two weeks. I can't deal with this now."

I got off the phone with my parents, walked back into the apartment, and sat down on the couch, placing my forearm over my head. "What's wrong?" Amy asked.

"Al Haramain was raided," I said.

We tried to talk it through. Should I approach the FBI? During the FBI interview at the Washington Field Office, it became obvious that they were investigating Al Haramain, but I didn't know why.

The newspaper stories provided more detail. Federal agents believed that Pete and Soliman al-But'he had smuggled about $130,000 out of the country to aid the Chechen mujahideen in March of 2000. Something clicked: I realized that this smuggling had occurred at the time that Soliman was passing through New York City, around the time that Pete had wanted me to meet with him at the airport.

Pete and Soliman had gotten $130,000 in traveler's checks from an Ashland bank. At first, when they asked for this much money, a bank employee told them that the branch didn't have that many traveler's checks on hand and suggested cashier's checks instead. Pete replied that the money was going to help people who couldn't cash cashier's checks. He was eventually able to get the money in traveler's checks.

Shortly afterward, Soliman left the country with the traveler's checks and failed to declare them at customs. An article in the *Medford Mail Tribune*, a local paper, explained:

> The IRS does claim Seda lied about the money in the foundation's 2000 tax return, reporting that the $130,000 went toward the purchase of a prayer house in Springfield, Mo. The government suspects the pair acted in such a way to avoid government scrutiny and retain the foundation's tax-exempt status as a charitable organization, the affidavit states. The allegations could lead to violations of federal tax and financial-reporting laws, felonies together punishable by up to 13 years in prison.

I didn't know before why Al Haramain was being investigated. I had thought (and wished) that this might be part of a wild goose chase on the government's part. But I thought about Pete's contempt for U.S. tax laws. I thought about his support for the Chechen mujahideen. And the allegations made sense.

I asked Amy if she thought I should get in touch with the FBI.

"You already said that they could call you if they needed anything," she said. "They probably would have gotten in touch with you if they thought you could be helpful."

All weekend, I could think about nothing but the Al Haramain raid. I wished I could go back to Thursday. Life was so much simpler when all I had to worry about was pleasing the firm's partners.

I finally decided to call the FBI. I knew I had information that might be useful. It had been my choice to hook up with Pete Seda and the Al

Haramain Islamic Foundation in the first place. The least I could do was try to make the right choices now.

I called the Portland Field Office on Sunday, and said that I wanted to talk to someone about the Al Haramain investigation. I was told that the Medford Field Office was handling the case, but that nobody would be there until Monday.

On Monday, in my Boies Schiller office, I made the call. My office door didn't have a lock, but I shut it anyway and sat at the desk. The phone felt like a lead weight in my hand. I dialed slowly.

A woman answered. I stumbled through my introduction. "Um, I know that the FBI raided the Ashland office of the Al Haramain Islamic Foundation last week. I thought I could provide some useful information because I used to work for them."

"Who are you?" she asked.

"My name is Daveed Gartenstein-Ross. I worked for Al Haramain back in 1999."

"Oh," she said. "I know who you are."

I know who you are? That single comment triggered every paranoid thought I had over the previous two years about the FBI carefully monitoring my every move.

But I pressed on, telling her that after learning about why Al Haramain had been raided, I realized that I may have information that could be useful. As I began to describe Abdul-Qaadir's e-mail list that had been used to spread propaganda for the Chechen mujahideen, she told me she was going to hand the phone to another agent who had more experience in dealing with technology. And she handed the phone to Dave Carroll, who had written the questions that I was asked in my first interview with the FBI.

Our conversation lasted over an hour. I was nervous that the door would burst open in the middle of my talk with the FBI. At the end, I told Dave, "You know, I spent a long time trying to decide whether to call you guys. My wife thought that I shouldn't. She said you probably would have gotten in touch with me if you thought I could be useful."

He burst out laughing. "I'd like to come out to Westchester," he said. "I want to sit down with you face-to-face, ask you some questions, spend a day with you."

My reaction was probably unusual for someone whose former employer was raided by the FBI, and is told that an agent wants to spend a day with him and ask questions. I couldn't wait.

I felt a great sense of relief. My transition wasn't yet complete, but it had begun. I had once worked for an Islamic charity that conspired to fund terrorists abroad while spreading radicalism at home. After that, I never understood how to explain this unusual episode to others, nor how it would affect my present life. But that was changing.

Now, for the first time, I was no longer trying to simply wish away that part of my life. I was beginning to embrace all that had happened to me—my conversion to Islam, my radicalization, my association with Islamic extremist figures—and to realize how it could be used for the good. Just as I knew that I was journeying into a new world after I became a Muslim in Rimini, there was another new world before me now, one far less charted.

fourteen

REUNION

It was a bright, hot day, and I felt nervous.

June 5, 2006, was the first time I set foot on Georgetown University's campus. I was walking toward the Intercultural Center. My pace was slow because I was twenty minutes ahead of schedule, but I was nonetheless focused on my destination.

The small details weren't lost on me along the way. There was a smell of fresh-cut grass that, appropriately enough, reminded me of Wake Forest's quad. Some of the summer session students were outside. A few, wearing backpacks and clutching new textbooks, were headed to class. Others stood around talking with the nervousness typical of the newly acquainted. A few students smoked—but not as many as I remembered puffing on cigarettes a decade ago in the tobacco mecca of Winston-Salem.

Using the campus map that I had printed off the Internet, I spotted the Intercultural Center. It was an ugly, square brick building with windows set far back in the walls that gave it the appearance of a parking garage. I entered through the plate-glass double doors and walked through the student common area, past a coffee stand that had just closed down.

The room number that I had jotted down was located in the basement. The building had thick metallic stairs, and each footstep I took echoed ominously. When I reached the dimly lit basement, I made my way through a maze of hallways until I found the room I was looking for. It was partially hidden at the back of an alcove. I entered the classroom, took a seat near the back, and watched as the students trickled in.

A man walked up to the podium and introduced himself as the head of Georgetown's Arabic program. He was somewhat dismayed because this was the first day of class and the instructor was supposed to arrive early for orientation. Eventually the instructor did arrive, a tall man of Indian descent with a close-cropped beard and very thin mustache. It was my old friend al-Husein Madhany, whom I had not seen since his visit to New York City in late 2000, when he had tried to help me through my crisis of faith.

As I was struggling with the manuscript for this book, I felt compelled to track down al-Husein. I was surprised to learn that he was just across town, teaching a summer session of Arabic at Georgetown University.

I wasn't sure how al-Husein would receive me. *Is he now a moderate, or a radical? Is he still my friend, or has he left me behind?*

This was the first class that al-Husein would teach in the summer session. As soon as he entered, I took note of his quiet confidence coupled with an apparent humility. This was a change from our Wake Forest days, when al-Husein's confidence was louder and more gregarious.

I looked for smaller signs. I noticed al-Husein smiling a lot. When I last knew him, when he was moving deeper into the world of Islamic extremism, he looked much sterner, his expressions a mixture of scowls and intense stares. I wondered, though, if I could be sure. I wondered if he was just another smiling salesman for radical Islam; surely that was within his power and personality.

When the class ended, a few students stuck around to ask al-Husein questions about the course. I stayed in the back of the room, jotting down a few ideas in my notepad.

As the last student left, al-Husein walked toward the back of the room. "Bro!" he exclaimed, arms outstretched.

"Husein, it's great to see you."

We met in a warm embrace.

"It's been a long time," he said.

I asked al-Husein about his plans. He had earned master's degrees from Harvard's Divinity School and from Georgetown. He was now finishing up a Ph.D. at the University of Chicago, with his general exams coming up this fall. Liana was working as a lawyer in D.C. and al-Husein would move here as well.

"It'll be nice to have you here, bro," I said. "I'm really looking forward to catching up with you."

We both leaned against the wall slightly as we spoke, perhaps a sign of nervousness on both our parts. "Likewise," al-Husein said.

"So are you planning on looking for a teaching job in D.C.?"

He didn't know. He was put off a bit by the impracticality of academia. He said he was interested in "institution-building"—building up new Islamic institutions in America. "I'm interested in working with other moderate Muslims," he said. And by now I had no question that this is what he was: a moderate Muslim. I had been around enough of a diversity of Islamic practice that I had a good intuitive sense of who was genuinely moderate and who was not. But more importantly, although it had been years since I last saw him, I knew al-Husein pretty well. There was a marked difference between the man who stood before me now and the friend who I feared I was losing seven years ago. But still I wondered about the path he had taken to arrive here.

"Al-Husein," I said, "I miss the days when we used to talk all the time. You were an incredible friend. It would mean a lot to me to have you back in my life as a close friend."

Al-Husein nodded. "I agree," he said. "Remember that time I visited you in Oregon? Do you remember when we made loud *dhikr* on the beach?"

I smiled, thinking back to our time together. I thought back to how al-Husein told me, after we had finished making *dhikr* together, that I had learned how to be a brother that day. Al-Husein, I realized, was the only brother I had ever known.

"That's what this religion should be about," al-Husein said. "Forget these people who are trying to make it too difficult for anyone to follow. It should just be about pure worship of Allah."

"I can't wait to hear about where your life has taken you," I said.

The smile on my face then turned to a more serious expression. This was the reason I had tracked him down. "Did I ever tell you about what had happened during my time at Al Haramain?" I asked.

"Not really," al-Husein said. "Nothing good, I assume."

I gave a half-laugh. "Nothing good is right. The branch I worked for was designated a terrorist entity by the Treasury Department, and two of the directors were indicted. That's kind of why I'm here." Al-Husein said nothing, so I continued, "I'm writing a book about it."

It was hard to read al-Husein's reaction. I realized that I was moving quickly, but that's the way it had to be. I had my publishing deadlines, and didn't want the book to blindside al-Husein. But suddenly I felt something else, something that I hadn't felt in more than half a decade. I was overcome with the feeling that al-Husein, even after all this time, even after both of our religious transformations, was still my brother. And as my brother, he wasn't going to judge me harshly. So I pressed on with renewed confidence. "I'm sure you understand what a big part of my spiritual journey you've been. That's reflected in the book, bro. Let me put it this way: the book is dedicated to three people, and you're one of them."

Al-Husein still remained silent, but looked both touched and suspicious. Both reactions were justified, and probably wise.

"I'm editing the book right now, and I want you to see it," I said. "I want you to get a chance to see if my recollections are right, to see if I've included anything that you don't think should be in there."

"I'd love to see it," Al-Husein said, nodding.

I had gotten what I came for. "I'll e-mail the manuscript," I said. "You can look at it at your convenience. When you're done, I'll take you out to dinner. We can talk about the book, and we can reconnect. I want to do both."

"Me too, bro."

We parted with another embrace. I then walked out of the classroom, out of the Intercultural Center, back into the bright summer day.

Fifteen days later, I summoned the guts and sent al-Husein the manuscript.

And waited. And waited. And waited.

Eight days later, I opened my e-mail and found a surprise. It was from al-Husein.

He and Liana had finished reading the book together the night before. I skimmed through the first couple of paragraphs of his message, then seized on his thoughts about the book: "Overall, we both have positive feelings about your publishing it and including us in it. In fact, we are honored. There are, however, a few content matters we would need to clarify with you." He proposed that we meet up for dinner to discuss the book.

The fact that al-Husein wanted to clarify certain matters of content came as no surprise. Over the past several months, I had made an effort to show the book manuscript to as many people mentioned herein as was possible and wise. Even figures who played little role in the narrative could offer voluminous suggestions about small details that they remembered differently, or about what they had actually meant by remarks they made years ago. I would have been surprised if al-Husein *hadn't* wanted to the opportunity to clarify some things.

No, what I seized on was al-Husein and Liana's positive feelings about the book, and his affirmation that they were honored to be included. I was filled with a sense of relief and happiness. Relief because the book covered so many matters that were of clear import to me and al-Husein, but matters that we had never discussed over the years. Relief because I wasn't sure if, upon reading the book, he would be angry, defensive, hurt. And I felt happiness because, in seeing his reaction— one that was measured and reflective—I recognized the same friend, the same brother, whom I had known years ago.

I had dinner with al-Husein and Liana in mid-July, a few days before I handed this manuscript over to my publisher. We met at an Indian restaurant in D.C. (Both al-Husein and Liana would point out that they were the only people of Indian descent dining there; never a good sign for an Indian restaurant.)

It was at that dinner that I began to learn where al-Husein's spiritual journey had taken him. He said that the Salafi voice was at its peak for him in November of 1999; by the time I saw him at his wedding, that voice was receding—although it was still quite strong. Al-Husein was then experiencing a great degree of cognitive dissonance. On the one hand, Brother Taha's voice filled his head. On the other hand, there was lived reality.

The reason the Salafi voice had begun to recede for al-Husein by December 1999 was the meeting with Liana, their families, and the

Orlando imam in November. Liana and others who cared about al-Husein were concerned about the theological turn he had taken, and decided to confront him.

After this intervention, another significant event helped bring al-Husein out of Salafism. This was a conference that he helped organize at Harvard called "Islam in America," which was designed to examine the lived experience of Islam in the United States. In organizing and hosting the conference, al-Husein noticed that the Salafis refused to enter into dialogue with Muslim progressives like Asma Gull Hassan (the author of *American Muslims: The New Generation*; she graduated from NYU Law around the same time I did).

This obstinacy on the Salafis' part upset al-Husein, as did their tendency to deny the experience of Muslims who collectively lacked power, such as African-American Muslims. Al-Husein and I spoke at some length about Salafism's appeal. The Salafis have a logical approach to the faith that seems compelling. Even if your heart rebels against Salafism (as both mine and al-Husein's did), a key Salafi ideal teaches you to question your heart. Al-Husein suggested that there are two ways Salafism's hold on a believer may collapse. The first is when the believer sees its failure to provide the answers one needs for actual, lived reality—something that was made plain to al-Husein at the Islam in America conference. Also, its hold may collapse when the believer has enough knowledge of Islamic history, theology, and Arabic to assess the Salafis' seemingly powerful arguments more critically, from a position of confidence.

Our first dinner together in more than half a decade didn't give me the opportunity to learn all the details of al-Husein's spiritual transformation away from extreme Salafism, but I believe that he too has an important story to tell.

Al-Husein also offered a couple of interesting insights into what may have been going through his head during our parallel journeys toward and away from radical Islam. For one thing, he said that his own practice of Islam probably wasn't as extreme at the time of his wedding as it came across to me. The environment at the Ismaili-dominated wedding was the exact opposite of the environment I knew at Al Haramain. At Al Haramain, I was dealing with people who thought that Freecell and credit cards were *haram*; at the wedding, al-Husein was dealing with nominal Muslims who wanted alcohol at the wedding and urged him not to fast for Ramadan. The role you take often depends on the environment you're in, and al-Husein said that much of the stance he adopted at the wedding was a reaction to its ultraliberal Islamic environment. (Of course, Salafism hadn't lost its hold on al-Husein at that point. But neither was the hold as strong as it appeared.)

In particular, al-Husein said that when he showed me the photo of the Chechen mujahideen, it wasn't out of a desire to cheerlead for their jihad. Rather, he showed me the photo of the Chechens because it was a symbol of his own struggles in Orlando. There were the Chechen warriors with their fight, and here was al-Husein, thousands of miles away, with his own very different fight—struggling for a sound practice of Islam in an environment that tried to turn him away from it.

He also had an interesting remark about the conversation we had about an Islamic reformation, the conversation where I felt he was probing for deviant beliefs. At one point we had served as religious sounding boards for each other; by the time al-Husein asked if I still believed in an Islamic reformation, I felt that this was no longer true. While I felt that al-Husein was probing for deviance, he may have had a very different purpose: he may have been reaching out to me as a sounding board, hoping that I could help pull him from his own radicalism. That, sadly, is something I was unable to do for al-Husein.

We finished dinner around ten o'clock, and Liana had to get to sleep. Al-Husein and I ended the night in the Ritz-Carlton's lounge in Arlington, Virginia. We went through his thoughts on the book in detail, but our discussion went far beyond that. By the time I dropped al-Husein off at his apartment at two thirty in the morning, it reminded me of the nights that we used to have. Far-ranging conversation, staying up far too late, and regretting not a thing when we were done. It was an evening spent with the same friend, the same brother, whom I had known years ago.

What al-Husein's friendship meant to me over the four brilliant years that we were close cannot be overstated. He was my first brother; he was my first true mentor. I fondly remember our late-night talks and walks around the quad. I remember how al-Husein always had something new to teach me. Some of these were college-type lessons involving exercises in absurd left-of-center thinking. But other lessons remain with me to this day. When we were in Istanbul together, I pointed out to al-Husein that other people seemed to gravitate toward him while often almost completely ignoring me. That observation began a several-week-long lesson in how to dress and carry myself more professionally, how to build my presence. That was an example of al-Husein at his best: having something extraordinary to teach me, understanding what I needed far better than I did.

Al-Husein was the kind of friend that I never expected to have because I never knew that friendship like his existed. He once described ours as a "found" friendship. That is, there are some friendships that you work to cultivate for weeks, months, or years; after much effort, a friendship has been made. There are other friendships that you simply stumble upon and immediately realize that they had always existed. All you had to do was uncover the friendship in order for it to be.

In the past few years, I've gained a lot and lost a lot. But I'm surprised and delighted that the friendship I gained in al-Husein has not been lost.

He's still there, and so am I.

FRIENDS AND FUGITIVES

When I worked for the Al Haramain Islamic Foundation, I was overwhelmed by the rules and restrictions, and it slowly seduced me into a radical interpretation of Islam. I'm sure that radical Islam's dark undertow has dragged many unsuspecting believers into those deep waters as well.

In the West, we tend to see all religions as variations on a theme. But Christianity and Islam stand in marked contrast to each other. For example, in the West religion is private and primarily a matter of conscience. In the Middle East, religion is public and is a matter of ritual as well as conscience. These differences are reflected in the divergent ways that prayer takes place within both faiths. Prayer in Islam is more ritualized than in Christianity, with the believer praying in Arabic and putting his body through a series of standing, bowing, kneeling, and prostrating positions. These differences are reflected in the oft-repeated saying that Islam is "a complete way of life"—as Pete Seda once observed to me, it leaves no doubt about the smallest detail, from the proper way to eat your food down to how to cleanse yourself after using the bathroom. And these differences can be seen in the lack of separation between mosque and state within Islam.

Part of Islam's seduction is its otherness—how different it is from anything else. And it would be a mistake to shortchange how satisfying a life is inside radical Islam. As I descended into radicalism, I had a greater feeling of certainty than I had known before. I felt that for the first time, I could truly comprehend and follow Allah's will—and I knew that those who disagreed with me were just following their own desires. There was a sense of community that came with this certainty. I was part of an exclusive club composed of those who could see beyond the shallow Western liberal values with which I was raised.

People I met within the Islamic experience were pulled in many different directions. You've already learned about what happened to al-Husein. Here's what became of the rest.

My feelings about **Pete Seda** changed over time. At first I was taken in by his charm, and it took me a while to realize that there were two sides to Pete: a public side and a private one. While the public Pete could befriend local rabbis and put a good face on the Al Haramain Islamic Foundation, the private one had a very rigid view of Islam that was extremely critical of Jews, homosexuals, and even his own family for following the Shia branch of Islam.

A grand jury indicted Pete in early 2005 on charges of conspiracy to defraud the United States and file a false IRS return by a tax-exempt organization. The charges stemmed from Soliman al-But'he's March 2000 visit to Oregon—the one during which Pete tried to convince me to meet Soliman at a New York airport.

The indictment explains that in February 2000, an individual in Egypt donated about $150,000 to Al Haramain, writing that the money was given "as Zakat [charity] in order to participate in your nobel support to our muslim brothers in Chychnia." That individual then undertook a wire transfer to Al Haramain's bank account in Oregon. In early

March, Soliman flew from Riyadh to southern Oregon. There, he and Pete bought 130 thousand-dollar American Express traveler's checks (at a cost of $131,300) as well as a $21,000 cashier's check issued to Soliman from the local Bank of America.

Soliman then left the country via JFK International Airport in New York. He failed to file a Form 4790, Report of International Transportation of Currency or Monetary Instruments, as required by law when an individual leaves the United States with traveler's checks exceeding $10,000. The indictment alleges that Pete then tried to disguise the money sent to Chechnya by inflating the cost of a building that Al Haramain had bought in Springfield, Missouri, by $131,300—the price of the traveler's checks.

Rather than facing trial in the United States, Pete left the country and is now living as a fugitive overseas. I spoke with Soliman by phone in late 2005 and he told me that Pete is in Iran and not doing well there, lonely and almost out of money.

After Pete was indicted, the local press was filled with an outpouring of community support for him. Rabbi David Zaslow had long been Pete's biggest public defender, and was undeterred by the indictment. After it came down, he was quoted in the *Medford Mail Tribune* saying that Pete has "been an outspoken spokesman against violence and terrorism, and he has earned my respect."

Probably the most ridiculous defense of Pete and Al Haramain that I have seen is a column published in the *Washington Times* in late November 2003 called "Stereotyping Hurts the War." Written by Lynne Bernabei, a Washington, D.C.-based attorney who represents Al Haramain, and Georgetown law professor David Cole, the column describes Al Haramain in the following manner:

> [T]he Al Haramain Islamic Foundation, Inc. of Oregon has been unfairly accused of links to terrorists. Al Haramain Oregon is a Muslim

charity dedicated to distributing Islamic information and Qur'ans to Muslims throughout the United States, and to educating the public at large that Islam is opposed to terrorism in all forms. Its mission, in part, is to spread the word that true Muslims abhor violence against the innocent. It would, therefore, seem to be a natural partner in the war against terror. Its articles of incorporation, filed with the Oregon Secretary of State in 1998, provide that it is dedicated to peace and the fight against terrorism. One of the group's most vocal supporters is a local rabbi, with whom Al Haramain has engaged in joint public education activities. As an Islamic charity, however, Al Haramain (Oregon) has been suspected and labeled as a terrorist by many who accuse first, and find out the truth later.

Having been on the inside of the group, I found the description of Al Haramain as "a natural partner in the war against terror" downright laughable. Lynne Bernabei is a paid advocate for Al Haramain; David Cole has no similar excuse for such slovenly research.

Soliman al-But'he was indicted along with Pete. Although a fellow fugitive, Soliman seems to be living a much more comfortable life. When I spoke with him in late 2005, Soliman was living in Riyadh and had just earned a promotion to assistant general manager of Riyadh's parks and recreation department. The one downside for Soliman is that he's no longer allowed outside of Saudi Arabia.

I don't know what became of **Dennis Geren** and **Charlie Jones**. From what I've heard, it seems that both men left town. Charlie may have gone to Wisconsin and Dennis may have moved to Portland, Oregon; but my information here is far from reliable. For all I know, both men are still going to the gym. Charlie may still be talking about how miraculous it is that someone who was once a sperm can lift as much as he does, while Dennis may still be correcting young Muslims whose shorts reveal a bit too much flesh.

Abdi Guled and **Mary Foster** are still living in Ashland. Mary had been a public-school teacher, and Oregon's generous public employee retirement system allowed her to achieve some small piece of the American dream: she retired while still young enough to enjoy her retirement.

Abdi, Mary, and the remaining congregation in Ashland weren't untouched by the legal troubles that Pete and Soliman found themselves in. They were once able to pray in a beautiful Musalla on the south end of town, but when I last spoke to Mary she told me that she and Abdi would hold services in their house on Saturday nights. Mary graciously invited me to these services the last time I was in town, saying that I was welcome even if Islam wasn't "my thing" anymore. (Alas, my schedule didn't allow me to make it out there.)

Mary told me that she had recently spoken with Rabbi David Zaslow, who suggested that perhaps the Muslim community remaining in Ashland could use the local synagogue for their *juma* prayers.

There is one sad note related to Mary and Abdi. They had always loved traveling together. I remember back in 1999 they showed me videotapes they made of various exotic locations they had visited, ranging from Africa to the Middle East. When I last spoke with Mary, I was saddened to hear that traveling had become far less joyful for them because she and Abdi seem to be on a watch list. Mary said they would be selected for extra security screening whenever they flew. It had gotten to the point where whenever Mary spoke with Abdi about traveling, he would reflexively recoil. Much of the fun and adventure of the experience, it seems, has been lost for him.

Then there are the friends and family who played such a big role in my life when I was being radicalized and deradicalized. **Mike and Amy Hollister** are still happily married. They have three kids with a fourth on the way as of this writing. They attend services at a United Reformed Church near their home in the Bellingham, Washington, area. Mike is working as a successful investment adviser.

When al-Husein and I visited Mike in Bellingham back in 1997, it struck me that the connection Mike and I once had was fizzling and might soon be lost. That has turned out not to be the case. Mike is again one of my closest friends; as with al-Husein, Mike's is one of the few "found" friendships that I've known in my life.

My **parents** continue to live in Ashland. Whenever I return home, their love for each other and the serenity they feel in their relationship with God is apparent. Although I was initially nervous about telling them that I had become Christian, they immediately accepted this new spiritual change—just as they have unconditionally accepted most of the choices that I've made in this life.

My dad is now semiretired and working in real estate.

Amy Powell had a brilliant career as a law student. She was among the top ten students in her class academically after her second and third semesters of law school, made it onto the Law Review, and earned a prestigious clerkship on the United States Court of Appeals for the Second Circuit. Amy is now beginning what will almost certainly be a similarly brilliant career as an attorney; she currently works as a trial lawyer for the Department of Justice.

Since Amy was never baptized as a child, she and I had the pleasure of being baptized together in the summer of 2003.

Amy and I celebrated our fifth anniversary on June 3, 2006, just before the final push to finish writing this book began. Whenever I take the time to think about the role that Amy has played in my life, I cannot believe how strongly she supported me every step of the way. It is a quiet yet strong kind of support that she continues to bless me with to this day. Her love is something that I could not possibly deserve.

As for me, today I work as a counterterrorism consultant. I work with federal law enforcement and local police departments in several capacities, including providing analysis of Islamic extremism and possible terrorist activity, and providing training to agents and officers. I am also an explainer of radical Islam to the public, not just through this book but also through articles and television and radio appearances.

The public, I find, does not have a good understanding of radical Islam because most Americans have trouble understanding how people in other parts of the world view religion. They have trouble understanding religion as an ideology and a true political force rather than a private relationship between the believer and his god. While many people are curious and open-minded, both the press and the government have done a poor job of educating Americans about this pressing issue.

On balance, I don't have any regrets about my year inside radical Islam. I learned a lot about myself, and a lot about the seductive pull of an ideology that is today America's deadliest foe.

I hope this book will be useful to anyone who has been or knows someone who has been drawn into the orbit of radical Islam and is trying to find the way out. There is hope that it can be done.

ACKNOWLEDGMENTS

I would like to thank all of the sources who were willing to discuss the substance of this book with me. These include Suzi Aufderheide, John Foote, Mary Foster, Mike and Amy Hollister, al-Husein Madhany, Amy Powell, Liana Sebastian, Susan Thorngate, and my parents. The manuscript was also reviewed by several federal law-enforcement professionals, both currently active and retired from service, with firsthand knowledge of the Al Haramain investigation.

In writing this book, I was blessed with two fantastic editors. I would like to thank Sara Carder at Jeremy P. Tarcher for her excellent work on the manuscript. I would also like to thank Richard Miniter, author of *New York Times* best sellers *Losing bin Laden* and *Shadow War*, and one of the handful of "found" friends whom I have known in my life. It would be difficult to overstate how much Rich taught me about writing and the art of storytelling during the editorial process. Rich: the book mentions that al-Husein was my first true mentor. You are my second.

I would also like to thank the many people who reviewed all or part of the manuscript and gave me editorial or substantive feedback: Amy Beard (a very competent editor and a high school classmate of mine who was surprisingly unfazed upon learning my story), Jennifer L. Davis,

Glen Feder, Jeff Panehal, Raphael Satter, and Maria Sliwa. I would also like to thank Mark Pezzo, an assistant professor of psychology at the University of South Florida and the man who first introduced me to self-perception theory; he graciously helped jog my memory while I was working on this book. Abdu Murray, a brilliant Michigan-based lawyer who is himself a former Muslim, provided valuable insight into framing my observations in chapter eleven.

I would like to thank my agent, Gary Morris, for believing in the project from the very outset and for helping it take shape.

I also appreciate the research provided by my assistant, Kyle Dabruzzi.

Last but certainly not least, Amy Powell displayed the same kind of extraordinary patience and forbearance while I was working on this book that she has shown throughout the entirety of our relationship.

GLOSSARY

adhan • Call to prayer.

ahadith • Plural form of *hadith*.

alayhi salaatu was salaam • Arabic for "upon him be prayers and peace";
   an honorific phrase said after Muslims speak the name of a prophet.

alhamdulillah • Arabic for "all praises due to God."

Allah • The Arabic word for God.

amu • Uncle.

aqida • Creed.

astaghfirullah • Arabic for "I ask Allah for forgiveness."

bida • Innovation in religion.

dawah • The Arabic word for invitation to Islam; roughly equivalent to
   Christian missionary work.

dhikr • Remembrance of Allah.

du'a • Supplications.

fatwa • Islamic legal ruling.

fi sabil Allah • Arabic for "for the pleasure of Allah."

hadith • One of Prophet Muhammad's sayings or traditions.

hajj • The pilgrimage to Mecca.

halal • Permissible under Islamic law.

haram • Forbidden by Islamic law.

hijab • Head scarf worn by Muslim women.

hijra • Prophet Muhammad's emigration from Mecca to Medina in 622 A.D.

imam • Person who leads congregational prayers and/or delivers the Friday sermons.

inshallah • Arabic for "God willing."

juma • *Juma* means Friday in Arabic; the *juma* congregational prayers, which occur on Fridays, are the most important prayers of the week for Muslims.

kafir • An unbeliever or infidel.

khutbah • Sermon.

kufar • Plural version of *kafir*.

kufi • Islamic skullcap.

madrassa • Islamic religious school.

masjid • Mosque.

mufti • An Islamic scholar who interprets *sharia* law.

mujahideen • Arabic for "those who strive"; a term used to refer to holy warriors engaged in battles throughout the world to advance their vision of Islam.

Mushrik • A polytheist or disbeliever in the Oneness of Allah.

Naqshbandi • A Sufi Muslim group that considers it vital to adhere to Prophet Muhammad's example.

nikah • Marriage.

riba • Arabic for interest.

sahih • The *ahadith* were evaluated based on the confidence that one can have in their authenticity; a *sahih hadith* is considered sound.

Salafism • A term derived from the Arabic word for predecessors or early generations, Salafism is an austere Islamic movement that claims to be returning to the pure Islam practiced by Prophet Muhammad and the first generation of Muslims.

salat • The Islamic ritual prayer.

shahadah • The declaration of faith; saying it publicly with two
   witnesses will make one a Muslim.

sharia • Islamic law.

shaytan • Satan.

shirk • The association of partners with Allah.

Sufism • Islamic mysticism.

Sunna • Prophet Muhammad's example.

sura • A chapter of the Qur'an.

tafsir • Explanation and interpretation of the Qur'an.

tajweed • Pronunciation during recitation of the Qur'an.

tariqa • Way or path.

tawheed • Islamic monotheism; belief in the oneness of God.

Ummah • The worldwide community of Muslims.

Wahhabism • Saudi Arabia's austere form of Islam, named after
   Muhammad ibn Abdul Wahhab (1703–1792).

wudu • Ablutions made before *salat*, the Islamic ritual prayer.

yahood • Jew.

yarhamukallah • Arabic for "May Allah bless you."

zakat • Charity.

BIBLIOGRAPHY

Cohn, Norman. *Warrant for Genocide: The Myth of the Jewish World-Conspiracy and the Protocols of the Elders of Zion*. London: Eyre & Spottiswoode, 1967.

Esposito, John L. *The Islamic Threat: Myth or Reality?* New York: Oxford University Press, 1992.

Fadiman, James, and Robert Frager. *Essential Sufism*. Edison, NJ: Castle Books, 1997.

Goldsmith, Joel S. *The Infinite Way*. Camarillo, Calif.: DeVorss & Company, 1979.

Lewis, C. S. *Mere Christianity*. New York: Touchstone, 1996.

Malcolm X and Alex Haley. *The Autobiography of Malcolm X*. New York: Ballantine Books, 1973.

McDowell, Josh. *Evidence That Demands a Verdict*. San Bernadino, CA: Here's Life Publishers, 1979.

Nu'Man, Muhammad Armiya. *What Every American Should Know About Islam & The Muslims*. Jersey City, NJ: New Mind Productions, 1994.

Philips, Abu Ameenah Bilal. *Tafseer Soorah al-Hujuraat*. Riyadh, Saudi Arabia: International Islamic Publishing House, 1997.

Smith, Huston. *The World's Religions: Our Great Wisdom Traditions*. New York: HarperCollins, 1991.

Zino, Muhammad bin Jamil. *Islamic Guidelines for Individual and Social Reform*. Riyadh, Saudi Arabia: Darussalam Publishers & Distributors, 1996.